Crossing the Data Delta

Turn the data you have
into the information you need

Pete Smith, Jason Edge, Steve Parry and Dave Wilkinson

Contents

Acknowledgements

The authors would like to thank all the people and organisations who have assisted us in producing this book. The list is so long that in general terms we will have to revert to the hackneyed 'You-know-who-you-are' coverall, though there are a few stand-outs who deserve to be recognised far more than we can say here.

Of all the many organisations which have worked with us over the years, and helped us form the key ideas behind 'Crossing the Data Delta', we have to give our special gratitude to the leadership, management and staff of the Abu Dhabi Systems and Information Centre (ADSIC). The Entity Group were appointed to work with them to produce the world's first comprehensive cross-governmental Data Management Strategy, which enabled us to crystallise much of the thinking that underpins the Data Delta concept.

We would also like to thank a number of individuals and organisations for allowing us to quote from them. We are particularly appreciative of Gartner Inc., Her Excellency Dr. Aisha Bin Bishr, Director General of Smart Dubai, and Helaine Olen of Slate Magazine in this respect.

In terms of the Entity Group itself, we would like to thank our directors Chris Finlay, James Wilkinson, and Richard Foskett for their unswerving commitment to this project. We are also deeply in the debt of Chris Buckett, John Harrington, and Preston Gregg, as well as Sam Thomsett and Chris Ruddick for all their expertise, ideas and support.

We need to give Aaron Zornes, chief research officer at the MDM Institute, and in so many senses the 'godfather of MDM' particular appreciation. Aaron's contribution to enterprise data management theory and practice over the years has been immense, and we are honoured that he wrote the Foreword to this book.

Our graphic designers Demographik made a massive difference to the appearance of the book and in making the many diagrams and graphics comprehensible. Last, but by no means least, our thanks go to our editor, Sarah Bacon, who rescued and resuscitated our prose.

Foreword

I am always pleased to see new publications developing and expanding upon our understanding of Enterprise Information Management (EIM) and its many constituent disciplines, particularly my own specialist areas of Master Data Management (MDM), Reference Data Management (RDM) and Data Governance.

My industry analyst firm has had the opportunity to proof and review numerous prior attempts to rationalize the complexity of IT architecture in regards to digital transformation – most of which have consistently failed to recognize either the need for culture-driven change, or the fact that IT is only *one* force in the change process.

However, the Entity Group team has significantly moved the goal posts with this exciting and original work, Crossing the Data Delta. A unique combination of theoretical understanding and hard-won practical experience pours out of every page of this book, with a blend of innovation and mainstream common sense that continuously rewards the reader. I was particularly gratified to read the authors' point of view that "reference data drives and enables data quality" with this point reinforced relative to the 'delta' conceptual model. Moreover, I found my personal investment in reading the primer to be rewarded with the authors' approach as a set of doggedly pragmatic/ deterministic principles (experience-based) to rationalize the heretofore pseudo-holistic approach to foundational/master data promoted by many other EIM architecture tomes.

Clearly, when IT practitioners move to the theory field, the work is often limited and constrained by personal experience. The four authors of this book all have impressive global pedigrees, from top-tier management in IBM and Cognizant to program lead roles within some of the world's most exciting MDM implementation projects. And now they've taken the time to step back and think about relationships, about causes and consequences, and about why they've succeeded and failed along the way.

The result is at the same time both thought-provoking and reassuring – and a fast-paced read. As an industry analyst/gadfly, I kept finding myself thinking: "I've been ranting about that [reference data, data governance] myself for a long time". But seeing how the authors link to a related topic which is expressed in a way I hadn't quite seen before is new, and it's different, but most of all the book adds a huge amount of relevant value to the debate.

In summary, this up-to-date EIM primer manages to simplify the morass of complex data dependencies confronting enterprise architects and related IT roles – from governance to meta data to reference data to master data.

In all seriousness, if I were a large enterprise about to invest in Big Data, BI, Data Governance or MDM, I'd call 'time out' until my key staff had read this book. It's a thought-provoking game changer that can help structure the necessary conversation about changing the traditional data culture in an organization.

I hope you will enjoy reading this as much as I did.

Aaron Zornes

Aaron Zornes, Chief Research Officer & Founder, The MDM Institute & Conference Chairman, The MDM & Data Governance Summit series (London, Madrid, New York, San Francisco, Sydney, Tokyo, Toronto).

1
Introduction to the Data Delta

Enterprise IT doesn't work.

At least, it doesn't work well enough to justify the massive investments most organisations – including, in all likelihood, your own – have made in IT over the past 50 years.

This book is about starting the journey to put that right. The 'big idea' behind this book is the concept of crossing the *Data Delta,* which is the gap between the data you have, and the information you need to help you make better decisions.

Bill Clinton famously ran his first US Presidential campaign in 1992 with the message, *'It's the economy, stupid'*, written on every wall in every meeting room that any member of his extensive campaign team might use. He believed the delivery of significant improvements to the US economy was the dominant concern of voters.

In the same spirit, this book embraces our mantra: *'It's the data, stupid'*. It is now, it always was, and it always will be. The authors of this book work for the Entity Group, the leading independent Enterprise Data and Analytics consultancy[1]. The Entity Group was formed, and more significantly, *named*[2] back in 1989. We knew it was all about the data then, and it has been ever since. The only real difference between now and then is the sheer quantity of data in the world today.

We want to demonstrate the use of the Entity Method to cross the *Data Delta*[3], and to enable you to turn your data into useful information; information from which you can derive knowledge and take action to transform your organisation.

---

[1] Naturally, we'll try to keep the self-promotion light, but once you've read this book, we hope you'll want to visit our site www.EntityGroup.com.

[2] Our name 'Entity' has a particular meaning in the context of data. Describing this can become somewhat self-referential. An entity is a thing about which there is information, and a data entity represents a proxy for that thing and provides the means for holding the information about the thing itself. An intriguing aspect of this is that the data entity is also an entity in its own right. It's turtles all the way down!

[3] *Data Delta* is a trademark of the Entity Group.

The *Data Delta* is a concept, an attitude, an approach, a method, and a context. It applies whether your data is structured or unstructured, whether your organisation is large or small, and regardless of the type of organisation for which you work. It's an agile, pragmatic approach to driving digital value throughout any organisation.

The Entity Group articulated the concept of the *Data Delta* and devised a method to cross it after working with data, information and knowledge for over 25 years. Our role in leading strategic data projects for major organisations around the world brought our thinking into focus. We have worked with banks and financial institutions, governments and government departments (including national security), transportation, healthcare, utilities, pharmaceuticals, the entertainment business, FMCG[4], automotive, not-for-profits and many others. The first time we were asked to document our entire thinking in one place was for the Emirate of Abu Dhabi. The Entity Group helped them produce the world's first comprehensive Data Management strategy at a pan-governmental level[5].

If the ideas of *Digital Disruption*[6] point clearly to the role of digital technology in revolutionising organisations as data changes their traditional value proposition, then our *Data Delta* model provides the blueprint that will enable you to unlock the potential of *your* digital data.

How can organisations survive the threat of digital disruption? Or an even better question, how can organisations exploit the phenomenal opportunity the digital age represents?

Data is the key link in a chain of components that define the helix at the heart of every organisation; it is a continuous spiral of events repeating over the passage of time.

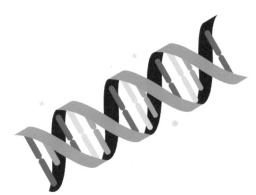

[4] Fast Moving Consumer Goods – eg dairy, shampoo, fish … products which move quickly off the shelves of shops.

[5] We were engaged as primary authors of the Data Management Strategy for ADSIC, the Abu Dhabi Systems and Information Centre, the central IT arm of the Abu Dhabi Government. One of the major outputs, the Data Management Standards, is published and available for all to see, thanks to the generosity and leadership of the Abu Dhabi Government: https://adsic.abudhabi.ae/adsic/faces/en/home/ publications.

[6] Clayton Christensen has led aspects of organisational thinking for nearly 20 years since his book, *The Innovator's Dilemma*, set out the concepts of *Digital Innovation*. His central argument rests on his observations that businesses were focusing too much on meeting the needs of today's customers, and not understanding the potential impact of technology on their core business proposition.
From *Innovation* bred *Disruption*. The demise of Kodak, despite inventing digital picture technology, and the rise of Apple's iPods, iPads and iPhones, at the expense of the traditional music industry, are often heralded as classic examples of this analysis.

Data originates from an action, perhaps a customer sale, or a citizen requesting a government service. That data can be turned into valuable information eg this is a repeat order for customer 12345. In turn, that information builds a repository comprising institutional knowledge eg that order is an example of customers over 40 responding better to the latest advertising campaign.

A core tenet of the Data Delta concept is that data is an asset.

And from that knowledge, an organisation can take further action; they could create a targeted campaign to reach out to the under-40 customers. That leads to more customer sales, more data, more information, more knowledge, more action. The cycle repeats.

Action ultimately drives more action, in a 'virtuous helix' of linked events with data as the ultimate building block. Data originates from actions and drives new actions. Action to data to information to knowledge to action. Repeats and repeats.

But every chain is only as strong as its weakest link. In this chain, the last 50 years of IT failures scream out that the weakest link is how data is turned into information. That is where the chain fails, and that is why Enterprise IT isn't working for you. No clever piece of software ensures you have the right amount of data of the appropriate quality, in the right place, at the right time, to help you derive the information you need.

Almost everywhere we look, we see a gap in the helix between data and information. This is a gap we have named the *Data Delta*. It's a break in the helix that your organisation needs to fix if it is going to survive and thrive.

The Entity Method is designed to help you cross the *Data Delta,* and fixes this weakest link in the chain. Examples of how the link can be broken include poorly defined data, data in silos, duplicate data, poor quality data, out-of-date data, insufficient data, even too much data. Our method rests on an enterprise-level approach involving people, processes and technology, implemented in an agile and pragmatic way. Only by crossing the *Data Delta* can you ensure data flows smoothly along your organisational helix, enabling you to take the right actions at the right time.

A core tenet of the *Data Delta* concept is that *data is an asset,* just like tables, chairs, cars, plant, buildings, employees and cash are assets. Organisations are usually quite effective at managing their physical assets. Most, for example, have roughly the right number of chairs, and the right number of cars, or computers.

It is someone's job to make decisions and conceive policy on the quality of each group of assets; they have established that some assets are critical and require substantial investment, whereas others are merely functional and less expensive. It's unlikely you suffer from physical asset thefts since your building is suitably secure. Someone in your organisation knows how long each type of asset will last, and hopefully has instituted a suitable cost-effective refurbishment, retirement and replacement policy.

Can the same be said of your data? Do you have the right amount? Too little or too much? Do you know the differing types of data; which data is more valuable and needs to be particularly well cared for? Is your data of the right quality? Do you know where your data originates? How it flows through your organisation? Who changed it? Who owns various components? Do you even know how to assess the quality of your data?

Let's be very precise in our language here. We are not using an *analogy* as to how data should be treated. It's much deeper than that. We are *not* saying data is *like* an asset. We are saying *data is an asset.*

The 'data is an asset' concept is so important to us, our aim is to convince you of its merit through dozens of examples and illustrations. Sometimes we use facts and logic; other times, analogies. We want to convince you, because ultimately, we want to convince everyone.

Let's try an analogy. Water is another useful asset to consider. Water in its entirety is an asset of immense value; without it, there would be no life on this planet.

But what value is placed on one cup of water? What is a fair price? How much would you pay for an Evian in a five-star New York hotel? How much would you pay if you were stranded in the desert with nothing to drink? What is a glass of tap water worth to you, right now?

The answer is clearly: 'It depends'. Just because something is difficult to value in small units doesn't mean, in aggregate, it isn't extremely valuable. The same is true with your data. The value to you of getting the data of one customer completely correct might not be much, but the data accuracy of *all* your customers together *is* worth a huge amount to you.

Data, like water, is a very valuable asset.

We believe that many of you don't treat your data like a *very valuable asset* today. If that's true for you, it needs to change. The concepts in this book – the core foundations of the *Data Delta* model – provide the tools and techniques to help you get from where you are now, across the gap to where your organisation needs to be. Understanding the *Data Delta* model helps turn this concept into measurable business value within your organisation.

This isn't about selling the latest product. It's not about a magic gizmo that suddenly makes those reports all add up to the same total across your organisation. It's about obtaining a deeper understanding of the gap between the data you have, and the information you need, so that something can be done about it. It's all about *actions* and the order in which you take them.

Our message is simple and it's not technical. It isn't about hardware. It has nothing to do with routers, servers, columnar databases, Spark, Hive, Pig, Storm, wires or cables. And it isn't about mobile, Cloud or even enterprise applications such as ERP, CRM or ECM or any other three-letter acronym[7] for the software at the heart of your business. *It's the data, stupid.*

It's about ownership of data, and planning a journey to improve your data so that it meets your evolving organisational needs. Your organisation's digital transformation is happening; like it or not. If you are not planning it, it is happening to you, and you and your organisation will be a victim of someone else's success. You need to take action to manage the digital transformation that's right in front of you.

Management theory of the 20th century focused on the realisation that *people* were an organisation's most important asset – and how best to manage the consequences of that reality. We at the Entity Group believe the 21st century is the era when *data* will be recognised as every organisation's most strategic asset. Throughout this book, we explain how data is turned into information, and from that information, knowledge is managed and appropriate actions are enabled. Digital transformation is a reality for all in the 21st century. Quite simply, it's sink or swim.

This book is written as a guide for everyone who recognises an urgent need to make accurate and deliberate decisions in support of organisational growth. Success requires a level of trusted digital agility to understand quickly and correctly the 'how and why' around key decisions. Effective management of data incrementally and effectively enables an organisation's transformation from one that treats data as a distraction and inconvenience, to a market leader that leverages data effectively to dominate their industry.

---

[7] Our editor overruled the authors and insisted we do not refer to three-letter acronyms as TLAs. At least, not in this first section, when we are trying to establish our serious credentials.

You are not all starting your journey at the same point. Every organisation has evolved a unique Data Management culture over the years. Each has its own digital landscape, created, most often, as a by-product of numerous business and IT initiatives and sometimes long-forgotten projects. An understanding of this individual landscape is crucial to the management of data and crossing the *Data Delta*.

Armed with that understanding, you can start to create and define projects that add very specific value to *your* organisation. Quickly, these small incremental improvements start to change and re-engineer the digital landscape, not by accident, but by design. The Entity Method is Data Management *by design*.

Dangerous and costly pitfalls are prevalent. Many have tried and failed. This book establishes effective Data Management techniques, and provides a proven approach and method for successfully crossing the unique *Data Delta* within your organisation. The Entity Method works for all.

In terms of structure, this book is written to be read cover-to-cover, but we realise some people will want to dive in and out. Here's a guide as to how it is organised.

Section 2 Customer Case Studies describes a series of examples from major organisations around the world that highlight the importance of the *Data Delta* model and the challenges everyone is facing. The message is clear: you are not alone.

Section 3 Crossing the Data Delta provides an overview of how organisations can move forward based on real-world experience of delivering success.

Section 4 Elements of the Data Delta Model provides a more in-depth introduction to each of the domains of the Data Management landscape and, crucially, the inter-relationship and dependencies between these domains. (There is a lot of useful information here that you are likely to keep referring back to after your initial read.)

Section 5 The Future looks at emerging trends, and how the context of the *Data Delta* is likely to change over the next few years, particularly as digital data increasingly shapes the world. Organisations will thrive, survive or fail by the transformational decisions they take.

Section 6 Putting it together reviews strategies for going forward, and provides information to help you choose the right path for your organisation.

The future is digital. Today is digital. All organisations must act now and continue to act through each future digital transformation wave. Reflect on how your experience of business life has changed over the last twenty years through the influence of digital technology. Do you even remember how you organised your personal life before the advent of social media, web calendars and smart phones? In reality, 'You ain't seen nothing yet'[8]. We are at the first stages of the digital revolution that will change our world as fundamentally as the technological advances that started the Industrial Revolution centuries ago.

This book helps you use the Entity Method to start crossing the *Data Delta* now, so that your organisation can take the right actions in the future. We hope you enjoy reading this book, but much more importantly, we hope you put these concepts into action. Let's get started.

---

[8] An optimistic perspective espoused by the philosophers Bachman and Turner in their seminal eponymous work.

2

Customer Case Studies

Houston,
we have
a problem

Let's start as we mean to go on.

Despite the quote on the poster that jogs everyone's memory, no one on Apollo 13 said, 'Houston, we have a problem'. As with many great movie quotes, this one is slightly inaccurate. Bogart, for example, didn't say, 'Play it again, Sam', and no one ever said, 'Beam me up, Scotty'. Gordon Gekko didn't quite say, 'Greed is Good'[9].

The dramatic pronouncement spoken by the real crew of Apollo 13, but changed for the movie, was 'Houston, we've *had* a problem'.

These little details are important. Getting the details that matter *right* is something we will come back to. Repeatedly.

The line, 'Houston, we've had a problem …' is, however, frequently spoken by members of the Entity Group consulting team about a week into each new project. Everywhere we work, we see examples of where there is a gap between the data an organisation has, and the information the organisation needs. The first action within the Entity Method is to help identify and understand this gap in your own organisation, so that you can do something about it.

Here are a handful of case studies from different types of organisations[10] we have worked with around the world. How many of them have elements of the *exact* same challenges that you are facing? These examples are important. Not only because there are lessons to learn from so many different sectors, but also to provide an important insight as to how we at the Entity Group came to devise the concept of the *Data Delta*, and very specifically, how to cross it. It didn't happen overnight, and it didn't happen as

---

[9] That famous speech went: 'The point is, ladies and gentleman, that greed -- for lack of a better word -- is good. Greed is right. Greed works.'

[10] The anecdotes we use to illustrate our points are an integral part of our story – without them, this book would end up as just another turgid theoretical tome wasting space on your Kindle or bookshelf. *Everyone* involved should be viewed extremely positively, whether we name-check them or not. Firstly, they realised they had a problem, and secondly, they decided to do something about it. Those are the first two difficult steps on any organisation's journey to cross the *Data Delta*. All credit to them, and to you too if, having read this book, you decide to follow a similar path.

a result of a theoretical exercise. Everything we have learned comes from trying to help our customers solve real-world practical problems that existed within their *own* data.

This book is equally relevant to those working in government institutions, to those in private companies, and in not-for-profits. In day-to-day life, you use a language and vocabulary that is very specific to your organisation. However, for reasons that will become clear, we ask you not to skip examples from areas outside your own organisations. We promise you will recognise very familiar problems – and, more importantly, *solutions* to your own queries – wherever you look.

2.1 A spider's web of Management Information

The transport industry is ripe for digital disruption. Business practices and processes that were devised a generation ago are still pervasive today. As an example, every year, more people take more flights to more destinations, while airlines find it increasingly challenging to make a profit. Many 'frequent flyer' business passengers see flying as a chore with few upsides. Loyalty points, though they may help defray the costs of the annual family holiday, are a meagre recompense for all those hours spent hanging around airports.

One of Entity's clients, one of the world's leading airports, conducted an investigation into the purchasing habits of the Business and First Class passengers passing through its departure gates. They discovered very few of these passengers actually bought anything from its extensive Duty Free outlets. Equally, can you remember the last time you purchased anything from that in-seat pocket insert while flying? Those department stores, tired brochures and trolley-sales are largely a sad reminder of 1950s retail.

Now take a step back and instead, consider the opportunity. All airline passengers have some level of disposable income. By law, those same passengers must also provide accurate information to verify their identity. Passengers naturally distinguish and segregate themselves by way of income – let's face it, there are no poor First Class passengers! Airports and airlines are able to command a captive audience of high-value potential customers for lengthy amounts of time.

Think about a Business Class passenger taking advantage of the complimentary chauffeur service when travelling to the airport. This passenger probably isn't inclined to fight their way through a department store shopping experience. They're headed straight to the peace and tranquillity of the Business Class lounge, for work, relaxation, or possibly both. How about offering a 'personal shopper' experience in their lounge, available as an app on their mobile device, to allow them to browse a wide range of goods – which will be wrapped for them and placed in the boot of their chauffeur-driven limo on their *return* journey? Or better yet, the goods are shipped directly to their home. No hassle, and no carrying involved. Perhaps the shopping selection is personalised based on Facebook or other social media information; a friend's birthday in a few weeks, a child who has just passed an exam, or a planned skiing holiday. Maybe it's as simple as if they ordered a gin and tonic in the lounge, they are subsequently offered a selection of high quality spirits.

It isn't hard to visualise an exciting digital entertainment and leisure experience that starts at the moment that tickets are purchased. Operators could charge a nominal fee on top of the ticket price to enable passengers to download new blockbuster movies, games and magazines onto their personal device, that become available as soon as they reach the Lounge. Personal notifications let travellers know the status of their flight, and when to leave their Lounge for boarding. The concierge network is there to answer questions and helps these privileged ticket-holders further customise their trip with services that span well beyond the mere flight aspect of their travels.

It's easy to figure out – *if you have great data*. The more you know about your passengers, the better the experience you can offer.

Always ask 'Why?'

When this world-leading transport agency engaged Entity Group to help them evolve their unique digital landscape to support completely new interactions and experiences they wanted to have with their customers, the project started with a basic question. 'Will moving from a traditional Business Intelligence (BI) tool to an analytics tool solve our reporting challenges?' Every month, different departments each came up with conflicting, and completely irreconcilable, figures. Surely there must be a quick fix?

We started with a basic analysis of their key monthly reporting pack, and demonstrated a resounding 'No' to the question stated above. Tools and technology frequently *aren't* the problem. BI and Analytics/Visualisation projects simply fail at shockingly high rates. A leading IT industry analyst estimated the failure rate of BI projects as high as 70%-80%[11]. Why? It's the data. Narrowly-focused initiatives targeting a specific technology or product keep the enterprise software market in business, but rarely deliver the *desired business outcomes*.

The following, highly anonymised, diagram illustrates the natural flow of data for this client's Monthly Management Board Report business process. As an early step, we asked members of their IT department and members of various lines-of-business about their role in producing this Report. Through each conversation, we documented what we learned using a simple map.

---

[11] If this seems incredible, try Googling *BI project failure rate*.

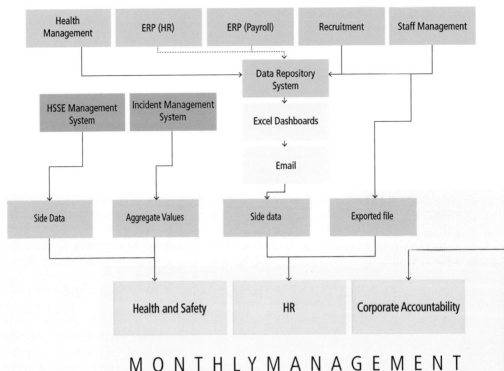

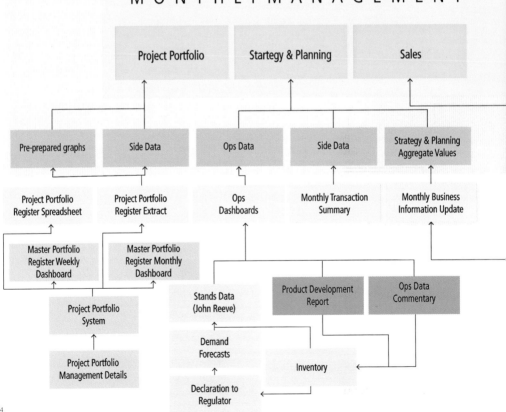

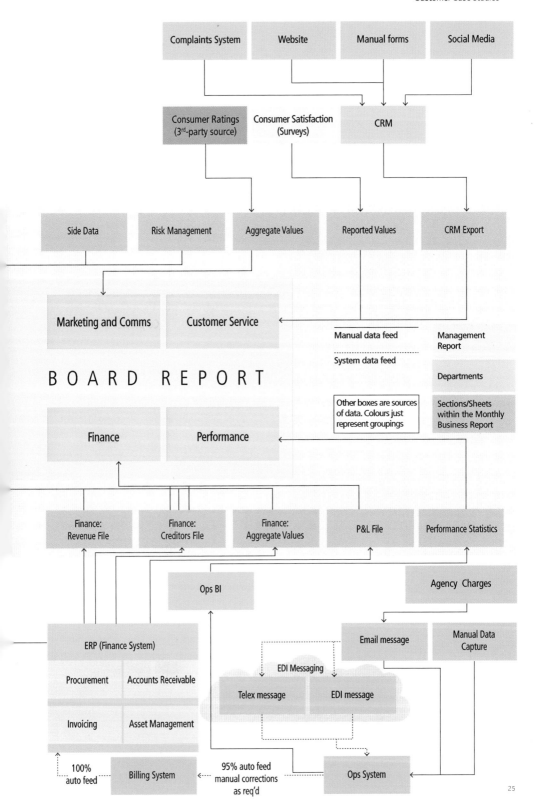

The box in the centre represents the Management Report (the focus for the intended BI replacement). Everything around the outside represents sources of data and contributors to the report. Each *dashed* line in the diagram represents a well-governed automated process (there are eight of these), whereas every *solid* line denotes a *manual* process.

There are over 60 ungoverned manual processes here. This is no surprise. This generic diagram represents what we find in most organisations. Neither traditional BI nor Big Data analytics solves data problems in real-world scenarios like this.

A 'spider's web' of manual intervention frequently 'supports' – if support is the right word – the key reporting activities for most organisations. When data is manipulated in so many different ways on a regular basis, no new BI or Analytics/Visualisation tool *alone* yields better quality information.

Later, we will address specific techniques to address this challenge. Sadly, it's not simply a case of changing 60 solid lines into dashed lines on a diagram! The *Data Delta* model for crossing your own *Data Delta* provides a series of clear principles to help prioritise the steps of your journey.

Always ask 'Why?' Why does an organisation need this level of manual intervention in its data collection processes? What creates this reality? How and why did it evolve over time? You will find many contributing factors. The resounding answer stems from noble desires to align and correct imperfect data to the best of one's ability. It's often politically beneficial to enhance certain data 'views' in the process.

Typical issues that create the need for manual interventions include:

- Finance and Sales have different interpretations of what comprises the sales figures for last month. What exactly is a 'sale' and what exactly was 'last month'?

- In government, perhaps you ask similar questions about taxes on income. What's the definition of income? What's the definition of employment? What's the definition of employment location?

- How many residents are there in your borough? Who exactly do you count, and when?

- How many customers do you have?

- What exactly is the definition of a customer? Or a resident? Or a supplier?

The consequences of struggling to define basic terms like 'customers', 'citizens' or 'patients' can be enormous. This can lead to significant wasted effort and, worse, can impact financial reporting, or drive a wedge through senior management relationships.

In terms of the diagram above, it's obvious the spider's web situation is unsustainable. This is never the best way to assemble a Data Warehouse[12]. Adding a different BI or Analytics tool in the middle won't improve this. If anything, it's likely to makes it easier to propagate pretty, but incorrect information.

From a Data Management perspective, this example covers many of the typical data issues we see.

Highlights to start thinking about include:

Who 'owns' this problem? Whose job is it to find a resolution?

Who owns the data involved? What does data ownership mean in practice?

How should the organisation establish a common 'dictionary' of key terms?

What level of data accuracy is required to answer the various information needs of the organisation? Does a duplicate person record mean you might make a life-threatening medical decision by mistake, or simply mean you mail two catalogues to the same household?

How should data be integrated? Where? By whom? Who decides?

How should differing types of data be classified, managed and measured?

What is the organisation really trying to achieve? How should success be measured?

In learning to cross your *Data Delta*, you need to work out the right answers to these questions – and many more – for *your* organisation. Think hard about priorities. Choosing what *not* to do is equally important to prioritising what you *will* do. Successful organisations force themselves to rapidly deliver tangible business benefits through frequent iteration.

Introducing concepts of the *Data Delta* model to your organisation does not require an army of consultants to descend upon you for a multi-year strategy study. A smart application of *Data Delta* principles will enable you to deliver incremental and measurable business benefit within a manageable timeline.

---

[12] Data Warehouses (DW or EDW for Enterprise Data Warehouse) are central repositories of integrated data from one or more differing sources. They store current and historical data, and are used for creating analytical reports for knowledge workers throughout an organisation.

2.2 Who am I?

The phrase, '360-degree view', (of a citizen or customer) is in grave danger of becoming a cliché, before the vast majority of organisations have got anywhere close to achieving it. It's an idea closely bound to many Data Management concepts.

The benefit of a 360-degree view[13] is clear. It's simply a way of pulling together everything you know about each person in one place. It's about breaking down all those different silos of information – separate buckets of data – that when looked at *together*, might tell a very different story about someone. Finance may assume that a customer is a late payer, but perhaps other systems make it clear you've messed up their last three deliveries. Or maybe a child has started to do badly at her local state school, but another silo knows her parent has moved six times in the last year. Is this a warning flag that should be reviewed in greater detail? Does someone need help?

If you want to obtain a *comprehensive* perspective, the first issue you might need to address is how to uniquely identify customers or citizens. Perhaps some form of ID scheme might help?

In the UK, a lively public debate over plans to introduce National ID cards has swayed back and forth for many years. Ideas for different schemes have come and gone, as the debate between cost and benefit, and between personal freedoms and governmental needs, has ebbed and flowed.

This is a little odd when you think about it, because the UK already has a national identity scheme in place. It has actually been operational for over 60 years.

The UK's national identity scheme works using the National Insurance (NI) number system, which was introduced back in 1948. Everyone born and resident in the UK receives their NI number before their 16th birthday. Or, if they are non-citizens or residents, they get their number when they receive permission to work. This number uniquely identifies each and every person. So that's that problem solved then … or maybe not.

The idea that the scheme works to identify people beyond its very limited, and specific usages would, to a UK citizen, be quite risible. If you were stopped by a police officer for a motoring offence, you'd be asked for your name, date of birth and address. You'd also

---

[13] The term 360-degree view – meaning all the information relating to a customer or citizen across all your silos – has a great deal of currency, although many people now argue it is a flawed concept. The term isn't particularly for us to challenge. We are fully aware that sometimes people are really looking for a 180-degree view, or at least a partial 360-degree view, and we will review some of the relevant subtleties in *Section 4.4 Master Data Management.*

be asked to produce your driving licence, but if you don't have that with you you'd simply be asked to take it to your nearest police station within a week. Never, as far as we know, has that conversation between a police officer and an errant motorist contained the question: 'Do you happen to know your unique National Insurance number?'

Most organisations have profound problems accurately identifying the people they deal with.

The NI system isn't used in this way. As a number without any linking information, even of age or gender, let alone more modern biometrics, it would clearly be wide open to abuse as the *core* of an ID scheme.

The reason why the UK's current 'ID scheme' is ineffective in allowing business and governments to accurately identify citizens and customers is perhaps because the scheme is simply too old; it pre-dated modern technology. The word 'biometrics' wasn't even in common parlance in 1948[14]. So let's look at a more modern scheme, one only a few years old, that is generally regarded as one of the best in the world. Here are two critical pieces of ID from the UAE; the graphic shows a UAE national identity card on the left, and a Dubai driving license on the right.

Name
Peter Julian Smith

Nationality
United Kingdom

Name
Peter Julian Smith

Nationality
Great Britain

---

[14] The term was first used we believe in a letter from William Whewell of Trinity College, Dublin in 1831, predating by over 40 years the more common first attribution to Moreau Morris in 1875. However, the word took another 100 years to enter mainstream consciousness, although elements of this topic, such as fingerprinting, were widely understood. Sherlock Holmes, for example, first discussed fingerprints in *The Sign of Four* as early as 1890.

Just as with that Apollo 13 quote, it's all in the details. If you look at the information above, you will notice that the driving licence has an incorrect spelling of surname, and a different – and in fact, incorrect – statement of nationality.

Both these pieces of ID are widely accepted in ordinary usage, such as checking in to a hotel. So when any hotel produces statistics of the number of unique visitors, the errors in the Dubai driving licence data are clearly going to give rise to anomalies. Of course, if it were just this one person with a record in error, this would hardly be an issue. And that's the problem.

No one in management cares about the data on just one record. It's just a little detail and almost everyone has more important things to do than sort out one record.

But look at this example again. If the most common surname in the western world is misspelt, how many others do you think might be *correctly* spelled[15]? And that issue with nationality? That's likely to affect every UK citizen in the country. In terms of the impact of this, one example would be to ask how accurate are statistics going to be that classify hotel stays by nationality, if there isn't a consistent view of nationality?

It is clear that even having a modern, well-organised compulsory national ID scheme is no 'silver bullet' to the problems of identifying customers and citizens accurately. There will always be exceptions and anomalies within individual records, and indeed groups of records.

Most organisations have profound problems accurately identifying the people they deal with, be they citizens or residents for governments, or customers for businesses. It is very common within an organisation to find a multitude of different *kinds* of lists of people in various departments. However, *none* of these lists is ever quite the same, and the owner of each one will carefully explain to you why their list is correct, while the others are not.

Finally, the focus on the above was about people and customers, but there is an even more complex set of issues around *suppliers* for some organisations. Most organisations don't value their supplier information nearly as seriously as their customer information. There is less profit for most in 'knowing your suppliers' than 'knowing your customers'.

---

[15] There are also language issues at play here. The Arabic version of the surname is spelt correctly – the English spelling is wrong. In an Arabic country, the system of record is naturally represented in Arabic, and English language spellings take second priority. The dialogue and record keeping in each hotel, however, will most often take place in English.

However, in certain industries
– particularly construction and
manufacturing – supply chain
management can be at the heart of
the business operation. In a complex
construction programme, it's not just
the need to manage the subcontractors
and vendors you deal with directly
(eg have they all got a current Health
and Safety certificate?). You need to
manage *their* suppliers too, right down
the supply chain. With the explosion
of joint venture companies and
complex multinational corporations,

The Data Delta model
helps an organisation
define context and
priorities so that the
correct relationship
between the detail
and the strategic
views can emerge.

it becomes critical to keep track of who exactly is supplying your goods and services to
your organisation. Everything we said above about customers still holds, with the added
dimension of the 'chain' of supplying organisations.Managing the data of customers,
citizens and suppliers is one of the major challenges facing businesses today. Data
held against each customer is highly likely to drive key BI and Analytics/Visualisation
reports; sales region, age, nationality, etc. This intelligence generates knowledge to your
organisation so you can decide what actions need to be taken. It's clear that if you can't
bridge the *Data Delta* from your data to the information you need, then there is no
guarantee that *those* actions are going to be the right ones.

Applying the principles of the *Data Delta* model will enable you to define a *context*
which will help you answer key questions. Consider how you and your organisation
might respond to these two statements:

- The data on a particular customer record is incorrect, and needs
  to be fixed

- The data on customer records isn't good enough to meet our
  sales and marketing needs

The first statement seems to be about almost inconsequential detail. The second scenario
is clearly a strategic concern that needs to be addressed with urgent intervention by
the senior executive. However, a moment's reflection will reveal that these are simply
two sides of the same coin. The first scenario is simply a practical manifestation of the
second. The *Data Delta* model supported by the Entity Method helps an organisation
define context and priorities so that the correct relationship between the detail and the
strategic views can emerge. Only then can an organisation choose the right course of
action to meets its goals.

2.3 Who are my customers?

The Chairman of one of the world's leading multinationals tried to give clear direction at a board meeting.

> *'I want our company to have great relationships with all our customers, particularly with the biggest ones. Everyone sitting at this board table should be spending a significant amount of their time developing key relationships with our most important customers. Let's say, at this table, we should be dealing with our top ten customers.'*

He then asked the key question:

> *'Who will tell me exactly who they are? I want some facts.'*

Silence ensued, until someone in the room was smart enough to pick up the phone and ask Entity how they might go about answering that question.

It was an exceptionally difficult question to answer accurately. This particular multinational traded with other multinationals in over one hundred countries around the world. Many of their customers belonged to complex groups, which were trading under different names in different regions. Sometimes, subsidiaries were fully owned, sometimes they were joint ventures, and sometimes the *other* partner in the joint venture was also a customer in its own right. These relationships weren't fixed, as companies continuously merged and separated over time.

Categorise your information so that you can resolve the important terms first and start using them to derive business benefit as early as possible.

And that's before some of the basic definitions involved were being considered. It seemed almost *everyone* in the organisation was happier using the word 'account' instead of 'customer', which is fine – you might think – except, we were able to identify *eighteen* separate definitions and usages of the word 'account'. These were all similar, all had merit, but they were different enough that they would result in a different answer to the Chairman's question: 'Who are our largest accounts?'

This particular organisation took a radical step. It simply stopped using the word 'account'. It banned the word from all documents and discussions, emails, policy guides, and even management meetings. It had become so poorly defined that there wasn't a chance it could be restored to a consistent usage across the organisation. This was the right step for this particular organisation; the equivalent action may or may not be right for you. What this story really brings home though, is how basic data challenges strike at the very heart of the effectiveness of one of the world's largest and most successful multinationals. If your top table doesn't know who your biggest customers are, you undeniably have real problems!

'Who will tell me exactly *who* our customers are?' is a classic Data Management question. If we expand the definition of customers to include citizens and residents so that we can refer to all types of organisation, this represents the most common question we receive. To answer it, an organisation requires an effective, practical Data Management capability that is integrated within its organisational strategy and *business governance* processes. One of the first topics that this area will need to address concerns 'modelling', where the business language of your organisation – such as 'What is a customer?' – is effectively defined. The positive news is that you don't need to do this for every term in your business at once. The Entity Method helps categorise your information so that you can prioritise and resolve the important terms first, and then start using them to derive business benefit as early as possible.

2.4 How much did we spend?

Sometimes links and causation are blindingly obvious. If your Cost Management and Finance departments have a different definition of the term 'month', they will arrive at different totals for costs by month. Sometimes links are more obscure.

Here's one: how can the *Data Delta* model possibly impact what is going on inside a refugee camp?

One of the world's most effective NGOs[16] works in over 120 countries on every continent. A typical project for this particular NGO in this era[17] might be running a refugee camp on the Syrian borders. The importance of such camps cannot be underestimated; they help keep ordinary Syrian people, the victims of religious and political extremism, alive. They also slow down the exodus of refugees embarking upon fraught journeys, through dangerous seas, across international borders.

Managing a refugee camp of, say, 25,000 people requires an exceptional range of skills. You might think it's comparable to providing local government services to a town of 25,000 people[18], but it's far more complex than that. You have to factor in that there is

---

[16] Non-Governmental Organisation (NGO) is a more precise term for 'charity' within the voluntary sector. 'Charity' is, in fact, simply a tax designation, and many organisations which wouldn't conform to the public perception of 'charity' (such as Eton College), are legally entitled to the special tax treatment afforded to charities. NGO is a more precise term, and it refers to the likes of Oxfam, Médecins Sans Frontières, Save the Children etc.

[17] At the time of writing (2016).

[18] If you are in the UK, that might be Skegness. In the USA, maybe Mason City, Ohio. Or perhaps Mundargi in Karnataka in India. Small, but hardly inconsequential towns.

absolutely no infrastructure. None. There is no housing, no sewage system, no transport system, no warehouses, no hospitals, no schools, no shops, no police force …

It should naturally go without saying that the individuals who make this happen are by and large extraordinarily talented people; they're not just doctors and nurses, but also those people who know, for example, how to build effective sewage systems for 25,000 people in a few days; the people who know how to support children who've seen both their parents die; and people who know how to get fresh drinking water into the mouths of tens of thousands of people within 48 hours.

Then there is the money. All those services somehow need to be paid for. Very little in this world is free – certainly not the food, water and medicines needed in a refugee camp. Funding comes from lots of different places. You may have personally given a donation to this type of operation, and if you have, that's great. Your money will go where it's needed, and all you need to know is that the organisation has received it. But the UK Government will have provided some funding too and, quite rightly, expects the camp to account for its expenditure. And so indeed will the EU and the US Government. As taxpayers, we would be appalled if governments were unable to explain their spending in detail.

So the challenge faced by the camp management is to account for their expenditure, not only against the agreed budget, but in terms of UK Government grants (in Pounds Sterling), EU grants (in Euros) and US grants (in US Dollars), when, all the time, the actual expenditure might have been in Syrian Pounds, or could have been on goods purchased internationally in US Dollars, or refer to the salaries of expatriate staff paid in Pounds Sterling.

The stakes are high. If anyone makes a technical mistake in all these multi-currency transactions, there is a risk that the press might run a story about NGO financial mismanagement which could impact donations.

To address this situation, the NGO needed to think very deeply about its data. It needed to rigorously define a whole set of financial terms – budget, base currency, spending currency, reporting currency, grant, earmarked money, etc – as well as some clear financial policies. For example, refugee camps are often in countries suffering from hyper-inflation, so exchange rate treatment in these instances becomes a major concern.

All this attention to the minutiae of *technical* financial data seems a long way away from the practicalities of running a refugee camp effectively, but without a clear focus on its data the NGO will absolutely fail to meet its objectives. Major NGOs have gone out of business because they haven't paid enough attention to these details, despite the brilliance of their fieldwork[19].

In *Data Delta* speak, we seek to provide clarity about the principle of *Description*[20], which incorporates key ideas such as a business glossary, but also 'Metadata Management' (managing information about data, such as who owns it, who can amend it, etc) which together give us the idea of *lineage*.

If you're looking at a financial report – whether it's the spend on a refugee camp, the sales figures in Manchester, or the costs of the A&E[21] department in the hospital – you need to be able to trust the information so you can take the right actions.

Central to the idea of 'trust' is the concept of lineage. If you can say, categorically, how a piece of information is derived, then it is more likely you will be able to trust it.

The same challenges are likely to exist within your organisation. It's not just about people in terms of customers or citizens; it's about every type of data, and just as importantly, it's about the relationships *between them*.

The Entity Method places significant emphasis on categorising the business terminology of your organisation – significant concepts and words – so that their relative importance is clear. It then helps you to take steps to define the most important of these; to the extent that they add value to your organisation.

---

[19] The British NGO 'War on Want' was placed into administration in 1990, despite having significant funds in the bank, because of the challenges of grant management. The funds it had in its possession were strictly designated for specific projects so, despite their large cash balances, they could not legally pay their staff.

[20] *Section 3 Crossing the Data Delta* will introduce the six principles of the Entity Method. The principle of Description is one of the most important of these six.

[21] The UK uses the abbreviation *A&E* to represent the accident and emergency function of a hospital. Other countries might refer to this as the ER (Emergency Room) or EW (Emergency Ward).

2.5 Pole dancing

No book on Information Management could be complete without a section on pole dancing.

No, not that kind[22].

POLE is an acronym widely used in law enforcement circles and stands for Person, Object, Location and Event. Experience has identified these elements as the key Master and Reference Data items that need to be managed especially carefully by police and security organisations.

Why is this important to you if you don't work in this field (other than the obvious point that you are the beneficiary of effective police and security forces)?

Requirements in this sector have driven solution development, both from a software vendor perspective, and from a Data Management standpoint. For example, security organisations have vast Big Data requirements in terms of volumes, and they work in multiple languages. The data they are dealing with doesn't just include typical human-error mistakes. A percentage of it they have to assume has been deliberately falsified. A small number of people are working very hard to deceive these organisations, and the effective management of data is a key tool in that fight.

The successful introduction of effective Data Management has helped law enforcement both from an operational perspective (eg who exactly is this person, and what do I know about them?), and in terms of analysis (identification of the potential relationships between people).

The ultimate role of both police and security organisations relates to crime *prevention*. Detection of what has already happened is, of course, important but we would all much rather those crimes didn't occur in the first place.

Has effective Data Management led to the detection of crimes? Yes, without a doubt. Probably the most famous example rests with the forensic accounting team that built the case against Al Capone for tax evasion, in 1931. We cite that example to point out that the *principles* of good Data Governance are *not* new, and actually pre-date the digital age. Today, all major police forces around the world routinely manage huge volumes of POLE Master Data, using advanced software solutions to help detect crime.

[22] No book on Information Management could be complete without a section on pole dancing. No, not that kind. Not entirely that kind, at any rate. One of our consultants was engaged with one of the UK's major retail banks on a project that encrypted data for their London-based staff. The team had written an app to scramble cached data held on a mobile device once it had gone into sleep mode. Our team was concerned as to whether this approach was sufficiently robust, so we had a confidential discussion with the bank's security unit to review the planned use cases.

The Security section leader patiently explained that none of the data allowed to be stored on a mobile device was in the least bit confidential; certainly, no client or account data would be permitted. So we asked, 'Why do you want it encrypted? Who are you trying to stop reading your Health and Safety policy?' Apparently, the bank was irritated by the embarrassment of devices being returned to their rightful owners via taxi the 'morning after'. Night club staff would frequently find devices when cleaning the next morning, turn them on and see which bank they belonged to, then return them via a complimentary taxi. The bank had decided that they would rather that their staff had to report the loss of the devices as it might make them more mindful as to what they dropped on the floor.

Database sizes are nowadays sometimes measured in terms of billions of records, and are critical to many areas of crime detection.

Has Data Management *prevented* crime? Again, it has. Absolutely, and without a doubt. For obvious reasons, examples cannot be put into the public domain, but would we have had more terrorist outrages without successful Master Data Management solutions helping security forces to highlight the links between people of interest? Yes.

2.6 Banking on success

Readers who are not involved in Financial Services might feel inclined to skip over this section. Please don't. If you are in the EU, trade with the EU, or considering the implications of leaving the EU, there is useful material here. And if you want an industry which is being revolutionised by a series of digital transformations, you need to look no further. After all, when was the last time you went to your local bank branch? Or deposited a cheque?

The Financial Services sector has a pressing need for robust Data Management. Western banks, in particular, are typically long-established organisations that have been through many mergers and demergers; acquiring and divesting swathes of customers and products along the way (which implies swathes of customer and product data too).

As an illustration, Barclays Bank was founded in 1690, whereas by contrast the National Bank of Abu Dhabi (NBAD) was established as recently as 1968. With hundreds of years' worth of historical data, it seems fairly clear that the data challenges facing Barclays and other Western banks are going to be particularly demanding when compared with the 'almost' half-century accrued by NBAD.

It should come as no surprise that those behind the management of banking data, and Financial Services data more broadly, have been at the forefront of Data Management practice and theory for many years. There are many different drivers within this sector, such as regulatory compliance, risk management, revenue generation, operational efficiency, customer loyalty, customer service, etc.

Complying with the requirements of Basel III regulations (especially BCBS 239[23]), as well as the data protection requirements of the EU GDPR[24] legislation alone would represent major Data Management challenges for any bank. However, these substantial initiatives are just one part of the tidal wave of digital transformation facing the

---

[23] As the name suggests, BCBS 239 is aimed at supporting transparency in the banking sector! More seriously, the Basel regulation is aimed at making holistic improvements in the aggregated risk management capability of major banks. At the core of this is the idea of moving towards a 'single view of aggregated risk data'; a concept very close to the heart of effective Data Management.

[24] The EU General Data Protection Regulation (GDPR) is far-reaching legislation with Data Management implications for many organisations across all sectors, not just Financial Services. It requires EU companies – and non-EU companies *trading* with the EU – to manage their customer metadata. For example, they must be able to *prove* they can answer the question: 'Who has the right to see this information?' This type of question cannot be answered without crossing the *Data Delta*. The upper limit of fines for non-compliance, defined as the greater of €20 million or 4% of global annual turnover, indicate the importance of this legislation.

Financial Services sector, as technology changes the way banks and their customers do business.

Many of these drivers rest on a customer-centric use case, as opposed to the account-centric nature of banking operational systems. A classic example would be that of the '360-degree view' of customers providing a definitive statement of current products and liquidity, providing information to determine the right time to try to cross or up-sell additional products. Or perhaps in corporate banking, using one of the leading third-party hierarchy information providers to obtain a clear view of the bank's aggregate exposure at group and total level. This aggregate view needs to properly consider the implications of trading with complex multinationals and joint venture companies.

We have worked with banks in the UK, mainland Europe and the Middle East, and a common theme is the size and complexity of their challenges, coupled with the organisational characteristic of a drive for perfection. This means that, for a bank, the challenges of *how* and *where* to start are particularly complex. There is so much to be done, and a bank's default position is likely to be that they want to do it all.

Within the last few years, we've dealt with two banks in particular which were considering implementation programmes that had been devised by their IT functions, and were scheduled to last more than eight years. In both instances, the direct consequence was an almost *immediate disengagement* from the process by the Business functions of the bank. We'll provide some specific advice on how we believe these challenges should best be addressed in *Section 3 – Crossing the Data Delta*.

Finally, it is worth considering another aspect of Financial Services – the impact of credit rating systems on our personal finances, which covers everything from mortgages and loans to credit card limits.

Helaine Olen, a columnist for Slate, wrote[25]: '*We live in an age of quantification, of bits of data we believe can take previously unknowable facts about us and use them to both track and predict our behavior*'. She was writing in the context that three different US credit agencies provided materially different credit scores; not only because of differences in their algorithms that analysed data (which is to be expected), but because of the quality of the personal data each agency collected. Hardly anyone informs a credit scoring agency when they move – agencies deduce that event from publically available records. However, in today's complex world, where, for example, a growing number of parents find themselves paying the first mortgage on behalf of their children, just how accurate is that deduction process?

---

[25] Helaine Olen's entire article is worth reading. It is available here:
http://www.slate.com/articles/business/the_united_states_of_debt/2016/06/what_is_a_credit_score_and_why_is_everyone_so_obsessed_with_them.html

We will talk more about the importance of algorithms in *Section 5 The Future,* as there is no doubt that high-quality algorithms will become as important as high-quality data to successful organisations in the future. But the challenges of correctly identifying people and events are critical now to every organisation, and it is only by crossing the *Data Delta* that you can ensure you are gathering information of the accuracy and trust levels you need *today.*

2.7 Summary

These case study examples should *begin* to provide an insight into some key issues that are addressed by the *Data Delta* model. Who are your customers? What are your products and services? Where are you spending your money?

These questions have enormous implications to any organisation. If you can't agree on how many residents or customers or suppliers you have, if you can't agree on the definitions of these terms, and if you can't agree on your cost or revenue in any specific period, then you will have significant problems. As that multinational Board Chairman demanded to know in the example in *Section 2.3 Who are my Customers,* how could he possibly develop the right relationships with his most important customers if he didn't know who they were?

This might sound bad enough, but the reality is even worse. Such challenges would be concerning if the world were standing still and we were all trying to manage the status quo. But that game is over and, whether we like it or not, the era of digital transformations is upon us. It's not that Amazon and Google and Uber are here to stay. It's that cinemas and bookshops and taxi ranks *won't ever be what they once were.* Your organisation, and the way it delivers its products and services, could well be next.

It's not about the Bucket

There are lots of people intent in selling something to you that will make this problem go away. In truth, they are only selling solutions for a small part of it.

A useful analogy might be to consider how you go about washing a car by hand. You need a number of items to do this; water, soap, a brush and a bucket. A moment's reflection would suggest that there are genuine quality issues about three of these – the water, soap and brush. You need the right amount of the right sort, and if you don't have them, the quality of your wash will suffer.

But the bucket? Well, it's got to be roughly the right size of course, but in all honesty, that's about it. It's just where you hold the water, in roughly the same way as various IT storage devices are where the data is stored. The bucket has to be the right size for the amount of water you need, but that's it.

It isn't too much of a stretch on this analogy to point out that having more water than you need actually makes the task harder. It's about having the *right* amount of water, and it also needs to be of the *right* quality. No one is suggesting you wash your car using Evian mineral water just because we talk about water quality. For this particular job, the water needs to be of the right quantity, and also of the appropriate quality.

Just as with your car wash water: do you have enough data or too much? Is it of the right quality? Bucket sales people will always want to sell you a bigger, better, pricier bucket. But are you sure you need more water to wash the same-sized car?

You'll find we'll return to various water analogies several times throughout this book. We think there's a powerful comparison between many aspects of water and data. How do you value it, measure it, assess its quality, and decide if you have enough?

In concluding this review of what our customers are facing, it is clear that the pace of digital change will be relentless. The only way to face the waves of digital transformation that are inevitably crashing upon us all is by taking an holistic approach. The Entity Method uses people, processes and technology to enable you to cross the *Data Delta* by providing a firm foundation of Data Management. Only when operating from this foundation can your organisation turn its information into useful knowledge and manage its digital transformation.

3

Crossing the Data Delta

So the problem is clear. The gap between data and information is the weakest link within your organisational data chain. The fault line between the data you have and information you need has expanded and is now, in many organisations, a yawning chasm. With huge amounts of new data being generated within your organisation every day, that chasm is only going to get wider unless you do something about it.

We've already said that an understanding of the *Data Delta* would show how you can go about bridging this gap. We've said before that *Data Delta* is a *concept*, an *attitude*, a *method*, an *approach*, and a *context*.

The next five subsections of this book will put some meat on each of these ideas.

3.1 Data Delta - A Concept

You have a lot of data. You need information.

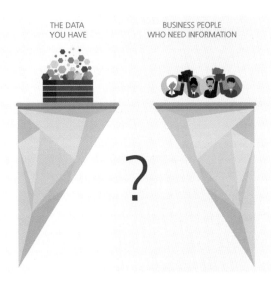

It's a common mistake to assume that by simply allowing the right people to look at your existing data – using the best available modern tools – they will be able to somehow perform a magical conjuring trick and work out the information you need.

If that's the approach you are planning to use, it's highly likely that *you will fail*.

We've already suggested that 70-80% of BI and Analytics/Visualisation projects fail to meet their objectives. And here's something else. Try Googling, 'Why do BI projects fail?', and you are unlikely to find a *single* hit for: 'We purchased the wrong BI tool'.

People – and not just BI /Analytics sales people – will argue with a frightening intensity that *this* BI tool is better than *that* one. Perhaps it is. Perhaps it isn't. The choice of BI tool alone is unlikely, however, to alter your chances of success in delivering valuable information to your decision makers.

What *will* make a massive difference is grasping the concept of the *Data Delta*.

In this context, we use the phrase *Data Delta* to represent the gap between data and information, represented here as a triangle, the symbol for the Greek capital letter δ delta[26].

THE DATA
YOU HAVE

BUSINESS PEOPLE
WHO NEED INFORMATION

DATA
DELTA

Data and *Information* are different things. Yes, information can be derived from data, but only when that data meets some specific criteria. For data to be useful, it needs to be:

Properly defined	We've already seen the challenges that arise when simple concepts such as 'month' or 'customer' are left to hang loosely in the air.
Complete	How do you ensure for example that a broadcast audience viewing total is complete, when there is so much variety nowadays in the way people view their chosen programmes?[27]
Sufficiently accurate	Which means we have to be able to *measure* the accuracy of the data, which implies a quantitative approach to quality management.
Meaningful	Which means we need to understand something about *context*.
Up to date	Or at least not 'out of date'.
Available	When it's needed, by those who need it, and in a suitable format.

---

[26] Just to be clear, we are using the word 'Delta' with two of its many meanings. Delta can mean 'gap' or 'difference', but is also the name of the fourth letter in the Greek alphabet, written in its capital form as Δ.

[27] There has, for example, been lots of discussion on the viewing audience of one particular award-winning BBC TV programme, *Top Gear*. At the time of writing, the BBC re-launched its award-winning motoring programme with a new team of presenters. There is much debate as to how many people are actually watching the new programme compared to the previous series. Getting an accurate total viewing figure, when there are so many different ways of watching the programme via the BBC's online services, is both particularly important *and* exceptionally difficult.

If your data doesn't meet those criteria, no matter who is undertaking the analysis, no matter what tools they are using, they aren't going to be able to produce the information that you need.

Suppose your Sales team currently calculates its monthly figures from the CRM[28] system. They know *these* figures are accurate, because they entered the deals and, as they form the basis for commission payments, a lot of care went into getting the numbers correct.

Your Finance department, however, uses the ledgers within the ERP[29] system to calculate its figures. They know *this* information is right, because it forms part of the audited record of the company. The financial ledgers within the ERP are indeed, legally, the system of record of your organisation.

Every month, the Sales and Finance teams produce their own reports because they need information on which to base business decisions, and every month, they will have a disagreement as to whose figures are correct, because the numbers never appear to agree. Giving each team a new BI tool will not change this. It will just mean they have prettier reports to argue about!

How do you go about meeting those criteria for useful data? It's not about trying to reconcile those Sales and Finance reports. Quite possibly, you may try to do that already, and know how time-consuming and self-defeating that exercise can be. What is required is a first principle analysis that removes the inconsistencies, so that everyone is using, for example, the same definition of the *reporting period*, the same definition of *territory*, and the same definition of *sale* and *revenue* etc. Ultimately, everyone is running their reports off the *same* data.

---

[28] Customer Resource Management. The wide ranging applications covering potentially all aspects of customer management from the sales process through to support interaction.

[29] Enterprise Resource Management. A large and complex application covering most aspects of production and sales processing eg covering manufacturing processes, warehouse management, goods distribution etc.

At a conceptual level, there are six 'Principles' that make up the Data Delta.

The six principles define that:

1   Data must be Governed and Owned

2   There must be an agreed Description of data

3   Data Quality must be defined, measured and managed

4   Principles of Access need to be established; the data lifecycle, storage, privacy and security

5   How data is Used and Shared needs to be agreed; how systems are integrated

6   Data which needs to be Controlled, and how and by whom, needs to be established, so that business applications can be successfully Implemented.

Bridging the *Data Delta* within your organisation isn't going to be a job that can be tackled in five minutes once you've read this book. Equally though, it doesn't have to be a five-year job. Most importantly of all, however long it takes in your organisation, there needs to be a plan so that you accrue incremental benefits along the way.

Without effective Data Governance... Organisations become constrained and frozen within the constraints of legacy systems, silos and outlook.

We have heard stories of executives shying away from Data Governance – and, therefore Data Management – out of a misplaced belief that it would somehow restrict their agility. We fundamentally disagree. An agile implementation of Data Management will *increase* the flexibility open to your organisation's management; it will provide *more* options and capabilities to solve business problems. Without effective Data Governance, the opposite occurs. Organisations become constrained and frozen within the constraints of legacy systems, silos and outlook.

Proper governance is the *only* way of turning data into valuable information. Having accurate, meaningful and relevant information leads to knowledge. And what is the value of knowledge? Thomas Jefferson[30] wrote in a letter to George Ticknor in 1817 of '*the important truths, that knolege [sic] is power, that knolege is safety, and that knolege is happiness*'. If you want power, safety and happiness, you need Data Management. The case is as simple as that.

To cross the *Data Delta*, the six principles of Data Management need to be understood in much more detail, and addressed with solutions that are right for your organisation. The principles are the same, whether you are a multinational FMCG, a government department or an NGO. However, the solutions for every organisation are different. Your own journey will be unique.

The key message is that crossing the *Data Delta* is the *only* way you are going to get the information you need to run your organisation effectively, and to gear up for the *Digital Age*. This entire book focuses on shortcuts, practical advice, and tips to get you there as quickly as possible. In our opinion, there *is* no other way. You mustn't shy away from it, but equally, anyone who is trying to sell you a magic 'black box' that will do all the work *for* you simply hasn't grasped the problems you are facing.

---

[30] Thomas Jefferson was, of course, the 3rd President of the United States, and the principal author of the US *Declaration of Independence*. Despite being a man of many original ideas, this isn't one of them! We are going to tease you now in that we'll reveal the true origin of this quote much later in this book, in section 4.15 Landscape Summary.

3.2 Data Delta - An attitude

'Never doubt that a small group of thoughtful, committed citizens can change the world; indeed, it's the only thing that ever has.'[31]

This maxim applies to governments of all political persuasions, from the most autocratic to the most democratic. It also applies to organisations. Every type of organisation.

To successfully cross the *Data Delta*, you are going to need to change attitudes within your organisation. That isn't an easy thing to do, but every revolution – indeed, every change – starts somewhere. The smallest group of thoughtful, committed citizens comprises just one person. This could, quite possibly, be you. Our advice though, is to get a few co-conspirators on board as quickly as possible.

Never doubt that a small group of thoughtful, committed citizens can change the world; indeed, it's the only thing that ever has.

The change in attitude will be achieved when your organisation accepts that *data is an asset*. Once that simple but powerful message is in place, the floodgates are open for a revolution. Everything we argue for in this book represents a series of logical extensions from that simple idea.

That *data is an asset* is an indisputable *truism*.

Consider two companies with the same turnover, the same-sized customer base, the same product portfolio, the same-sized branch network. One of them has superbly managed data, knows exactly which customers have which products, has taken 'data ownership' away from IT, and instead, the whole business manages data with a passion.

The other company has twenty enterprise systems and no Data Management strategy. As a result of multiple marketing mail-outs and misdirected orders, customer complaints occur every day. No one has any idea which customers have which products. It simply depends on which computer screen or report is being examined at the time.

If these two companies were for sale at the same price, which one would you buy? Well, you *could* buy the one with superb data, because the better-run company might be easier to integrate with your own. Or perversely, you could purchase the other one, because if they are doing *that* well with their appalling approach to data, they could do so much better, once you've sorted all that out.

---

[31] This quote is most often attributed to the American cultural anthropologist, Margaret Mead, and sometimes to Lenin. Neither attribution can be verified, and as you should know by now, these little details are important to us.

Either way, you made a rational choice of the value of the organisation, based solely on the quality of its data. And you can quantify that value. How much extra would you pay to buy the company of your choice?

Anything which impacts the value of an organisation – especially in terms of the hard cash you are prepared to pay for it – *must* be an asset.

Once it is truly accepted that data is an asset, a whole succession of beneficial questions can begin to flow: do we have enough of it or do we have too much? What's the cost of ownership? Is it of the right quality? Is it complete? Who is responsible for it? Does it support our strategic objectives?

For your specific organisation, the answer to these questions can only be framed in the context of looking at the much broader challenge: 'What *information* does your organisation *need?*'

This is a really interesting topic to consider. Firstly, *who* within your organisation can address it? There is perhaps a seemingly obvious answer to that question – IT – but that's definitely not correct. Not to disrespect IT people – they are, typically, a very smart collection of folk – but their role in relation to data needs to be seen as *custodians/enablers*. That isn't, of course, to deny them being part of our group of *'thoughtful, committed citizens'* plotting the revolution. Indeed, with their expertise in data it is quite likely this area will be a potential hotbed of early recruits to the cause. But this group of people cannot be responsible for the definition of your organisation's information needs.

'Information needs' can only be assessed by those people responsible for making the business decisions within your organisation. Without exception, these are 'Line of Business' responsibilities; the people in Marketing, Sales, Service Delivery, Production and, to some extent, corporate support functions such as Finance, HR and IT in relation to their specific roles as well as their group support responsibilities.

These 'Line of Business' functional areas will doubtless have competing, if not conflicting, requirements, which in most organisations can ultimately only be resolved by going upwards through the management hierarchy.

This helps identify the primary targets for changing attitudes – it's at the very top of your organisational tree. Only when that person, or group of people, are truly committed to the idea that *'data is an asset'* can your organisation change.

How do you get that key person or group to change? Well, all the arguments you will need can be found in this book, so you could always ask them to read a copy[32]! More seriously, you know the critical people involved, and their drivers and objectives. *You* are the best person to change your organisation. Read the rest of this book, and then get on with it.

3.3 Data Delta - A method

If *Crossing the Data Delta* ended at this point as a concept and an attitude, you could probably file this book safely alongside all those 'best practice' manuals that fill up the business book sections of libraries and *Amazon*. Of course, they are great, and yes, they champion the right way to do things at a theoretical level. The question, though, is how actually, practically, do you go about it? Where is the pragmatism?

We are going to give you lots of ideas on how to cross the *Data Delta* using the Entity Method. This approach was specifically designed, not as a general-purpose consultancy methodology, but as a framework for addressing the *Data Delta*. We believe it is the most comprehensive approach, offering a complete solution in this space.

The strategic problem definition is top-down, whereas the solution implementation is agile, with a strong 'bottom-up' emphasis.

The following model lies at the heart of the *Data Delta*. It explains in a single picture exactly what topics you need to address to help you get to the information you need, based on the data you have.

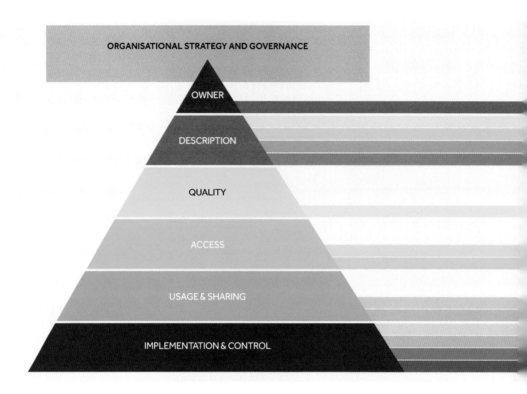

Firstly, you'll notice how the main triangle matches the shape of the gap in the previous diagrams we've used: it represents the gap between the data you have and the information that you need. That's the key point. If you do all the things in this triangle, you *will* cross the *Data Delta*. This list of topics is both 'necessary' and 'sufficient'. Moreover, let's again state that there is *no* other way of doing this. If anyone in your organisation even starts to mutter 'Hadoop'[33] at this point, get them to go back and read this book from the beginning.

Do you have to do *everything* inside the triangle? Over time, the answer to that question is that you probably do, but certainly *not* all at once. Precisely how much effort, resources and money you will spend in each area will vary greatly in accordance with your needs. You'll get some pointers on that in the coming sections.

With this in mind, it should be clear that the model provides a *top-down* definition of the *Data Delta* landscape. That's very important, and something we will come back to on several occasions, but there is one essential point to make clear at the outset. The Entity Method is NOT a 'waterfall' top-down methodology from an *implementation*

---

[33] Hadoop (named wondrously after a toy elephant) is an ingenious technology that allows large volumes of data to be carved up and distributed to lots of computers so they can all work on processing it at the same time. If you use the internet, there's every chance that you have made use of Hadoop, even if you were unaware of it. If your organisation is dealing with Big Data (and so many will be in the future if you aren't already doing so today), you will almost certainly need Hadoop, or one of the many technologies that have been inspired by it. However, it's just a technology layer. Go back to all those business problems we discussed at the outset. How many of those will Hadoop, on its own, solve? None. Hadoop actually sits inside our *Data Delta* triangle. Despite the marketing dollars being spent, and despite the fact that it is seriously clever and you may well need it, if 'Hadoop' is the entirety of the answer, you've asked the wrong question.

perspective. The *strategic problem definition* is top-down, whereas the *solution implementation* is agile, with a strong 'bottom-up' emphasis.

3.3.1 Data Management Principles

The *Data Delta* model comprises a series of 14 areas that we refer to within the Entity Method as Data Management *domains*. We will review each of these in turn in the next section, but for now you should notice they are grouped together within the six Data Management *'principles'*. We've already mentioned these, so let's expand on them now with a little more information.

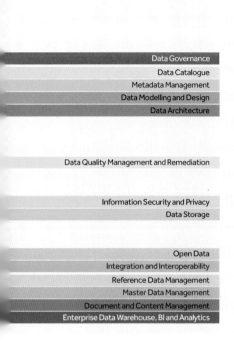

Data Governance
Data Catalogue
Metadata Management
Data Modelling and Design
Data Architecture

Data Quality Management and Remediation

Information Security and Privacy
Data Storage

Open Data
Integration and Interoperability
Reference Data Management
Master Data Management
Document and Content Management
Enterprise Data Warehouse, BI and Analytics

These six principles assist in the understanding of the overall Data Management landscape, and the chain of dependencies that exist between them in terms of hierarchy and sequencing.

Principle 1 – Ownership

You need to be very clear about *who owns* which pieces of data at the various levels within your organisation. Who in the management chain is accountable, and who is responsible for taking action? Most people in your organisation will be pretty good at doing things when they are clear what it is they have to do. Instead, it's all the material filed in the 'too difficult' tray that typically doesn't get addressed.

You will need a Data Governance Steering Group to declare categorically who owns accountabilities and responsibilities for your data, and *then* to provide the appropriate authority to resolve disputes as and when they arise. When you ask for clarity on who owns, say, the definitive 'revenue' figure or the 'cost' figure, there will be disputes. That's great. Have the disputes, and then sort them out. Once.

And after they are resolved, many of those distracting tensions will start to dissipate. It's also essential to write down what you agreed. There's nothing more frustrating than having to revisit a tough call you've already resolved once.

When we go into more detail in the next main section of this book, everything relating to this principle will be found in the Data Governance domain (*Section 4.1 Data Governance*).

Principle 2 – Description

There's a great deal of work to do to describe your data properly and usefully. Everything needs to be geared towards how to make data more valuable. Gaining clarity over what exactly you have and don't have is essential. Sometimes, the value of having such clarity is that it enables you to see more easily what you are missing. At other times, it can just be more of a question of clearing up confusion.

For example, let's suppose your Financial Year runs from January to December, and on April 1st your Sales team closes a 12-month rental contract netting $1,000[34] per month for a deal with an immediate start. They receive the entire payment in advance, and consider it to be a $12,000 sale. The problem is that the figures in your Financial system only show a *revenue* of $9,000[35]. We have experienced situations where the lack of clearly-defined and properly communicated terms has resulted, not only in an argument but, worse, the Sales team actively devoting time and resource to the upkeep of their own figures because they don't agree with those maintained by Finance.

That's a very important point. People and departments *will* undertake unnecessary work because they, like us, are genuinely passionate about wanting to 'get it right'. What *you* need to do as part of crossing the *Data Delta,* is to unlock that passion, and give people the right tools to do the right job. In that way, the total amount of work being undertaken inside your organisation stands a good chance of *decreasing*.

You need to describe data in a manner which is standardised and simplified. This will facilitate more effective sharing and will prevent unnecessary duplication. By reducing the number of copies of the same data, you move towards improving consistency as well as the quality of your data. But best of all, by describing data *properly*, you take a key step in turning it into useful information, allowing people to interpret it and use it as the basis for taking action when appropriate.

As we look towards the future, this topic will become even more important than it already is today. It's clear that the correct definition of terms will enable machines to develop the sort of 'semantic' understanding that underpins human thought and choice. Machines, however, will be able to do so using huge quantities of data, which is well beyond human capability.

Describing your data properly isn't just about getting your pen out and making a list. You need to think carefully about the *format* in which you want this information, so that it becomes as useful as possible to your organisation. For example, let's consider

---

[34] These quanta can relate to any currency you choose. We thought it might be too contentious to decide between Sterling or Euro as the default currency for the book, so we hedged with a Dollar sign instead.

[35] Using standard accrual-based accounting, revenue represents income (not cash) relating to each financial year. In this example, $9,000 would be showing this financial year calculated as $1,000 per month for the nine months from April to December inclusive, and $3,000 would appear in the accounts as revenue for the following financial year.

that you're describing the data of your customers or citizens. You might foresee that, although your organisation *today* describes gender using only the values 'M' and 'F', it would be worthwhile allowing additional values to be used in the future (already the case on Australian passports, which also allow for the value of 'X'). If you describe the data flexibly – and with the right tools – then making a change to the list of allowed values becomes an administrative change, as opposed to a whole raft of costly system changes.

Describing data properly, using the right tools, can lead to lower Total Cost of Ownership in the future.

The principle of Description is a significant one, and is covered across four Data Management domains in the sections that follow, namely: Metadata Management, Data Catalogue, Data Modelling, and Data Architecture (*Sections 4.11* to *4.14* respectively).

Principle 3 – Quality

Once data is properly described, it becomes possible to measure its quality objectively, moving away from the subjective language we hear so often in comments like: 'The Finance system data is very good; it is our system of record, after all'.

What does 'very good' mean, and why focus on the 'Finance system'? Is this really where you hold your definitive customer information? Would your Sales or Customer Support teams agree with that position?

In terms of quality, not all data is of equal importance, and we would expect to see different quality standards and targets established for different classes of data. The Entity Method will help you develop a consistent language to define the different types of data, so that you can choose the quality standards that are right for your organisation.

We are often asked what good quality data represents. There's no easy answer to this, because to do so requires an understanding of what your organisation needs from its *own* data. *You* need to determine whether you need to hold twenty or fifty critical pieces of information about customer or citizen. *You* need to determine whether having data that is only 80% accurate is acceptable, or if various data items should be at a quality standard of 95%, 97%, 99%, or indeed 99.999%. Of course, before you can think in terms of measurement, you need to establish the basis for making those measurements, and implement a method for capturing the information.

There's a cost to maintaining high-quality data, but there's also a cost associated with holding onto poor-quality data. All our experience is that the true cost of ownership of poor-quality data is *much* higher; it really could stop you reaching your business objectives. How much is that worth to you?

The Entity Method is especially focused on building processes, and employing technologies that encourage a culture of continuous improvement. Good today; better tomorrow.

The principle of Quality has its own domain described below: *Section 4.10 Data Quality Management and Remediation.*

Principle 4 – Access

This principle is about allowing authorised people to access data securely, and in a way that has the correct level of control and audit suited to the nature of the data in question. You also need to provide adequate protection for the privacy to individuals whose information is being accessed or shared.

The Data Access principle is probably the most technical of all, in the sense of being related to activities undertaken by IT staff. However, this IT-centricity doesn't let everyone else off the hook in terms of accountability. It's just that a lot of the responsibility for 'doing' work in this area will largely fall to your IT function.

As an example, IT will have a role to play in ensuring your data is appropriately stored. They will provide the technical capabilities for archiving, and eventually possibly deleting data. However, it is *not* IT's remit to decide *what* data gets archived, and *when*. The responsibility for these decisions lies with the Data Owners within the respective Line of Business. *They* will need to understand what is at issue here.

Data needs to be stored in a format so that it is readily accessible to *authorised* users.

Remember though, that we are using the term 'Data' in a very wide sense. This doesn't just mean ERP data in neat tables and columns, but also that mass of unstructured and semi-structured data, stored in the form of emails, documents, web content and even audio and video. This represents ever-increasing volumes, variety and velocity of flow for data.

You will need to make sure that data and information systems are stored and hosted in environments that are secure, robust and resilient. This is the part of the *Data Delta* model where we need to consider IT strategies such as *Cloud* and *Virtualisation*.

Are you a non-IT person reading this? Excellent. We are delighted and impressed. It is important that you understand at least the *principles* of these concepts. No one is ever going to ask you to set up a service in the Cloud, but you do need an appreciation of what this is all about. Not knowing this sort of thing within your organisation is like not knowing what the gears do in your car.

Yes, you can still drive it perfectly well in 'normal' conditions. However, you will get far less value out of your car if you don't know why you should change gears[36]. And when conditions deviate from the norm – for example, when there is a sudden snow storm – it really helps to understand the principles involved.

Finally, you need to consider physical data protection, not simply in terms of good housekeeping, but increasingly, where disaster recovery is concerned. Whether we are talking in terms of climate change or terrorism, whether the disaster is man-made or natural, it seems clear that in the future, there are going to be more threats than ever before. Could your organisation survive without its data? If you understand that data is an asset, you should know the answer to that question.

The principle of Data Access, including basic ideas on *Cloud* and *Virtualisation*, is covered below in the domains of Data Security and Privacy, and Data Storage.

Principle 5 – Usage and Sharing

Authorised people can now access your data, but there are key considerations for you to address concerning how they actually use and share the data.

A significant focus of this principle is one of reducing complexity – data should be created and managed using as few processes and systems as possible, and these should be applied consistently. Furthermore, the capture and *use* of data should be directly related to supporting the needs of your organisation.

We encourage you to take another look at how you currently *maintain* data from the perspective of how you *use* it – and ensure that you are only capturing data that is necessary, reasonable and proportionate for your needs.

---

[36] Or the car itself should change gears, if you drive an automatic!

This makes it easier to share data between processes and information systems inside your organisation, but also with external parties, such as customers or citizens, partner organisations and regulatory authorities, etc, where it is appropriate and warranted.

We strongly encourage the practice of making data services available via a strategic integration platform, such as an Enterprise Service Bus, as a means of sharing and re-using data. Undoubtedly, this requires more initial effort than some form of point-to-point method of sharing, but each service implemented in this way will increase the 'agility quotient' of your organisation, and will lay the groundwork for being responsive and customer-focused in a 'digital' context.

Related to this is the subject of whether you are going to publish anything as 'Open Data'. This is the idea that data is made publicly and freely available for *anyone* (internally and indeed, externally) to use as they wish. There are many benefits to Open Data. Some are expressed in terms of creating opportunities and contributing to an expansion of the 'digital' economy, while others relate to enabling people to build useful applications. Still others might accrue to the *providers* of the Open Data themselves, in that they benefit from the exposure gained by providing such as service. Governments are leading the charge in this area, and many now have legislation requiring more data to be made 'Open', but other types of organisations are also recognising the opportunities of contributing data to the wider community.

Principle 6 – Implementation and Control

If you've addressed all the other principles adequately, when you arrive at the implementation and control level, your life should be a great deal more straightforward, and your chances of successful delivery should be considerably higher. However, there are still key considerations you need to get right, and we have seen people misdirect their Master Data Management and Data Warehouse efforts to such an extent that they actually widened their *Data Delta*. This shouldn't happen at all of course, but if your organisation goes about it in the wrong way, you can end up with extra data silos, which will make that 'single version of truth' more difficult to achieve than ever.

Critically, we want to emphasise the relationship between this principle and the five above. Very specifically, we are saying that you cannot address this principle in isolation, which is an approach nevertheless still attempted by many organisations. A BI project on its own? An MDM project on its own? These will, in all likelihood, fail.

We explore the key domains of this principal – Master Data Management, Reference Data Management, Document Content Management, and Data Warehouses, BI and Analytics – in significant detail in the first four sections of the next more technical chapter, *Elements of the Data Delta Model*.

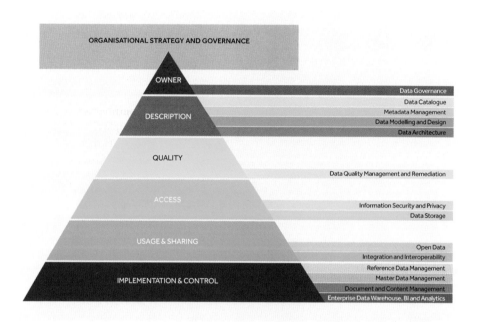

As an example, let's use our *Data Delta* model to examine why so many BI and Analytics/Visualisation projects fail. The IT industry has been running BI projects in various guises for many years, with 'report generators' preceding the embryonic BI tools that developed into today's more sophisticated products. Over the course of that time, the repeated failures of BI projects were most often attributed to the law of 'supply and demand'.

The argument most commonly cited was that whilst the 'Supply' side of report production was within the IT function, and the 'Demand' side of report requirements was within the Lines of Business, demand would always outstrip supply, causing an inevitable backlog and failure. The benefit of the reports being produced was realised within the operational departments, while the cost was borne by the IT function, which had a finite budget.

This led to a desire to find some way to balance the costs and the benefits. An obvious solution was to move report production away from IT to the Lines of Business themselves. Each successive generation of BI technology got closer to this goal, and by 2016, it's fair to say that some BI and Analytics/Visualisation tools[37] are genuinely delivering this capability to end users.

And yet, BI projects continue to fail.

The various reasons why well-run BI and Analytics/Visualisation projects fail are all[38] represented inside the *Data Delta* model, and there are lots of them. For example, it's not uncommon that two people will run similar reports and arrive at different totals based on basic figures such as revenue, cost, or headcount. Very quickly, this leads to a lack of confidence among senior executives, who have neither the time nor the inclination to get involved in the inevitable debates as to 'Who is right?'

Why does this happen? Well, let's rule out the tools. In this day and age, they *all* do their job. And it's also relatively safe to rule out the people: the tools are now sufficiently advanced that the level of technical skill required to produce a BI report is not especially demanding.

Which leaves us with … the data itself. In fact, *it was always the data*. It's just that the other issues used – or *were* used – to camouflage the root cause.

This might mean that the data isn't defined properly eg what is the definition of a 'Sales month'? Perhaps it isn't of sufficient quality eg different functions are using different codes to denote regions or countries. Maybe there's some flaw in the basic integration model as to how, or indeed when, data arrives at the BI tool. There are many possible points of weakness, but every one of them will be addressed as you go about crossing the *Data Delta*. Equally importantly, if you *don't* cross the *Data Delta*, then you have no chance of ever addressing the underlying problems.

Don't be tempted to believe there's a silver bullet in the shape of the latest 'intelligent' software package. No component or suite of software is going to solve this for you. If your reports don't add up now, and you replace them with a modern BI or Analytics/Visualisation tool, you will have an array of pretty reports that still don't add up, but probably run a lot faster.

---

[37] Tableau and QlikView would be obvious examples, but the traditional vendors, such as IBM and Oracle, are fast playing 'catch up'.

[38] A *well-run* BI project is one which is properly planned, where the requirements are clearly identified, where there is appropriate time etc. It is sadly true that in 2016 a few BI projects are still failing because they do not meet these basics, and are not well run. These however are the distinct minority in our experience.

3.3.2 Data Management Domains

There are 14 domains of Data Management that make up the *Data Delta* model.
The Entity Method guides you through addressing each of them. We are going to dive into much more detail in each area in *Section 4 – Elements of the Data Delta Model*, but firstly, here is a brief overview to help you select where you would like to read more, if you aren't up for going through all the domains in detail.

There are 14 domains of Enterprise Information Management that make up the Data Delta model.

One word of caution though which we will amplify at key points. We have already discussed the relationship between the domains, and later in this section, *Section 3 – Crossing the Data Delta*, we will discuss implementation strategies. What is very clear from a *Data Delta* perspective is that these topics must *not* be tackled in isolation. It is only by understanding and acting upon the complex dependencies involved that you will succeed.

Before we break into individual domains, a further key point on the relative importance of data needs to be established. *Not all data is equal*, and data can be classified in this context into useful *categories*. The following diagram helps to identify seven different categories of data.

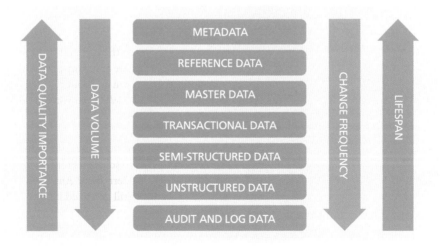

This diagram considers data in the following categories:

- Metadata – information about data such as its name, purpose, owner, date created, status, security classification, expiry, etc.

- Reference Data – relatively static data that is used by other data records – usually lists such as country codes, customer codes, statuses, categories, etc.

- Master Data – information that has organisational importance, such as customers, citizens, suppliers, products, assets, etc.

- Transactional Data – specific details of an occurrence such as on-boarding a new customer, raising an invoice, making a payment, recording a measurement from a sensor, etc.

- Semi-structured Data – that mass of data outside of your tightly-defined transactional systems that relates to key parts of your organisation eg customers, products, services, etc. A typical example might be a customer complaint email. The actual text within the body of the email is unstructured in that there is no formal schema describing the pattern of the words. Given that natural language text expresses inherent rules (ie the grammar), it is usually possible to extract elements such as the customer name, the date, and probably the product or service that is the subject of the complaint. Semi-structured data is often regarded as a part of Big Data.

- Unstructured Data – we consider this to include types of data where extracting meaningful information requires more advanced analytical techniques, for example images, and audio or video streams. Another example might relate to chatter across specific social media sites – responding to a political campaign or a terrorist situation. Even in these cases, the data is actually presented at the lowest technical level in a highly structured format, but the meaning itself cannot be determined by machines using standard processing capabilities. Significant effort is being invested to develop 'Machine Learning' systems to cater for this type of data. Unstructured data is regarded as a part of Big Data.

- Audit data – information about the transaction data such as who triggered the transaction.

The arrows pointing upwards in the diagram indicate that data within the higher categories have longer lifespans and are important, because they have impact on data in the lower categories. Clearly, efforts to improve the quality of data should be prioritised to target first the data in these categories.

The arrows pointing downwards in the diagram indicate that more data is generated in the lower categories, and that such records change more frequently.

For example, consider a typical cash withdrawal transaction from a bank. Let's say that you withdraw a small sum of money from your bank (eg $10[39]), but the transaction is recorded as a significantly larger amount, that of $1,000. Clearly, on a personal level, this is naturally of big concern to you. However, from the bank's perspective, this is simply one erroneous transaction amid the many millions it handles, and it is a straightforward exercise for them to rectify it. There is no potential risk to them, other than perhaps losing you as a customer.

Imagine however, that the bank had recorded key Master Data customer information incorrectly. Mr Brown of 123 Acacia Avenue might be a fine upstanding citizen, but Mr Brown of 231 Acacia Road might have defaulted on previous loans and represents a well-recognised credit risk. If the data is recorded incorrectly, the confusion of the two Master Data records for these similarly-named customers could have a knock-on effect on all their future transactions. Not only is there the risk of losing a good customer, there is a serious concern that they may have lent money they aren't going to get back.

This example shows the importance, from the bank's perspective, of getting its Master Data right. And as it is for them, so it's also for your organisation. It is even more important to get Master Data right than it is your individual transactional data.

Here is a brief overview of the 14 domains of Data Management. More detail on each can be found in *Section 4 Elements of the Data Delta Model.*

Domain 1: Owner – Governance

When data is governed effectively, a balance of forces will arise that shapes the way the whole organisation treats its data, in a positive and beneficial manner. In other words, it simply becomes easy to work with data as an asset, because everything is in place that helps you do just that. These guiding forces will work to orchestrate the people, processes and technology in support of your organisation's overall strategic objectives in the context of a new culture.

---

[39] Again, these amounts can relate to any currency you choose.

The cultural aspect relates to a pervasive, institutional awareness that *data is an asset*, and therefore needs to be treated, measured and managed accordingly. Such a cultural transformation needs to affect conversations and behaviour as staff work to optimise the value of their data assets. You're launching a new product? Great! As part of that process, people need to shout: 'What does this mean in terms of data?'

This will require genuine and committed support from the executive level of your organisation. They should commission a Data Governance organisation to oversee the organisation-wide transformation, and to weave effective Data Management into the cultural fabric of your organisation.

From an individual perspective, there is a need to define new roles and responsibilities – such as those of a Data Steward – defining what it means to be the curator of data. Obviously, you will want to ensure *all* your people are aware of and, where necessary, trained in relation to their Data Management responsibilities.

In terms of processes, there's a need to define and implement revised ways of working, such as how data is maintained. Once implemented, these processes need to be measured and monitored on an ongoing basis.

There is likely to be a need to introduce new or enhanced technical solutions to enable or strengthen your organisation's capacity to unlock *value* from its data. Most of the issues facing organisations trying to get control of their data stem from the belief that technology *alone* represents the panacea.

This is a false belief: it has not been true in the past, and neither will it be in the future. There is *no* substitute for a culture-driven change, and technology is only one force in the change process.

You should not attempt to introduce every aspect of Data Governance for all your data at the outset.

It's important, therefore, to ensure that technology is introduced in such a way that it supports and reinforces an overall Data Management strategy and policy. This includes ensuring that wherever there is misalignment, there is a path to migrate the existing solutions towards this strategy, and also that the architecture is sufficiently flexible to accommodate future requirements and technical developments.

One of the key points that we shall explore later is that you should not attempt to introduce every aspect of Data Governance for all your data at the outset. Experience tells us that taking this approach will not deliver value to your organisation quickly enough.

Instead, you should look to do an initial classification of your data assets, including information systems, based on criticality, data hierarchy, and the importance of those assets to your organisation as a whole. At a conceptual level, the right approach involves identifying a relatively small scope of particularly *important data* to begin with, and introducing Data Governance processes specifically for that. Over time, work to extend Data Governance piece by piece to cover all your data.

If your organisation takes all of this on board, it will be well on the way to crossing the *Data Delta*, but don't forget to communicate what's going on, every step of the way. With all that we have outlined above, and irrespective of the size of the initiative that might act as the trigger for improving Data Governance within your organisation, we hope it's clear that the impact is likely to be organisation-wide. Indeed, it *should* be organisation-wide.

We would urge you to treat any data-related initiative as part of a broad programme, so that the widest set of implications can be properly considered – people, process and technology. There is already some excellent best practice advice available about managing and communicating with stakeholders within the realm of a programme[40], and we vigorously support this advice.

Domain 2: Implementation & Control – Enterprise Data Warehouse, Business Intelligence (BI) and Analytics

Most people have a good understanding of this particular Data Management domain. Expressed formally, the disciplines of Data Warehousing, Business Intelligence and Analytics relate to the planning, implementation and control activities to provide information and support for knowledge workers engaged in reporting, query, analysis, and decision making.

The vast majority of failures in an organisation's approach to Data Management manifest themselves as problems with Business Intelligence. Suffice to say, there is every chance that the BI system itself is not at fault.

To be a little more specific, Data Warehouses allow storage of data in ways that are optimised to support trend analysis and forward planning. It's important to understand that the way data is held to support such analytical requirements is *very different* from holding data that is used by your live operational systems.

Operational database management systems are concerned with holding data in a highly efficient and tightly controlled form, so as to maintain integrity, and respond to the demands of intensive read-and-write operations. Data Warehouses typically contain snapshots of data that are organised in ways that makes sense to business users (so that they can find the information they need).

BI and Analytics provide the tools that allow business users to find the information they need from within the Data Warehouse. This includes capabilities for generating reports and creating dashboards, and carrying out advanced predictive analyses. There is no doubt that recent years have seen exciting developments in this space, with the long-heralded arrival of true self-service tools for end-users becoming a reality for many organisations. The buzz around Big Data extends the scope of this domain to include so-called 'intelligent' analytical tools that are capable of analysing large volumes of data that can be both structured *and* un-structured.

The term, 'structured data', relates to information that is held in a controlled format, and it uses a schema to determine what each piece of information represents. We talked earlier about Metadata, and how this exists to *describe* data, and so give *meaning* to that data. In this sense, a schema is a type of Metadata – it effectively says 'any data stored in this place is the name of a person, or their address, or their gender' etc.

> The vast majority of failures manifest themselves as problems with Business Intelligence … there is every chance that the BI system itself is not at fault.

By contrast, 'unstructured data', such as free-text documents or content from social media sources, does *not* use a schema. Instead, there is a reliance on more sophisticated analytical methods to derive meaning from the data.

Such methods are based on statistical models of how people use language to express themselves. However, as we explore later on in *Section 4.3 Document and Content Management*, there might be more short-term value in focusing on *semi-structured* data; for example, a customer complaint letter is itself unstructured but contains information about a customer, and probably a product or service.

There is a tendency for 'the market' to promote a message that Big Data somehow obviates the need for good quality data. This is a dangerous myth. In fact, we would go as far to say that, for the unwary, because of this misunderstanding, Big Data represents a danger. Prior to Big Data, decisions were largely based on facts derived from data stored in a structured or known, and therefore *controlled*, format. In the world of Big Data that clamours for 'predictive analytics', there is a genuine concern that decisions are made on the basis of 'facts' that come from *significantly* less controlled data sources.

Let's be clear, we are not anti-Big Data in any way. That would be preposterous. However, we urge caution in the face of all the beguiling marketing hype. There is no substitute for prudent Data Management, *especially* in the context of Big Data, as painful a message as that may be to digest. Big Data is *not* a substitute for robust Data Management. Indeed, if your organisation is making business decisions based on Big Data 'facts', we would argue that this only increases the need for implementing robust Data Management approaches so as to validate the analysis and the business decisions which will arise.

Clearly then, this domain needs to draw upon and extend other key Data Management domains such as Information Security and privacy, Metadata, Data Catalogue, Data Quality Management and Remediation, Data Storage, and Reference and Master Data Management.

Domain 3: Implementation & Control – Document and Content Management

Document and Content Management relates to the lifecycle of content not held in a structured format. This also includes a consideration of repositories used to hold and 'publish' these types of information. This should not be regarded as any less important than data held in more systematised formats, such as records in a relational database. For instance, unstructured documents might describe the contract terms between your organisation and its customers and suppliers, or corporate policies and standards, standard operating procedures, employee terms or CVs, or even content published on your corporate website.

It is important that documents and other types of content are carefully managed. This requires consideration and implementation of related policies and standards, the consistent use of Metadata to describe content, appropriate repositories for collecting, maintaining and making the content available to those who need it, and suitable workflow processes to manage it.

Domain 4: Implementation & Control – Master Data Management (MDM)

Master Data Management (MDM) is concerned with the planning, implementation and control activities of data relating to key entities – typically, but by no means exclusively, customers and citizens, sometimes products, sometimes other 'things' – to ensure timely consistency of data within a 'golden view' of contextual data values.

Why do these data items need special treatment? There are many arguments, but here are two. Firstly, MDM provides the ability to link relevant related information across different silos, perhaps belonging to customers or products. For example, it will facilitate a consolidated view of all the data about a specific customer or vendor in one place, no matter that the data is held in many separate silos.

Secondly, is the idea that if you have an error with Master Data, its implications can be far reaching, far more so than a simple error in a transaction. Muddling up two customers or citizens can mean you try to sell a product to someone who has already bought it from you, or if you are a bank, perhaps you give someone a credit card who shouldn't have one. Or if you are the police, you could arrest the wrong person and let a guilty person remain free. Master Data errors tend to have significant consequences, so it's sensible to use special techniques to get Master Data right.

Sometimes this 'golden view' is, in fact, a physical record, which may or may not be replicated across all data sources in the organisation. Sometimes, it is a 'logical view', a representation deduced from other physical records.

Master Data concerns key information that changes over time, typically citizens, customers, vendors, students, patients, products, assets etc. It is distinct from transaction data, such as orders, invoices etc. Master Data can form the basis for aggregation and dimensional analysis of data in BI and Analytics/Visualisation.

The purpose of MDM is to arrive at a 'single version of truth', based on a 'golden view' of the data that can be trusted throughout your organisation.

Domain 5: Implementation & Control – Reference Data Management (RDM)

Reference Data relates to lists and code systems that are likely to be in common use throughout your organisation, such as lists of countries, customer types, status codes etc. Its concern relates to the planning, implementation, and control activities of such contextual data values.

The fundamental idea is that this data is important because it is used in the definition of other data, such as marketing segments defining bands of customers. Getting your reference data wrong will potentially have a negative impact on many other records. It therefore needs to be identified and then managed robustly within your organisation.

This data is important because it is used in the definition of other data, such as marketing segments defining bands of customers.

An example, used in several sections of this book, highlights the difficulties that arise from a typical reference data inconsistency whereby the nationality of a person might sometimes be referred to as 'United Kingdom', and other times as 'Great Britain'. This is a *reference data issue*.

Not only will getting your reference data wrong potentially have a serious impact on management reporting and analysis. This is also likely to result in missed opportunities which could otherwise 'add value' and meaning to data.

Finally here, managing Reference Data centrally is important for organisations that require multiple language support; the ability to standardise on the most important terms within an organisation that can sometimes be 'lost in translation'.

Domain 6: Usage & Sharing – Integration and Interoperability

Data Integration and Interoperability is about managing data as it moves, and making sure that it is readily shareable and re-usable. Clearly, this needs to be within the bounds of properly controlled access – just because you have the capability to move data in a controlled and effective way, does not change the security and access issues involved. The objective is to design the ability to share high-quality data inside your organisation *and* between your organisation and external stakeholders, such as customers or citizens, partners and regulators.

This is a wider issue than simply having the right set of technical tools in place[41]. If people are going to make sensible use of data, that data needs to be made available in formats that make sense and have some meaning to people and/or machines. It follows that you can very quickly get into a situation where data is being shared in so many different formats that it becomes almost impossible to keep track of everything. It's

---

[41] Examples of such capabilities include an Enterprise Service Bus (ESB) providing real-time services, or Extract-Transform-Load (ETL) tools to transport batches of data between data sources.

tempting in this context to create yet another format to suit your particular purpose, rather than determine if something suitable already exists.

Another tendency is to create a direct share of data between two points ie point-to-point, rather than going to the effort of using a potentially more flexible mechanism such as an Enterprise Service Bus (ESB) to mediate in the communication.

> Sharing data effectively is fundamentally important. It reduces the tendency for users to maintain entirely separate and entirely unnecessary additional silos...

Getting the sharing of data under control is one of the most fundamental enablers for unlocking additional value for your organisation, but is often largely ignored, or else restricted in the scope of data or services it covers.

Sharing data effectively is fundamentally important. It reduces the tendency for users to maintain entirely separate and entirely unnecessary additional silos – silos which cost money, but ultimately add no value, had the data been effectively shared.

We see some shocking examples of this, such as processes built on people emailing personal, financial or corporately sensitive data between one another in plain text or via unprotected documents. Practices like this are all too commonplace, but highlight a disregard for data security, quality, traceability and control in general. How could anyone be sure who is viewing data, or what they are doing to it along its journey? And this isn't just about people with malicious intent. Controls are also there to prevent errors, accidents and omissions.

Hopefully this demonstrates that there is real value in taking a step back to consider whether your organisation is benefiting from its sharing capabilities. Do you have the right tools, and are these supported by effective policies and standards? But above all, are your people aware of the risks and costs of searching for 'quick fix' solutions?

Domain 7: Access – Data Storage

Data Storage relates to how data and systems are stored and hosted so that they can sustain operational and availability targets, whilst withstanding technical failures and outages, and at the same time remain secure against unauthorised entry and malicious attacks.

'Virtualisation' allows hardware resources to be defined and configured using software. In this way, one computer resource such as a server can be logically split into many. This has a direct cost saving in terms of hardware purchased, but also greatly simplifies maintenance, reducing further the total cost of ownership.

'Cloud Computing' largely enabled by virtualisation, allows for the shared use of computing resources, usually hosted within datacentres and accessed via a network. The level of shared access can be secured and restricted so that the use of the resources within a 'Cloud' is constrained to a tightly controlled group of people. In such instances, the Cloud is described as being 'private'.

In the future, with increasingly more people and devices connecting to the internet, there is likely to be a strong trend towards the use of storage and processing that is distributed among the devices themselves. This is known as 'Edge Computing'.

Your organisation is very likely to be relying on virtualisation and Cloud computing today. Even if not as an officially sanctioned matter of policy or IT strategy, there is every chance that Cloud resources or applications, such as internet storage or services delivered via a 'Software-as-a-Service'/SaaS model are used somewhere within your operation.

Then there's Big Data, which introduces the concept of 'data lakes', which are repositories of data held in raw formats. Some will tell you that this is all unstructured data, but that's unlikely to be the case. The key point about a data lake is that the structure of the data it contains does not need to be known at the point the data is *added* to the lake. When you later come to use the data, it becomes the job of the processes used to do the searching or analysis to work out what the data means.

It's important, not least from a business continuity perspective, that you get a handle on all the various data storage methods used, and how this maps onto the lifecycle of data as it flows through your organisation. You should aim to take stock of your current data storage capacity, along with a measure of its utilisation, and so predict how prepared you are in terms of future needs.

It may be that you could derive significant benefits by using more centrally managed and virtualised Cloud resources in preference to buying and maintaining hardware and software that's widely dispersed across the estate.

It's not sufficient to audit resource usage as a one-time exercise. You really need to establish the means to monitor your operational usage of data storage and processing resources on an ongoing basis, and so improve, maintain and fix issues related to availability, stability and security as necessary.

The storage of data is clearly a key aspect of the overall information lifecycle. You should get into the position of being able to track and document the passage of data through all the stages of its lifecycle. This includes a consideration of when data should be retired – to a secure offline or near-line archive – or disposed.

The overriding concern is to comply with all regulatory requirements relating to confidentiality, privacy or conditions of use. For example, many legal jurisdictions will require that you can justify why you hold personal information about an individual, and that such information is discarded when there is no longer any justifiable purpose for keeping it. Many organisations are currently ill-equipped to respond to such regulations, even when the personal data they hold is contained within structured databases and data warehouses. This becomes especially problematic in the context of Big Data, where personal data is potentially floating around in the depths of a less rigorously controlled data lake.

Aside from the regulatory requirements, all 'live' data and content carries inherent risks and cost of ownership, and data retirement needs to be considered in terms of minimising these. Therefore, all data that is deemed to be approaching the end of its useful life should be considered for retirement.

Data retirement, then, requires special consideration at the policy level, and the policy needs to take account of both business and prevailing regulatory requirements.

Then there is the need for coping with information going astray.

As part of the approach to resilience, your data storage should be protected by 'back-up and restore' and disaster recovery capabilities. These are part of a wider discipline known as Business Continuity and Disaster Recovery (BCDR)[42]. It is critical that this facility is tested regularly. You don't want to find the weaknesses in your back-up provision after some precipitating event has caused your online data storage to fail.

Domain 8: Usage & Sharing – Open Data

Open Data relates to the idea that data is made publicly and freely available for *anyone*, internally or externally, to use as they wish. There are many benefits to Open Data; some are expressed in terms of creating opportunities and contributing to an expansion of the 'digital' economy, while others relate to enabling people to build useful applications.

---

[42] It's impossible to do justice to BCDR in this type of book. Readers are encouraged to refer to ISO22301 – Business Continuity Management (http://www.bsigroup.com/en-GB/iso-22301-business-continuity/) and also the UAE's Business Continuity Management Standards (http://www.ncema.gov.ae/dassets/download/b6f229f6/AE_SCNS_NCEMA_7001_2015_ENGLISH.pdf.aspx).

Still others might accrue to the *providers* of the Open Data, in that they benefit from the exposure gained by providing such as service.

From a governmental perspective in particular, data is a valuable resource to the wider community, and publishing government data in a form that is available, discoverable and usable, helps promote transparency and efficiency. There is also significant credible evidence that Open Data has the potential to create economic opportunity[43].

Open Data can bring benefits for the private sector too, both as providers and consumers of Open Data. Publishing Open Data is an effective way for organisations to demonstrate value, and to create an ongoing relationship with potential customers.

Open Data requires finding the balance between data you wish to share, and data that you need to keep confidential, both inside your organisation, and between your organisation and the outside[44]. Although this topic takes a slightly different emphasis depending on whether yours is a public or private organisation, all enterprises today need to be looking for opportunities or requirements to publish data beyond their firewalls.

Part of this question of balance is bound up in the quality of the data being offered. In some cases, inaccurate or incomplete data might carry risks, and in other cases there may be arguments that some data is better than none at all. Key to this is that data should be made available with a statement regarding its quality, allowing potential users to determine whether the data is suitable for their requirements. However, this is not necessarily that easy to accomplish, as many organisations struggle to articulate how confident they are about their data. Resolving this is a key aspect of crossing the *Data Delta*.

Domain 9: Access – Information Security and Privacy

Your organisation has most likely invested considerably in information security already, and the good news is that everything you've done will be useful from a *Data Delta* perspective. Our experience shows that even in those organisations demonstrating a general low awareness and maturity in Data Management, staff can point to the importance of information security, and their own part in upholding it.

This is largely due to the availability of comprehensive international standards coupled with often stringent regulatory requirements.

---

[43] There is a huge amount of documented evidence on the internet from international bodies and national governments. A good place to start your research would be the UN site of the Public Administration and Development Management, Department of Economic and Social Affairs covering Open Government Data and Services at https://publicadministration.un.org/en/ogd

[44] 'Personally Identifiable Information' (PII) is explicitly excluded from the scope of Open Data.

Within the context of Data Management, data security encompasses the holistic security classification of data, data ownership, confidentiality and risk, as well as access control and auditing.

Data Privacy is an area where you might need to think *beyond* your current information security provision. This has emerged as a central aspect of data security, but is not so directly targeted by the recognised industry standards. Privacy requires acknowledgement that data owners are custodians of data on behalf of individuals, who have a reasonable expectation that their data will remain private.

A generation has grown up which *appears* more open in terms of the data they choose to publish about themselves (eg in terms of holiday snaps), but those same people still have expectations and increasing rights concerning the privacy of, for example, their medical data that is held by others.

Domain 10: Quality – Data Quality Management and Remediation

Very few would disagree that it's better to have high-quality data than data which is lacking in some way. What's interesting is that when we ask people within an organisation questions like, 'How would you rate the quality of your data?', we almost always get subjective responses such as 'Poor', 'Patchy', 'Okay' or, sometimes, 'Fine'. We have yet to identify an organisation where anyone is able to support their opinion with an objective, qualitative response.

The focus is on identifying what 'good quality data' means in the context of your organisation, and establishing the right metrics to measure and improve that quality on an ongoing basis.

What we *do* find is that if we ask a few more questions about Data Quality, we get a very helpful picture of where an organisation stands in relation to the *Data Delta*. Data Quality is a key 'indicator' domain where we look, over time, to identify shifts in the way an organisation speaks about itself. Here, the language in everyday use is a useful bellwether for how data is regarded and managed.

To bring about improvements, the Data Quality Management domain should focus on planning, implementation and control activities, and the application of suitable measures to quantify, improve and ensure the fitness of data in support of your organisation's strategic objectives.

The focus is on identifying what 'good quality data' means in the context of your organisation, and establishing the *right* metrics to measure and improve that quality on an ongoing basis. This is likely to include consideration of metrics related to elements such as accuracy and validity, integrity, redundancy, relevance, completeness and consistency.

By far the most effective way to improve the quality of data is to find meaningful ways to measure it. This enables targets to be established, and solutions – in the form of a blend of people, process and technology – to be introduced to improve data quality.

Domain 11: Description – Data Architecture

Data Architecture is part of the wider consideration of your organisation's Enterprise Architecture (EA) as a whole. It considers the overarching strategic objectives and the overall value chain of your operation, and then defines how data will support those objectives and the operation.

Data Architecture lays down the blueprints for enabling information to flow freely around your organisation. This includes how data relates to other types of EA models, how it is stored, how it relates to your organisation's business systems, and how various technical components combine to support your data-related capabilities.

Part of this involves providing both business-level and formal technical definitions of related data items such as Customer, Vendor, Account, Contract, Project, Programme etc. Having a comprehensive understanding of the data your organisation uses is essential for being able to use the information successfully eg to support Business Intelligence and Analytics.

It's important to view Data Architecture as a business-led concern, and at the strategic and operational levels. This provides your IT function with the information it needs to support and enable the aims of the business from a Technology viewpoint.

This more detailed view, in turn, will ensure that all the system components are in place – along with the connectivity between them – to provide the optimum technical architecture for your organisation.

If your organisation has not adopted an architectural framework, then this should be addressed. The framework will help determine *how* best to model and document your data capabilities, including which artefacts are to be produced (see Data Architecture in the next section for examples).

All Data Architecture methodologies will lead you through a similar journey. You'll need to baseline your current data architecture, describing your current data landscape. From here, you can move forward to define your target architecture, representing the desired data capabilities across your organisation at some point in the future.

With the target in mind, the trick is to work out a roadmap for all the stages in between or the so-called 'transitional architectures'. We advocate developing a reference architecture – a blueprint containing all the major technical components that support the Data Management landscape. This helps to ensure that as technical decisions are taken over the course of the journey to cross the *Data Delta*, these are not taken at the expense of future flexibility.

Even where there is no clearly identifiable 'architecture' function within an organisation, the fact that you work *with* information means that you do *have* an architecture. The task is then to pull together a description of it, and ensure you have a roadmap to establish the technical architecture comprising all the components to underpin your data capabilities.

Domain 12: Description – Data Modelling and Design

Data Architecture and Data Modelling are easy to confuse, and this is not surprising as they are closely related. Data Architecture represents the link with the business context – its drivers and requirements – that determine the data capabilities required to support its overall goals, but also, the way that these data capabilities are modelled and documented (including which artefacts are to be produced). Data Modelling represents the activities to physically produce these model and design artefacts.

There are several standards and supporting tools for modelling data. Whether you choose one of these, or decide to establish your own standards, the important thing is to aim for a consistent approach that will be applied to all the modelling assets you produce. You need to manage these within a suitable location, preferably one of the purpose-built repository tools.

Your central modelling repository will contain all solution artefacts including new and work-in-progress designs, as well as approved and implemented designs. It will allow authorised users to search and re-use models that are in any state of completion or approval.

Your data modelling activity is intended to ensure your data is fully understood, and that this understanding is documented in the most effective way possible. The collection of modelling information is discussed in some depth in the next section (see *Data Modelling and Design*). This relates to identifying key data entities (such as Customer, Citizen, Supplier, Product, Asset, etc), usage of these entities, descriptions of their data attributes, and also the key datasets that relate to these entities.

All of this information will be useful in terms of building your Business Glossary, your Data Dictionary, and other assets related to documenting an understanding of your data.

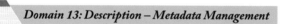

Domain 13: Description – Metadata Management

Metadata is essentially 'data about data'.

It can be helpful to think about this as the column headings in a spreadsheet, where the rows are representing the data being described. For example, if the rows of our spreadsheet represent a list of data files, then the columns might be 'Filename', 'Date Created', 'Owner', 'Purpose', 'Status' etc. Metadata Management is about planning, implementation, and control activities so that the way Metadata is used adds value to your organisation's data. This translates into controlling the way that data is described in a *useful* and *consistent* way.

Metadata Management applies controls for describing the structure and semantics of the information that's important to your organisation. This can be useful in several ways, not least when you need to allow data to be exchanged between applications or between the various business functions within your organisation. Making use of consistent Metadata allows the quality of data to be maintained, if not improved, as it flows around from place to place.

> Metadata Management applies controls for describing the structure and semantics of the information that's important to your organisation...Metadata is a key part of the 'glue' that binds the domains together at a practical level.

Metadata exists at both a business level *and* a technical level. For example, business Metadata might take the form of a Business Glossary, where terms such as 'Best-Consumed-by Date' can be defined precisely and unambiguously, but using language that makes sense to non-technical people. Whereas technical Metadata might describe how the 'Best-Consumed-by Date' is represented inside a data repository, such as the name of the field used to hold the data, the field type, the length of the field, validation rules, such as 'this date must be greater than the Production Date'.

Metadata is a key part of the 'glue' that binds the domains together at a practical level. It may include data from other domains, for example metadata about access controls for a service, from the *Data Security and Privacy* domain, or data quality metrics for a published dataset.

Domain 14: Description – Data Catalogue

Data Catalogues represent powerful repositories where key artefacts relating to the Description principle are stored. Our conception is that a Data Catalogue allows *all* the information – the Metadata – about the data that is of importance to your organisation to be managed and shared, with access controls, and from within a centrally accessible place.

This has widespread benefits that touch many of the other Data Management domains. In essence, a Data Catalogue should be the 'go to' place to discover anything about the data used by your organisation. This might include information about the way a certain type of data is stored, such as data about customers/citizens, contracts, vendors, products, services, or information about actual physical data extracts or BI reports that have been generated. An example of this might be allowing you to answer questions such as, 'Where can I find the latest data about our top 10 customers?'

Establishing such a capability helps you find useful information more easily.

3.4 Data Delta - An approach

Before we start to look in detail at the scope that the *Data Delta* model addresses, it's important to establish how *Data Delta* thinking should be applied to your organisation. Make sure you give thought to developing an achievable roadmap that's realistic, and that will deliver value to your organisation.

Firstly, the most important point is to determine what represents a credible and feasible change programme in terms of where your organisation stands today. Unless you work for a start-up, your organisation will not be a stranger to change, and there is likely to be a significant amount of resistance, or worse, cynicism, associated with change programmes.

When looking to find the correct roadmap for your organisation, we would strongly advise that you base your programme strategy on the following:

a) *You need a plan*

This might sound obvious, but we have seen organisations which realise they have a huge amount of work to do, but just dive into the parts they best understand. There's an overriding sense of frustration, so people are keen to start more or less anywhere. That's never going to work in the absence of an overriding strategic direction. Don't just start with a pilot project and just hope for the best.

What does a plan comprise? Well, firstly let's separate a plan from a schedule. A schedule is a list of tasks at a sensible level of detail, showing the estimated duration of tasks and their interdependencies. You need one of those as *part* of a plan.

A plan is a written document that describes what it is you have to do to succeed. There's no point re-stating standard project theory here, so if you want a list of topics it should contain, use Google for any standard reference material store such as PMBOK[45].

Two points are worth particular emphasis. Firstly, you will need to define success. That requires some serious thinking, as in an enterprise Data Management project you will have many stakeholders with differing objectives. One standard technique to flesh out the objectives is to ask stakeholders to complete the sentence: 'I'll know we will have succeeded when …'

Secondly, another key ingredient of a Data Management plan is a reference architecture. A qualified person needs to describe how all the 'moving parts' of your solution will fit together. This isn't easy, and mistakes at this level can have severe consequences. One useful test is whether the technical architecture team involved can communicate their recommendation in language the business can understand.

b)   *You don't know the future*

That might sound contradictory to 'You need a plan', but it isn't. Consider the game of chess, as played at Grandmaster levels. No matter how clear your strategy is, your next move will change on a tactical basis as the game unfolds, and your opponent plays their move. Your strategic objective remains largely unchanged, but you will end up getting there in rather different ways to those you originally planned. However, if you were *only* to react to your opponent, they would control the game, and you would most likely lose. 'Tactics without strategy is the noise before defeat'[46].

In terms of Data Management, it is very common to see business users wishing to change direction once the first few steps of the plan unfold, and they are often right to do so. A classic example is the business leader who decides to change priorities upon seeing tangible benefits derived from undertaking initial steps towards a 'single view of customer/citizen' across all the disparate systems. Having a timely and accurate common view of customer/citizen data throughout your organisation is such a game changer that the priorities of objectives often need to be adjusted.

It might be that the business now sees the value in investing in improved business processes, or one particular part of the technology roadmap might now come very clearly into focus. Different organisations will choose a next step depending on what is right for them but, in our experience, it is frequently in a direction very different to that originally planned.

Your plan needs to be flexible and agile enough to cater for radical changes in direction as you begin to cross the *Data Delta* and people are able to take more informed decisions. Going back to the chess analogy, every move should focus on getting your most important pieces into a better position. If you consistently do

---

[46] This is a great quotation, though no one actually knows who said it originally. Although commonly attributed to Sun Tzu in 'The Art of War' – and certainly sounds like something Sun Tzu might have said – this is not the case. That doesn't mean, however, that it isn't a useful insight!

that, then in time, a direction to win the game will emerge. You could not have foreseen that particular winning direction at the outset. Indeed, you would have lost the game, on time control, had you tried to plan out the whole game in detail before making a move.

Effective business leaders of today know better than to invest in plans where it takes five years to deliver results. Your programme would be squashed before it got off the ground. Agile[47] approaches to this challenge are the only credible way forward.

c) *You don't need to do everything*

In our experience, certain types of organisation have an institutional characteristic that strives for administrative perfection. Obvious examples can be found in the banking industry. It's not uncommon to find organisations with 20 or 30 strategic enterprise-level systems. We have worked with organisations which had over 500. If we stay with the 'single view of customer/citizen' example, banks often begin by planning to standardise key customer information everywhere, across *all* these systems.

On paper this is laudable, but it is expensive in practice, and likely to take longer than anybody is really willing to wait. All we can say is that, after doing this for over 25 years, we have never *once* come across an organisation that has reached an endpoint, where 'everything' was done. That said, almost all the organisations we've worked with in this period have succeeded in crossing the *Data Delta* to a much better place.

When you design your programme, as well as taking into account the organisational needs and logical dependencies, you also need to plan to deliver value points every six months or so.

d) *Deliver regular incremental benefit*

So, if five-year programmes are out of consideration, where is the dividing line? What about two years?

Irrespective of the overall length of your programme, we have found that *six months*, give or take a month or so, is the longest any organisation can tolerate before seeing

---

[47] The 'opposite' of 'agile' in this context would be 'waterfall', implying a highly structured top-down plan. There are many elements of waterfall working that can and indeed should be bought into an agile approach eg clear definition on deliverables. The essential difference between these two styles is one of attitude to change. In an agile approach, a change in direction for sound reasons is welcomed. In a waterfall approach, the top-down structure usually tends to discourage change.

a benefit from the programme. Any longer than this, and the organisational 'belief' and momentum in their programme will fade away.

This fact should be regarded as a *design criterion* when shaping what you need to do, and may well influence your first and subsequent steps. There is an important concept of 'value points', specific events at a point in time which drive value to a stakeholder. When you design your programme, as well as taking into account the organisational needs and logical dependencies, you also need to plan to deliver value points every six months or so.

Your organisation may turn around and say: 'No, we realise this is complex and this step will require significant foundational activities. Why not take a year to do it right?'

Don't let this happen. We would argue for a plan that targets benefit realisation in six-monthly increments. Once a promise of a twelve-month gap is articulated, in all likelihood, it will soon be forgotten. People and institutions have very short memories.

This will almost certainly mean that your steps turn out to be that bit shorter than you might prefer in an ideal world. Nevertheless, we advise that you to go for the smaller steps. If you promise to deliver something in six months *and achieve it*, then your next six-month plan will be accepted much more readily.

What if the amount of work is so large that it is going to take five years, no matter how it is divided up into smaller projects? You might *suspect* this to be the case, based on your deep understanding of the organisation and the amount of work required, and you might very well be right. However, we would advise you to remember the chess analogy: do you really know your second project, or in truth, is that more of an informed opinion? And do you know at the outset how many moves it will take to win the game? You can safely and prudently estimate the potential investment from a budgetary perspective, but there is a considerable likelihood that the individual work packages are going to evolve in different directions along the way. You have to remain agile.

For this reason, it is potentially misdirected effort to plan future phases and stages in too much detail when they might not unfold in the way you forecast at the outset.

In general terms, one approach that has proven successful is to define an endpoint that represents not the completion of an enormous programme, but instead one that achieves critical progress within the overall scope of that challenge.

Mechanisms, processes and people are then established, through which further work can be undertaken on a continuing 'business-as-usual' basis. It is very common that key staff in the various business functions will change their minds about the relative importance of particular challenges as you help them cross the *Data Delta*.

e) People, Process and Technology

Every single domain within the *Data Delta* rests on introducing change to people, process and technology. There is no doubt that there are many traps in this. We see organisations put far too much emphasis on technology and end up with IT-led initiatives that are doomed to fail. But we also see process-led approaches fail – typically, those led by non-data management specialists, who simply don't appreciate the complexity of the technical solution.

Getting the balance between people, process and technology is part of the *art of programme management*. We produced this graphic as a conversation starter: the figures were simply subjective assessments from a group of our top consultants on their recent projects. We don't claim this is scientifically based, but it is steeped in pragmatism.

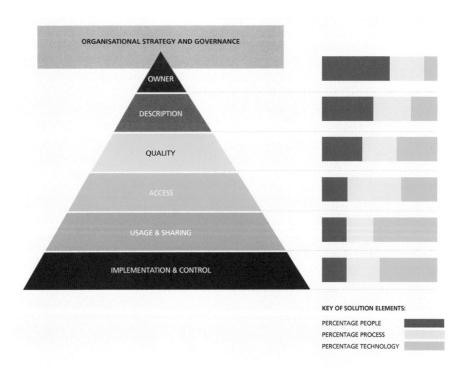

3.5 Data Delta - Finding the right context

Finding the right initiative to start your journey across the *Data Delta* is far from straightforward. Here are some approaches that seem fine in theory, but are unlikely to work in practice:

Top-down Implementation	You could, in theory, start at the top of the apex of the *Data Delta* model, put in a Data Governance regime and start working your way down through all the principles and domains, building your organisational capabilities as you go. We have seen this approach recommended and attempted a number of times before, but in every instance we know of, it has failed. The lead times before any business benefit becomes realised are simply too long. For example, a Data Governance function established in isolation from an operational Data Quality Management capability is at grave risk of 'paralysis by analysis', and can very quickly become nothing more than a 'talking shop'. Using this approach, your organisation may well lose interest long before it starts realising true benefits.
Look at all your Data	Similarly, any implementation programme that attempts to cross the *Data Delta* for all your data in one go is also going to fail, no matter what sequence you choose. This is almost bound to represent too big an undertaking and again, you would be unlikely to be able to deliver tangible, bankable business benefit in acceptable timeframes. That naturally leads to a discussion of data *prioritisation* which needs to start with an understanding of the categories of data (eg master data, reference data, transaction data etc).

The following diagram is key to understanding how to cross the Data Delta.

In some senses, it represents the summation of quite literally hundreds of years of project experience as we have tried to help organisations for the last quarter of a century. The trick is to find a small 'slice' of your data, which if you addressed every aspect of it, would make a significant improvement to the organisation.

Consider this thin arrow slicing vertically through the Data Delta model:

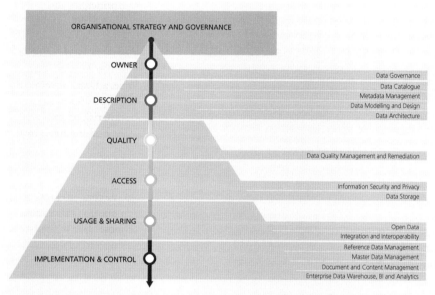

An implementation approach that delivers business benefit by addressing related domains for a small amount of data can succeed

The idea of this diagram is that you can identify a small amount of data and apply *all* the Data Management principles to it. You probably need to stop and think about this for a moment. The diagram has profound implications, and could be the key to *your* drive across the *Data Delta*.

It should give rise to lots of questions. We will try to answer many of them here, but some of the answers will be specific to your organisation.

Understanding the implications of data categorisation can be extremely helpful in determining a plan for improving data quality. For many organisations, an effective tactic is to focus on a small slice of their Master Data. This is likely to be customers or citizens, or perhaps other specific types of Master Data first eg suppliers, assets or products.

In the first instance, the key is to identify the smallest subset that will add real visible value to your organisation. This might perhaps be as small as 500 of your most important customers.

It is important that, as part of this first project, the Data Governance capability is established, even though this is only going to manage a relatively small amount of data at the outset. This means addressing *each* of the Data Management principles and related domains eg Data Description, Data Quality Management, Access and Storage, etc. Getting your Data Governance in place early on allows you to be sure that *every* concern can be approached in the right way. This provides an opportunity to consider introducing new information technology (eg software, hardware and infrastructure), allowing time for it to 'bed down'.

Be realistic about how much you can achieve in this first instance. For many organisations, this will amount to crossing the *Data Delta* for a key subset of your data, perhaps, delivering a single 'golden' read-only view of certain of your customers/citizens within six months. One place to start for a bank, for example, might be Large Corporates/Financial Institutions. Resolving just a few hundred key customers into a consistent and trusted system of record can deliver real business benefit, if done properly. Take a step back and consider that your organisation could finally have one authoritative timely repository of the most important data for your key customers/citizens.

It's highly unlikely that within six months you can integrate that view into every key business application in use in your organisation. In fact, you might be well advised to steer away from integrating the Master Data back into any of your source systems to begin with. Providing the design is properly architected, it should be straightforward to move from read-only to read-write in your second, or other subsequent, project.

And what is your second project? You know we are fond of water analogies, so let's now consider the following picture of a delta. This is an image of the Nile Delta in Egypt. In many senses, the Nile Delta is the most valuable part of the country. 95% of the people live here, though it represents only 5% of the land. Deltas are very valuable resources.

Eventually, all the water in the Nile will find its way through to the Mediterranean Sea. However, any two water molecules that are adjacent for part of their journey could end up finding very different routes to the sea. Likewise, two similar pieces of data might have very different lineages back through your organisation.

It's not a matter of 'better' or 'worse', but of finding the right direction for each drop of water, or rather, for every piece of data.

Hopefully, it has become clear that you cannot yet know your second project *for sure*, though you absolutely need a plan, if for nothing else, then for the necessity of the annual budgetary process. It's like asking the chess grandmaster what his *second* move is going to be. You must have a plan, but you need to be flexible and agile as to how that plan is implemented as circumstances evolve. There are many possible options, just as there are many ways for the water to flow across the Nile Delta. You might decide to take your initial data, and do much more with it. Perhaps you could start integrating it back into some or *all* of your enterprise systems. Or you might look to take a second slice of data, and follow the exact same route. And then a third.

Your organisation will learn so much from undertaking its first *Data Delta* project that at the outset, you should only plan subsequent steps at a high level. You can be confident, for example, that Data Governance will move from being a vague concept understood by only a handful of people within your organisation, to something of value that your organisation actually does.

At some point, you will want to move from taking 'vertical slices' through the principles of the *Data Delta* model, and focus on building out capabilities within certain horizontal layers. This equates to activating that particular principle for all your remaining data entities. There's no requirement to do this for all the principles at once. You might target a specific domain first, such as Data Storage or Reference Data Management. In the final analysis, how you choose to fit the pieces together should relate to supporting the strategic objectives of your organisation.

Finding the right path for your organisation is not easy. Creating these tailored strategies is one of our specialisms at Entity. You'll find our contact details at www.entitygroup.com.

3.6 Data Delta - Summary

By now, you should have a good overview of the concepts of the *Data Delta* model and our approach towards crossing it. We don't want you to think this is all lightweight theory, so the next section (*Section 4 – The Data Delta Model*) contains substantial information about each of the 14 domains we have established.

But equally, we must not understate the importance of the conceptual positioning of *Data Delta*, and there is a very important reason for this. Most organisations around the world are suffering from frustrations related to their data. As these frustrations grow over time, organisations become more and more desperate to find the 'silver bullet' that can solve their problems. It is a sad fact, evidenced by history, that solution vendors in the IT sector are all too eager to take advantage of this.

Please don't misunderstand us. The latest generation of BI and Analytics/Visualisation tools really is very impressive, and genuinely does allow data-literate business users to access data of real value. Furthermore, the technologies underpinning Big Data are truly remarkable, allowing your organisation to manipulate millions of records *in seconds* in ways that were inconceivable ten years ago. Most organisations, almost certainly including yours, will need to make significant investment in these areas as their data volumes, variety and velocities expand. This is discussed later in *Section 5 – The Future*.

However, taken in isolation, these technologies are *not* going to solve your problems, despite the hyperbole. They might well be *necessary* elements of your solution, but they certainly are not *sufficient* on their own.

The concepts of the *Data Delta* are critical because they represent the *only* way your organisation can address every aspect of its current, and indeed, future, data challenges. Writing out a multi-million-dollar cheque for the latest piece of technology, however 'big', 'smart', 'intelligent', 'advanced' or 'digital' is still not going to do it.

So let's recap.

Symptoms of the problem are all around you. You see time being wasted in meetings, where the question of whose figures are correct are being endlessly argued. You know there is real frustration at not being able to get to authoritative sources of basic information. There are too many *basic* unanswered questions: Who are our best customers? How many citizens live here? What products do our customers have?

These problems are only getting worse. With more and more data each week, it seems there's just too much data for it ever to get sorted out.

The solution starts with an idea. *Data is an Asset.*

If you genuinely believe that data is an asset, you will start behaving differently; just as last century there was a shift towards recognising that people were an important business asset which changed so many entrenched management positions. The fact that *you* believe that *data is an asset* is great, but what's needed is for the entire 'top table' in your organisation to believe it too. Whether or not you sit at that table yourself, your most important role is to make that group of people converts to the cause.

The good news is that it's a simple message at this level. Senior people are, by definition, concerned about value.

They want to understand it, and they want to know how it can be measured, managed and developed. By treating data as an asset, you immediately start talking their language.

The basic theories of Peter Drucker[48] have stood the test of time. If you want to manage something, the easiest way forward is to figure out how best you can measure it. You need to *measure* the quality of data so that you can *manage* it. If you manage it, you can increase its value. Data *can* become useful and actionable information. Information brings knowledge, and knowledge, as Mr Jefferson said, brings power and happiness.

Once you understand what measuring the quality of data means, then questions such as, 'Is our data good enough?' move from the abstract to the tangible.

An obvious first step is to categorise your most important data, and then start measuring and managing that data. This involves a whole panoply of activities and disciplines: Data Governance, Data Description, Data Quality Management, Master and Reference Data Management etc.

There are many targets for your most important data, though most organisations settle on a subset of customer or citizen information (other data candidates include products, assets and vendors, and certain sectors such as Construction and NGOs might place their focus on projects).

You need to find a way for an initial project to take these ideas and deliver *real* value for your organisation. You might consider the six-month time stipulation to be an

---

[48] Peter Drucker – the American management consultant (b 1909 – d 2005), regarded by many as the founder of most core modern management theory.

unnecessary restriction. Our opinion is the exact contrary: it is the key *enabler*. If you can convince senior executives of your argument, you can negotiate a six-month window to prove your case. You don't need to deliver perfection, but you *do* need to deliver a substantial improvement. If you do that, then you absolutely will have the ear of those senior executives when discussing what to do next.

Therefore, from a programme perspective, you need to address the top-down *Data Delta* principles with a bottom-up agile implementation approach. That isn't the easiest trick in the world to achieve, but we have helped lots of organisations undertake this. It is certainly possible.

Finally, it is important to keep the big picture in mind. Crossing the *Data Delta* is the *only* way to exploit the phenomenal opportunity of the digital age.

The existence of the *Data Delta* represents a break in your organisational data helix.

Data is the key link in the chain of components that make up the helix. Data always originates from an action, and can be built into valuable information. In turn, that information drives the institutional knowledge of facts and insights. Based on this acquired knowledge, an organisation can take effective action.

Data originates from actions, and drives new actions. The risk in the chain is the weakest link, and that relates to how data can be turned into information.

The Entity Method to help you cross the *Data Delta* **targets** this weakest link in the chain. It rests on an enterprise-level approach involving people, process and technology. Only by crossing the *Data Delta* can you ensure data flows smoothly throughout your organisation. And only then can you take the right actions at the right time.

4

Elements of the *Data Delta* Model

The purpose of this section is to provide a more in-depth introduction to the *Data Delta* model, and each of the 14 Data Management domains will be explained in more detail.

To help in this endeavour, we've created a fictitious company called *GoDelta* which has completed the initial stages of its journey across the *Data Delta*. We will use the past exploits of *GoDelta* to animate the picture of how effective Data Management has a positive impact on all areas of organisations.

Choose for yourself the best approach towards this section, where we dissect and explore each Data Management domain in detail. There's every likelihood that you will have less interest in some of the domains at any one time, so by all means skip around, and we'll all join together again in *Section 4.15 – Summary of the Data Delta Model.*

However, before you take your own path, please remember the overriding advice from the Entity Method of taking a 'thin slice'. You really shouldn't be considering any of these sections in isolation when you move towards implementation. If you read the MDM or BI sections, for example, you'll find lots of great advice as to how to implement these areas. But if you don't think about the governance of your data, how it is described, and its quality managed, you will, in all likelihood, sadly fail.

Indeed, it is worth underlining that as you break your data away from its current silos where security is usually effectively managed by trusted business applications, you may well need to think through enterprise security and privacy considerations too. It's a jigsaw. Study the individual pieces, but never forget their only *real* value is as part of the whole picture.

The 14 Data Management domains are defined in this key graphic of the *Data Delta* model:

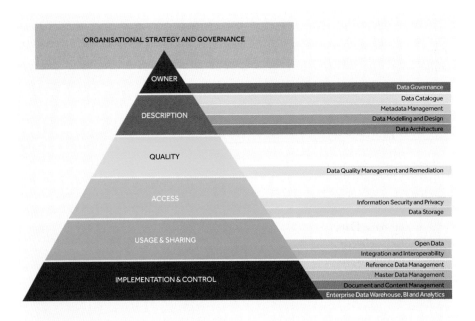

- Governance
- Enterprise Data Warehouse, BI and Analytics
- Document and Content Management
- Master Data Management (MDM)
- Reference Data Management (RDM)
- Integration and Interoperability
- Data Storage
- Open Data
- Information Security and Privacy
- Data Quality Management and Remediation
- Data Architecture
- Data Modelling and Design
- Metadata Management
- Data Catalogue

4.1 Owner – Data Governance

The word 'Governance' has, in some organisations, developed something of a bad press. It has become associated with consultants, mega-projects and inflexibility; perhaps because in many people's minds, it's a poorly defined term. In this section, we want to dismiss those negatives altogether.

We want to give not only a very precise definition of what Data Governance is – by way of twelve specific elements – but we will lay down a blueprint of the relationship *between* those twelve parts, and create a journey for success.

With our 'agile' hats on, we will explain that you do *not* need to do everything with all the twelve elements at once. Data Governance is not a 'binary' concept in that you either have it or you don't. In fact, you will probably start your journey by introducing *parts* of several of these twelve elements for a relatively small, but rather important, subset of your data. Data Governance is *not* one monolithic mega-project. It's a series of initiatives, each delivering real business value. Anything else, and you're probably going about it the wrong way.

It's also true that many software vendors are bringing out 'Data Governance' products. As you will see from our definition, these usually address only fairly small aspects of governance. Each of the fourteen domains that make up Enterprise Information Management are about people, process and technology, and quite possibly Data Governance is the one *most* about people and process.

Yes, some software tools will help certain aspects of Data Governance – which is great. However, in truth, in many instances calling a product 'Data Governance' is just a case of vendors over-labelling their products. This won't be for the first time, and we are fairly confident it won't be the last.

We want to be clear as to what governance is, and what governance is not. Let's get the 'nots' out of the way. It is not a talking shop. It is not an excuse for inertia. And it most certainly isn't something that can be entirely addressed with software products.

In many ways, Data Governance is the most important of the Data Management domains. It's about people, processes and technology working together to make a reality of the concept that *data is an asset*. If the HR function has, in its widest definition, responsibility for 'people as an asset', then the Data Governance function has responsibility in the same broad sense for the *data assets*.

The important thing to remember is that governance needs to reach as high and as far as possible within the organisation. Without governance, data oversight and decision making will be ad hoc, with no alignment of strategy or responsibility.

Data Governance serves to dissolve the silos between data domains, and between departments and business functions. It's about you working together as one organisation as far as everything to do with data is concerned.

So let's define it.

4.1.1 Features of Data Governance

We often refer to Data Governance as the 'glue' that binds together a series of data initiatives. By building an embryonic governance structure as part of an early delivery project, you can prove its value and subsequently, widen its scope across the organisation. It's essential to use good agile principles, even in this domain; use the agile 'Sprint'[49] concept to deliver value within a fixed time interval.

We have identified a path that defines the relationship of the twelve elements of Data Governance. By the time you've fully crossed the *Data Delta*, these steps need to be in place so that all your stakeholders can use their data with success.

Where possible, we use industry-standard tools and language in their definition (for example, we use RACI[50] when describing roles and responsibilities), whereas other elements will be entirely new. We don't, for example, expect you will have existing policies and standards documents covering all the Data Management domains.

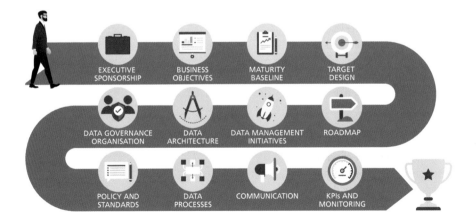

In our experience, these twelve elements are both necessary and sufficient to drive an effective Data Governance capability. You need to think about how best to implement them within the context of your organisation. Addressing the *Data Delta* is no different to any other agile approach. It's a question of doing *first* the things that will add most value to your organisation. Don't try to do everything at once.

Here are the twelve elements:

Governance Element 1. Executive Sponsorship

We said earlier that the key to success was forming *a small group of citizens* committed to changing your organisation. A vital mission for this group to achieve early on is to convince the Senior Executive group of the case to cross the *Data Delta*. You're going to need money, people and the ability to change business processes – even its cultural philosophy – and the only people who can enable that are those *right at the top*.

One obvious first question is: 'Who should lead this?' There isn't a black-and-white answer to that. In the world of Data Management, there are two main *opinions*, and they both have merit.

You could take the view that this will be steered via a new executive position – a 'Chief Data Officer' (or CDO, if you like) – and closely aligned perhaps, to the functions of a Chief Risk Officer. Some of the world's top banks have successfully gone down this road.

We are more inclined towards the second view however; that this is an additional responsibility for a very senior Line-of-Business[51] executive; ideally, this individual has *most* to gain by the success of crossing the *Data Delta*.

It might be a Chief Marketing Officer, or perhaps a Director of Services in a governmental function. On balance, we feel that for most organisations, it's more important for Data Governance to be aligned with the core Lines of Business, rather than engaging another specialist or dedicated executive.

To get a clearer idea of who should undertake this most important role of Executive Sponsorship, let's consider what they need to do. As an executive, they will clearly not be involved in day-to-day decision making and processing. Instead, they need to articulate and communicate the vision, allocate the required resources, and put an appropriate

---

[51] 'Line of Business' is used here as a generic phrase for all your operational departments. In a typical commercial organisation, these would include sales, marketing, production and distribution. In a government department, these would relate to service provision.

monitoring regime in place to ensure that the essential processes are being undertaken to the necessary standards.

What does a healthy level of Executive Sponsorship look like? And what is the impact of *not* having it? Let's take two examples from the Telco Sector to illustrate the differences.

First, a positive model. One of the world's largest telecommunications providers implemented a Data Governance regime with senior Executive Sponsorship. The organisation had an enormous footprint in the market for digital services. Internal requests for new systems and, increasingly, changes to existing systems were being generated at an average of 50 per week. The value of a single request could range from $30k to $10m.

All of these system changes were bound to impact the data of the organisation. The challenge for the executive was in how these changes should be governed.

The senior executive in question was widely experienced, and inherently suspicious of most forms of gateway[52] process management – whereby initiatives could only proceed from one stage to the next after certain stated criteria had been met. His experience was that middle-tier managers were experts at 'playing the system' to make sure their favoured initiatives were given a green light, whereas other projects mysteriously stalled (bureaucracies have a deep understanding of administrative systems, and how to bypass them!).

This executive asked the Chief Architect to design a simple governance protocol that focused on the one point in the process that couldn't be bypassed – the allocation of funding. A simple rule was introduced: without approval from the Chief Architect (evidenced by an allocated approval number), no data-related purchase orders could be progressed by the Procurement function.

These numbers were only ever issued following a weekly review meeting that considered all current applications. Though this represented a standard gateway technique, it exploited access to the financial coffers to give it real teeth. In addition, the application process was itself streamlined so that a standard set of artefacts was required to be produced in each case. No one could claim ignorance of what they had to do, and when they had to do it.

---

[52] Gateways represent a standard device to conduct reviews at key project stages to ensure all is proceeding to plan, and that future plans still make sense. The art is to make sure you have the right number at the right times. Too few, and you might find the project out of control; too many, and you will lose all project momentum.

Was it perfect? No. Inevitably, there were a small number of data-related system changes that didn't require an external purchase order, and these weren't immediately identified by this process. However, in reality these accounted for less than 10% of all changes. The key to any agile approach is to take the 90% win and leave the other 10% for tomorrow, rather than spend time staring at a flowchart trying to figure out that potentially elusive all-encompassing and perfect solution. As Voltaire said, in what is the clearest maxim for the justification of the entire agile movement: *'the best is the enemy of the good'* [53].

If you're wondering what the senior executives had to do to make this happen, their activities were senior leadership actions. They certainly didn't get involved in the weekly review process. They knew what was required, they set the challenge for the Chief Architect, and most importantly, they communicated to their peers to ensure cross-organisational awareness that there was no way around this. No one, no matter how senior, was going to be allowed to break this rule. By articulating the benefit of managing the risk to their data, the executive was able to bring everyone on board.

Let's contrast this positive application of senior leadership with the activities of another national Telco, which had an exclusive monopoly role as a provider for a significant group of islands, comprising a small country. These islands had a hurricane season, but that wasn't the most disruptive part of their weather pattern. During the hot summer season, the demand for air conditioning was permanently at risk of outstripping the grid supply. The untested theory was that if the islands' telecoms system were to drop completely, it would take thirty days to restart it. In other words, the islands would be without any telecommunications for the best part of a month, which would mean as well as general chaos and inconvenience, the economy would miss out on the lucrative international roaming fees from passing cruise ships – a key part of this island group's economy.

Then one hot day, the inevitable happened. A critical component on the main distribution panel literally exploded. And 'Murphy's Law' – the only truly reliable law of management theory! – kicked in. The part that blew up wasn't stocked on the main island … or any of the others.

Emergency procedures were invoked, and an ageing generator came online. Frantic calls were made to determine whether a replacement part could be flown in. And then someone realised that no one knew how long the generators would last.

Everyone always said they believed the generators would be 'Good for 24 hours', but the hardware had been through several upgrades *subsequent* to the original requirements being specified, and in all that time no one had thought to revisit the emergency provision. A check on how fast the generators' batteries were being drained concluded

---

[53] There really is very little new in this world. Voltaire made this insightful remark in both his French and Italian writings, the earliest dated 1770. Whilst the Voltaire quote is the most famous, even that wasn't new. We've traced the saying back 150 years earlier to *'Proverbi italiani'*, by Orlando Pescetti, but suspect it may be much older.

that their capacity was significantly less than 24 hours, and possibly only a matter of minutes!

In the event, the batteries did hold out, and disaster was averted when the replacement part was flown in and quickly fitted. A post-mortem revealed that the island economy had survived by 22 minutes. Just 22 minutes later, the batteries would have failed, the entire telecom system would have crashed, and chaos would have ensued.

It's easy to spot the impact of the lack of executive sponsorship here. How much executive time would it have taken to issue an instruction that the infrastructure recovery procedures had to be re-drafted and tested once a year? It would have taken five minutes for a senior person to write the memo, and then another twenty to check the executive summary of the annual report that should have been produced.

Doubtless, the executive would also have needed to consider the budgetary implications of procurement decisions as the infrastructure was upgraded, but again, this could readily have been built into a 'business-as-usual' model.

Effective executive sponsorship of data issues does not take much time at all. As soon as you recognise and acknowledge that *data is an asset*, you begin to lay the groundwork for establishing proper procedures to secure its supporting infrastructure. After all, corporate management theory is geared towards effective management of assets – and so organisations are built on the basis of maximising the assets on the Balance Sheet, the 'workforce' and fixtures, fittings, equipment and stock.

It's worth noting that all the decisions that underpin conventional asset management are based on information – and yet most organisations struggle with managing that information. Crossing the *Data Delta* means managing data – and therefore information – as an asset, and this can only benefit the management of other assets.

Governance Element 2. Business Objectives

It's fairly safe to assume that by now your organisation has developed some reasonably well-defined business objectives that the senior management team, at least, has subscribed to and understands. They are likely to be well-documented and broadly up to date[54].

The reasons are obvious: if you *don't* know what it is you are trying to achieve as an organisation, your chances of success are extremely slim.

---

[54] If not, what have you been doing on all those management away-days in those rather comfortable rural conference centres?

Assuming that you *do* have a series of well-considered business objectives, have you looked at them from a data perspective?

By way of an example, let's suppose that you have an objective to grow the number of new customers by 20% per annum over the next five years. In the first instance, this implies a quality standard on your customer volumes; you need to be sure you are accurately measuring the number of customers you have at any moment in time.

However, and possibly more importantly, it is highly likely that you'll achieve your growth in customer numbers based on a series of marketing initiatives, and these, in turn, will be based on the data that's currently available to you.

Perhaps you plan to undertake some targeted advertising using the demographics revealed by the postcodes of your customers. Perhaps you intend to analyse the channels through which you first engaged with existing customers to see how repeat promotions can be made more effective. You might have another objective to sell more product to more customers (or – in a government context – deliver your services to more citizens).

However you decide to approach this challenge, it begins with analysing *which* customers have *which* products or services, and this is a central Data Management concern that relates to how you manage your master data.

Given that you have well-defined business objectives, a fundamental part of your journey to cross the *Data Delta* is in reviewing them from a data perspective, both initially, and as they continue to evolve. They will be a key part of working out the right sequence of activities.

Governance Element 3. Maturity Baseline

Every journey should begin with a clear understanding of *where you are now*. There are lots of ways you might pursue this, and we have put a lot of thought into this particular step as part of the Entity Method.

A noticeably bad idea is to start with an audit! It's perfectly obvious you are going to 'fail' an audit – otherwise, why would you want to set out on your *Data Delta* journey in the first place? And audits, especially IT audits, are usually nothing more than 'tick-box exercises', where dramatic conclusions are seemingly proclaimed on 'evidence' that is often particularly flimsy.

For example, by now most organisations have perfectly reasonable Change Control processes for their Production IT environments – often based on ITIL or some other widely-recognised standard or framework. An audit will look for documentary proof of this, and if any weaknesses are identified in the documentation, it's likely to conclude that your process itself is ineffective. The problem is that an audit will almost always focus on the detail and miss the big picture. It's also likely to make your people defensive and discourage open dialogue.

The alternative approach to an audit is a Capability Maturity Assessment (CMA)[55].

In contrast to an audit, where the objectives centre on 'omission' and fault-finding, the purpose of a maturity assessment is to establish your current status in a *broader sense*. This involves talking to a wide range of representative people to assess their viewpoints, and will also include a review of existing documentation. However, in the case of the document review, this is not undertaken from an audit (and fault-finding) perspective, but rather to aid understanding.

It's very likely that there will be a difference between how well a process is actually undertaken, and how well it is documented – sometimes one will be better; sometimes the other. Because of this, a maturity assessment should be undertaken by seasoned people who can form an opinion based on their experience of other comparable environments. It's inevitable that there is an element of subjectivity in the way the method is applied.

A Maturity Assessment results in an overall score within the range of 1 to 5; where '1' acknowledges that even though there may be pockets of 'best practice' this is not replicated generally, and '5' recognises capabilities that are repeatable, measurable and continuously improving, and as such, they are a part of your organisation's DNA.

Organisations with the highest level of maturity, will not take *any* business decisions until they have considered the potential impact from the perspective of their data (for example, would this decision contravene our Data Management Policy in any way?).

The Entity Method considers Maturity Assessments for each of the Data Management domains and similarly, your own Maturity Assessment needs to provide a baseline measurement at this level. However, experience tells us that if, for example, you ask a

---

[55] The original capability Maturity Model was developed at the Carnegie Mellon University, which holds the registered service mark for this term. It was originally developed for the US Department of Defense.

filing clerk a direct question about 'metadata', or your VP of Strategy and Planning about 'Interoperability', you're unlikely to get a very warm reception.

Because of this, when preparing to interview representatives from across an organisation, we structure our questions around a broad group of themes that have meaning to business and technical people alike.

After each interview, we go back and determine what their responses tell us about the maturity of the various Data Management domains.

Getting the baseline assessment correct at the outset is critical to crossing the *Data Delta* successfully, so it's worth outlining the main themes here. We've identified nine themes to discuss:

a) Business Objectives, Drivers and Requirements

Make sure you cover the theme of 'Business Objectives, Drivers and Requirements' – and ask each of the people you decide to interview for their views on the vision, mission, strategy and role of your organisation (or their department within the organisation).

Related to this is the idea of 'Business Performance Monitoring, Management Information and KPIs or SLAs'. The point is to capture the nature and scope of the 'management information' used by leaders to steer the direction of your organisation. Questions here should be directed both at those who rely on and use this information, and those who may contribute to providing it.

b) Business Risk Management Through Data

You should ask about the role of information in helping leaders to manage and mitigate risk. Risks are often categorised in terms of 'financial', 'operational' and 'compliance'. We call this theme: 'Business Risk Management Through Data'.

And on the subject of compliance, be sure to probe into any 'Regulatory Compliance Requirements' in order to help build a picture of the regulatory framework in which your organisation operates. These questions establish the types of regulation either imposed on your organisation from *outside*, or imposed by *you* on other organisations. It also considers the role of information in helping the organisation comply, and provides evidence of compliance with any relevant regulation.

c) Data Availability, Timeliness and Reliability

The next theme is usually where people start to identify some real areas of pain related to 'Data Availability, Timeliness and Reliability'. This is where we look at the accuracy and format of information, and the ability people have to access information when they need it. Ultimately, the answers received here will feed into how best to deploy your people, processes and technology to both improve and *maintain* acceptable levels of data quality (including any data remediation required).

d) Data Ownership and Stewardship

'Data Ownership and Stewardship' determines how accountability and responsibility for data is currently apportioned across the organisation (if at all). Don't forget to ask questions to check whether people feel they understand who owns which bits of data, and who they should approach if they have a question, or should they identify a potential problem.

e) Data-related Risk

This next one – 'Data-related Risk' – comes from a different perspective, and looks at any risks inherent to the data itself. In other words, any risks introduced because the organisation actually *has* data. An example would be the risks related to personal data being misused.

f) Data Security and Privacy

Of all the Data Management domains, 'Data Security and Privacy' is likely to be the one with which people are already familiar. You need to inquire as to how people ensure information is kept appropriately secure, about the controls around who has access to it, how the information is used, and for what purpose. You need to build a picture of your organisation's overall ability to maintain an audit trail covering the lifecycle of all data, and to monitor all data activities carried out by individuals and systems.

g) Data Governance/Management Policies and Standards

It may be that your organisation already has 'Data Governance/ Management Policies and Standards' in some form or another. We can usually find pockets of excellent (or even 'best') practice, even within organisations that tend towards the lowest extreme of Data Management maturity, and it's important to highlight such practices so they can be replicated more widely.

This theme relates to the Data Management principles, policies and standards for governing *how data is used and managed* across your organisation. Your assessment needs to consider the people, processes and technology that already contribute to supporting this.

h) Architecture

The theme of 'Architecture' is most likely to relate to your IT function. However, it is well worth asking business people about the effectiveness of the systems they use, and also whether they have any input into the definition of data models, a business glossary, a data dictionary, or maintaining a catalogue of the data used within the organisation.

This is also the time to ask if people are aware of any formal approach your organisation might have towards Enterprise Architecture (EA) modelling (Data Architecture is a component of EA).

i) Data Sharing and Interfaces

Finally, the theme of 'Data Sharing and Interfaces' relates to how data is made available for use, and how it is shared around your organisation (and beyond). This is where we often unearth horror stories of people blithely emailing unprotected spreadsheets containing commercially sensitive or personal information.

Ask about how people use data day-to-day, and how they get access to, or share this data. Also consider data that is 'published'. What data is made available inside the company on shared drives or 'intranet' portals, via web services or via a public-facing 'web page'? But also consider your organisation's stance on 'Open Data' (this will be described in more detail later in this section).

We recognise that this brief survey of themes for a Capability Maturity Assessment may seem a little overwhelming at first sight, but we think you will find this exercise to be a liberating, empowering and hugely valuable experience when you actually come to undertake it for your own organisation. It represents a fabulous opportunity to expose long-standing issues – devoid of any blame – that may have festered for too long. A Maturity Assessment exercise, conducted well, provides the opportunity for stakeholders to feel they have a platform where they are being heard, and it sows the seeds for encouraging them to buy into the idea of Data Governance and Management, as well as to related changes down the line.

Governance Element 4. Target State Design

Having established the objectives of your organisation, and its current state of maturity with regard to Data Management, the next stage is to address questions like: 'Where do you need to be?' and 'By when?' These can be surprisingly difficult questions to answer, and all too often we see programmes fail because organisations approach these issues in the wrong way.

Strangely, it's often *not* the pace of change that's usually difficult – we find we can frequently move organisations forward much faster than they think; the key concern is how far to go. Exploring these questions will help to form a vision of the state of maturity at some point in the future. We refer to this as the *target state*.

The trick here is to assess what represents an achievable programme target based on current maturity levels within your organisation, knowing, as you do, the challenges of introducing change within it.

This is the place to consider all the capabilities and 'features' of your data platform in the widest sense of the word. What do you need in order to put the right information into the hands of the people that need it and thus support your organisation's strategic objectives?

A clear understanding of the features will lead to a consideration of the solution options. Include in your thinking the benefits of each option, how long they will take to implement, the technologies that might help, the processes that will need to be introduced or enhanced, who will be impacted – and how – and the costs involved.

Of course, the primary driver for your targets must be those 'business objectives'. They should dictate *what* aspects of *which* data you need to establish as your priority.

At the Entity Group, we actively conduct research on the latest developments around the world across all the domains of Data Management. When designing a target state vision on behalf of our clients, we like to reference the targets we propose against our knowledge of international best practice.

This is powerful, in that it allows you to benchmark your organisation's Data Management capabilities, both now and in the future, against the 'state-of-the-art' in the wider marketplace.

Governance Element 5. Roadmap

So now you know where you are and where you want to go to, and this means that we can produce a roadmap for the journey. As the King said in Lewis Carroll's 'Alice in Wonderland': "*Begin at the beginning and go on till you come to the end: then stop.*"

It's important to produce the roadmap, using the correct level of detail at this stage. Roadmaps are fundamental communication tools, and you're going to need a significant number of people within your organisation to 'buy into' your roadmap. This is not a time to reach for a detailed Gantt[56] chart in Microsoft Project, or cousins such as Oracle's *Primavera*. Such tools are great for down-in-the-trenches detailed planning, but the output isn't immediately accessible for most people.

Your roadmap needs to communicate when key organisational capabilities will be delivered, and how this translates into tangible business benefit realisation over time. The key here is to illustrate this as a single 'roadmap-on-a-page' picture. If you struggle to represent information using pictures, consider asking someone in your design department to help.

Governance Element 6. Data Management Initiatives

Once you have established a roadmap, it needs to be evolved into a detailed programme of Data Management initiatives. These initiatives take the form of implementation projects, and are the vehicle for introducing new or enhanced Data Management capabilities to support the organisation's business objectives.

During the design of these initiatives, there is often a tendency to place most of the emphasis on introducing technology capabilities, but it is important to keep the dimensions of people, processes and technology balanced within the overall programme. If new technology is being implemented, consider how this might affect people or

---

[56] Henry Gantt is recognised as the founder of the technique of representing a project schedule graphically, showing tasks down the left-hand side of the paper, and a time line going across. He formulated this style in about 1910. We now know that a Polish engineer, Karol Adamiecki, was using the same technique in 1896, but his work was not published at the time. There is no suggestion that Gantt copied Adamiecki's work; this is simply a case of two people having the same idea at roughly the same time.

processes, and whether any new roles, responsibilities or processes need to be established to support the technology.

The definition of an initiative should provide a comprehensive view of the costs involved and benefits to be realised. Each initiative needs justification in its own right, and as you progress on the journey to cross the *Data Delta*, the value of some of your programme elements will inevitably shift.

This is an important point to reflect upon. By definition, in crossing the *Data Delta* you are making an organisational-level change. It should therefore be *expected* that the new organisation may well have different priorities to the one at the start of the change process.

This is not an excuse to skip planning plan at all, but it is a reason to plan with caution and insight. Plan your future initiatives at a reasonably high level; objectives, deliverables, likely resources and of course anticipated costs and benefits. Don't however develop complex detailed plans showing, for example, minor task dependencies within the project at too early a stage.

Governance Element 7. Architecture

Data Architecture is a wide-ranging subject and should be considered within the context of an overarching Enterprise Architecture (EA) approach. This is deliberated at greater length later, as Data Architecture is one of the Data Management domains.

From the perspective of contributing to the success of Data Governance, however, it is necessary to state that any technology that contributes to the data platform – whether existing, new, or to be acquired – needs to be presented in the form of an evolving technical architecture.

We advocate starting with a reference architecture – a blueprint containing all the major technical components that support the Data Management landscape – and comparing this to your *existing* environment to help identify any possible gaps.

The following list will give you an idea of the type of components we have in mind (this list is not exhaustive). We have grouped the tools according to how they relate to the Data Management principles of the Entity Method:

Ownership (including Governance)

- Governance, Risk and Compliance Tools (GRC)

Description

- Business Process Modelling (BPM)
- Business Rules Engine
- Data Catalogue
- Business Glossary
- Data Dictionary
- Data Modelling/EA Tools

Quality

- Data Discovery Tooling
- Data Quality Tooling (DQ)

Access

- Data Security (Data Masking, Test Data Management, Data Loss Prevention Database Activity Monitoring, Access Control, Firewalls, Intrusion Detection, etc)
- Network Accessible Storage (NAS)
- Backup and Restore
- Archive Management
- Network Infrastructure

Usage and Sharing

- Extract-Transform-Load (ETL)
- Enterprise Service Bus (ESB)

Implementation and Control

- Master Data Management and Reference Data Management (MDM/RDM)
- Document Management System (DMS)
- Records Management System (RMS)
- Content Management System (CMS)
- Big Data Componentry (MapReduce, CEP, Graph, Natural Language Processing – NLP)
- Enterprise Search Tooling
- Identity Resolution
- Enterprise Data Warehouse (EDW)
- Business Intelligence/Predictive Analytics (BI)
- Etc

For further details and examples, see the section on Data Architecture later in this book.

Governance Element 8. *Data Governance Organisation*

Treating data as an asset – and signing up to cross the *Data Delta* – means your organisation is going to start doing things differently on a day-to-day basis. You will need to set up an appropriate structure to ensure this happens.

Specific responsibilities relating to the ownership of data will need to be defined; from the executive level right down to the lowliest clerical positions.

The critical concern is to identify all the roles, new or enhanced, required to maintain your data capabilities, and then assign responsibilities, appropriately documented using a standard RACI matrix. These are the roles and responsibilities of your Data Governance Organisation.

There's usually some form of steering committee to oversee the governance of data. They should meet on a regular basis, and act as the final arbiter for all matters relating to Data Management.

Some roles amount to part-time 'additional duties', whereas others will develop into full-time activities. It's impossible for anyone to tell you which is which for *your* organisation based on a generic template. It will really depend upon your organisation, processes, and the nature and quantity of your data, in terms of for example its rate of change (its *velocity*, in Big Data-speak).

Central to any Data Governance function will be the role of Data Stewards, and 'Stewardship' is indeed a useful concept to consider when thinking about who will be responsible for maintaining data that is used by several different parts of your organisation. Examples of shared data range from highly-important, but rarely changing information such as country codes, through to data in support of business-critical processes, such as the change of address of a customer or citizen. Once you acknowledge the importance of shared data it's clear that someone will have to fulfil the maintenance responsibilities *on behalf of the whole organisation.*

Data Stewards will take responsibility for the lifecycle of your data as it passes through the various information systems and functional boundaries. This includes taking responsibility for the quality of the data under their stewardship, and cleansing the data as necessary.

Data Owners are accountable for particular datasets, and direct the work of the Data Stewards. They will be drawn from both the business and technical areas of your organisation, and will ensure the quality standards for their dataset/s are upheld.

Governance Element 9. Information Management Policies and Standards

The Data Governance Organisation will need a clear charter for undertaking its responsibilities. You'll need to produce a straight-forward policy and a supporting set of standards; only then can the Data Management principles be applied successfully.

Those principles are articulated throughout this book; ownership, clearly described and discoverable data, measured and thus improvable data quality, access (both in terms of mechanical storage but also security and privacy), availability and integration of data, and management of supporting tools to maintain and report on the data.

You are also going to need a policy and set of standards for each of the fourteen domains:

- Data Governance
- Data Warehousing, Business Intelligence and Analytics
- Document and Content Management
- Master Data Management (MDM)
- Reference Data Management (RDM)
- Data Integration and Interoperability
- Open Data and Privacy
- Data Security
- Data Storage
- Data Quality Management and Remediation
- Data Modelling and Design
- Data Architecture
- Metadata
- Data Catalogue

The policy should address the scope of your Data Management systems, roles, responsibilities, management commitment, the coordination required among your organisational functions, and their compliance obligations. It should also highlight the importance of

Data Management as a pillar of upholding high standards of data quality, and cover the Data Management lifecycle *end to end*.

The standards should support the policy and direct organisational functions and other stakeholders in how to implement appropriate Data Management controls.

Producing meaningful policies and standards across the entire Data Management landscape is not straightforward. At the time of writing, we're aware of over 70 relevant standards, frameworks, and bodies of knowledge. Some of these have the full weight of the ISO or other reputable standards agencies, and can be considered 'gold standard' whereas, at the other end of the spectrum, others are of questionable value.

For example, there are no standards in terms of Master Data Management, but there are *several* methods that we feel could be regarded as 'best practices' that stem from the leading MDM vendors in the Gartner[57] Magic Quadrant[58]. In particular, IBM and Informatica both have a huge amount of very useful advice, but it won't come as any great surprise to anyone that the scope of their standards bear an uncanny relationship to their respective, albeit excellent, product capabilities.

Our customers benefit from our templates for both policy *and* standards in Data Management. In each case, there needs to be some customisation to suit the needs of the situation, but the head start puts organisations at a significant advantage in terms of crossing their own *Data Delta*.

Governance Element 10. Data Management Processes

Something is probably going wrong if your Data Management programme doesn't result in the need for new or enhanced processes and procedures within your organisation.

These processes manage, control and monitor the use of information, information-related projects, and initiatives in line with the established policy.

Some of these processes will be carried out automatically using some form of technology, but this by no means covers all data-related processes; some will be entirely manual. It's important to determine what these processes achieve, who – or what technology – is involved, and how often they need to occur.

---

[57] Gartner is, in our opinion, a renowned research and analysis organisation with a focus on information technology. It publishes a number of 'Magic Quadrants' covering a variety of categories of technology, and these effectively determine the suppliers to be 'niche players', 'challengers', 'visionaries' or 'leaders'. Suppliers aspire to be in the latter group. For further details, see: http://www.gartner.com/technology/research/methodologies/research_mq.jsp.

[58] Gartner, Magic Quadrant for Master Data Management of Product Data Solutions, Andrew White, Bill O'Kane, Terilyn Palanca, Michael Patrick Moran, 12 November 2015. Magic Quadrant for Master Data Management of Customer Data Solutions, Bill O'Kane, Saul Judah, 11 November 2015.

And don't forget – as that old stalwart Peter Drucker tells us – for processes to be effective, we need to incorporate some way of measuring the outcome.

Going forward, it's crucial to update your Change Management[59] approach to ensure that *all* changes to business processes and procedures consider the potential impact on Data Management concerns; it would be a sad state of affairs to make improvements in Data Management, only to set things back by changing something that fails to take account of the effect it has on the data lifecycle.

With this in mind, all potential stakeholders should be kept in the loop of both possible and *actual* changes to business processes, even if these processes do not *seem* to have any relation to data.

All potential changes need to be checked for compliance with your Data Management policy and standards, and possibly also for regulatory requirements.

This all assumes that 'documenting processes' is something that your organisation does as a rule. However, we are well aware that this is often not the case. We cannot stress enough, though, how much value you'll derive from getting this information down on paper, which can only effectively take place after you've discussed the process at length with colleagues.

Once you have your processes mapped out, you have two choices.

Your own staff now understand your current operation in all its intricacies, so you can either teach them to produce 'As Is' (current) and 'To Be' (future) diagrams – which should take an effective trainer no more than a couple of hours. Or you can teach an external consultancy everything about your business, and they can produce the diagrams. This option will probably take several months and, in all likelihood, will involve an awful lot of cash!

The most direct – and therefore, arguably, useful – way to document processes is to use a 'Swim-lane' diagram. List down the left of the page the various parties (or 'actors') involved in the process you are documenting, each in their own 'swim-lane'. Time is represented by going across the page, left to right.

Using *this* format, you map the process flow as 'boxes' representing the activities (be sure to put the box in the swim-lane belonging to the actor doing the activity), and arrows showing the direction of flow between the activity boxes.

---

[59] There is an assumption in this sentence that you already have an organisational Change Management process. While that is true for the majority of Entity clients nowadays, it wasn't always true, and there are still some business sectors a little behind the curve on this. The idea is fairly obvious – since there are so many factors driving change in a modern organisation, the organisation should have an explicit capability to manage change.

Once you've tried this a few times, it becomes clear that *horizontal* lines on the swim-lanes are usually straightforward, and the vast majority of your business process problems are in the *vertical* lines (when a process moves, for example, from Sales to Finance). The vertical lines are where you need all your focus on Data Management controls.

There really is no mystery about process mapping, and here's something unexpected: it's fun!

Getting Purchase Ledger Clerks in the same room as Procurement Managers, for example, with some sheets of A1 paper, marker pens and 'post-it' notes, and asking them to map all your business processes, is a hoot.

The reason is obvious – most people genuinely enjoy talking about their job. And there are great 'light bulb' moments as people figure out how they help – and sometimes hinder – their colleagues down the line.

It's very noticeable that self-produced 'As Is' and 'To Be' process diagrams are significantly stronger documents than those 'manufactured' by external experts. All those little twists and turns – those strange exceptions that only occur once a year – they all flow out in a well-run process workshop. Just keep asking the question, 'Do you *always* do *that* next?'

So, a clear recommendation from us, if you can resource it, is to map your own processes, and do it yourself, with an experienced facilitator.

Governance Element 11. *Communication*

One of the most important aspects of Data Governance is communication. Delivering the 'data is an asset' message to everyone in the organisation takes time. No-one likes to feel they're being patronised, and governance – occupying a position above the departmental silos – risks being seen as issuing commands from an 'ivory tower'.

The best way to spread the Data Governance message is to use people already on the inside of the various business functions to take ownership of the message. This amounts to establishing 'Data Champions', who have a role 'evangelising' the benefits to the organisation, of ensuring that data is shared and standardised and, conversely, pointing out that shortcuts in Data Management *don't* help your organisation in the long term.

A communication strategy is needed to identify the key influencers in the various parts of your organisation, so the message can be delivered to them, and you can secure their buy-in for the benefits of crossing the *Data Delta*.

You could get the most successful Sales Manager on board by demonstrating that she could increase her bonus through joined-up data. You could help the Procurement team negotiate better prices with suppliers by understanding how different parts of the business make orders throughout the year.

Find specific examples of how embedding effective Data Management within your organisation will help individuals, and they will be happy to help you in promoting the benefits.

There's one more thing to consider when delivering 'the message', and that is with regards to individual responsibility. Every single person within the organisation is responsible for the quality, health and management of data. If someone finds a broken window, they will call someone from Facilities Management. If they have a broken laptop, they call IT Support.

If they find broken data, do they know who to call? Data Governance exists to ensure individuals understand their own responsibilities.

Governance Element 12. KPIs and Monitoring

The steps we've been discussing are all leading towards a place where you can measure your success. We have looked at objectives, CMA, targets, policy, standards, and processes (with built-in measurements).

If you've managed to get *all* of these elements in place for all the Data Management domains, you'll be well on the way to crossing the *Data Delta* from a governance perspective. What remains is to establish a practice of continuing to monitor all the measurements, and use this approach to improve your organisation's Data Management effectiveness.

There are many data-related aspects that can be measured and monitored, particularly at a Data Management domain level. Here are some high-level considerations to get your thinking started.

Of course, one of the most fundamental metrics is how quickly you can service data requests. How quickly can you retrieve data? How long does it take to turn around data changes?

This relates directly to your SLAs; how quickly is it *required* that your organisation can turn around the information requested by stakeholders, or else carry out a change to that data?

This is measured as the *elapsed* time from receipt of a request to completion of a change – not only individual changes, but also the end-to-end. Requests might be received by a system automatically via a user interface or an automated service call, or they may be raised manually. In each case, we are looking to implement mechanisms to measure the time between a request being made, and its resolution.

Having dealt with the time element, you need some means of measuring the accuracy of any changes being made. The idea is to capture the initial request, and ensure that the result is as expected. This can be applied to both automated and manual changes.

One approach is to take a sample of requests and examine the results by manual inspection. It's best to vary the size of the sample according to the data volumes for different types of data.

You're likely to have lots of changes to your customer records and therefore may decide to adopt a lower percentage of samples. But you will have relatively few changes to reference codes (such as lists of countries, regions, or customer types), so you will check more of these (this also takes into account the importance of reference data – getting something wrong here could impact lots of other customer records). By doing this, you're measuring the accuracy of both the systems and/or the people involved in processing data.

Measuring the quality of data is clearly of critical importance. There are many techniques for this, and any given organisation is likely to need to implement several approaches. Options range from simple manual checks, to automated scripts, right through to purpose-built Master Data Management solutions, and fully-fledged business rules engines to handle validation.

In general terms, you're largely checking for three things:

- 'Completeness' – are all the required fields on the data record populated?

- 'Correctness' – do the populated fields contain accurate values?

- 'Redundancy' – are there duplicate records?

This is where most of those who make it *this* far, stop. But there is still much that can be done to measure – and therefore *improve* – the way that data is managed and used to support your organisation's core operations.

From a Data Management perspective efficiency is all about optimising the productivity of teams and individuals involved in compiling or maintaining data. In doing this, you are monitoring activities carried out *across* the business, not simply within IT.

If you start to gather information on the number of people involved in maintaining information, and combine this with what you already know about request volumes and the time spent servicing those requests, then you can start to build a picture about how many requests each person can handle.

If you go on to combine this with the *cost* of your resources, you can end up with a good sense of the financial cost for each transaction. This can be useful for managing the overall costs of your service delivery.

It follows that if you estimate the load required in the future, you can make more informed projections about your forthcoming resource requirements. Are you working with a surplus? Do you need to be recruiting? Do you need to be scaling back?

Remember too, that the whole point of service delivery is to provide your stakeholders with the features they need, albeit at a cost that represents value to them.

You therefore need to establish some mechanisms to measure the satisfaction of your customers. Of course, we would hope to see improvements in these measures too, but primarily you need to guard against *declining* satisfaction. All the moves you have made to increase turnaround times, and reduce the resources required, could be having a negative effect on the overall quality of your service – as perceived by the customer – so you need a safeguard against this.

Putting all of this together makes it possible to plot performance and *projected* performance using real numbers.

The introduction of Data Management will deliver tangible financial and quality-of-service benefits. With an effective data model in place, supported by useful metrics, you can really begin to drive improvements in your organisation's value chain.

To do this, you need to acknowledge – and you need your executive sponsors to acknowledge – that data-related processes *are* measurable. But you should *only* measure those aspects that will lead to actionable information. It's also worth noting that, though tools can be helpful, the important thing is to get to a point where you are able to collect information, and if that means doing it manually, then so be it.

It may seem a strange thing for us to be saying, but precision is not the pre-eminent concern here: what you are looking for is trends and exceptions. It's more important to be consistent in the approach than over-analyse things, and delay taking action.

Our advice is to get moving on your Data Governance. The sooner you do that, the sooner you can get into a position of measuring things related to your data and so reduce waste in your value chain. You will also optimise your delivery operation, increase the satisfaction of your customers and, in short, unlock measurable value from your data.

4.1.2 Impact of Data Governance

There's no denying it, Data Governance will have a *political* impact within your organisation. Someone will try to own it; there will be mutterings about 'empire building', and of people trying to take control of data away from other parts of the organisation.

The thing to focus on is the overall impact and benefit that Data Governance brings. It allows your organisation to make decisions based on the evidence contained within the data, rather than 'hunches' or guesswork. It allows your decision makers to focus on building value-generating capabilities, rather than arguing about the validity of facts and figures. Most of all, it allows your organisation to treat data as a valuable asset, and thus give it the management time and space it deserves. No one is saying it will be easy though.

For each of the Data Management domains, we have developed a set of guideline definitions for determining the level of maturity, in terms of how each particular domain is implemented. These will be helpful in getting a sense of where your organisation currently stands, and we have included a set under each Data Management domain heading in this section.

The following definitions relate to Data Governance.

Level 1 – Initial: There is no evidence for consideration of Data Governance practice. There is no joined-up strategic management of data. Architecture (systems and data) practices are ad hoc. Across the organisation, little regard is given to re-usability and standardisation. Though some definitions may be agreed, these tend to be used by people for specific projects.

Level 2 – Repeatable: There is evidence of documented Data Governance practices, though largely at project or departmental level. Architecture practices are also documented at a departmental level. There is no guarantee that these practices are sufficiently comprehensive, or that there is any consistency of implementation across departmental or organisational boundaries. There is no evidence of governance thinking at an enterprise or organisation level.

Level 3 – Defined: Organisation-wide policies and standards are defined to provide strategic direction for Data Governance practice across all departments. An organisation-wide Data Governance Steering Group exists, with defined roles and responsibilities, and departments understand the processes for engaging with Data Governance. Architectural strategy provides direction for all data-related projects across the organisation, with checkpoints to ensure projects are consistently aligned with the strategy. Data-related processes and roles are clearly defined and understood across the organisation.

Level 4 – Quantitatively Managed: The Data Governance Steering Group actively measures itself and departments against a number of KPIs, with departments reporting compliance with Data Governance practice and standards. Enterprise Architecture is used as an enabler for improvement in people, process, and technology, with re-usable architectural building blocks and deliverables across the organisation.

Level 5 – Optimising: Data Governance practices are at the core of the organisation, with all tactical and strategic programmes feeding back metrics for KPI reporting in order to drive a constant cycle of Data Management improvement. Data Governance practice seamlessly crosses organisational boundaries, with departments modelling individual practice upon that of the wider organisation's Data Management ethos.

All projects and programmes are coordinated with the enterprise or organisation architecture function as a matter of routine. Change in one system or process is understood and evaluated across all impacted stakeholders across the organisation. There is continuous improvement to the Enterprise Architecture skillset. Systems and processes are clearly identified as strategic, tactical, or legacy. A strategic reference architecture is measured against the active current state architecture.

4.1.4 Value of Data Governance - Introducing GoDelta

Now that you have an understanding of the features of effective Data Governance, the ground is set to illustrate the value it represents.

For the remainder of this section, we'll make use of an invented but 'life-like' organisation to demonstrate various aspects of crossing the *Data Delta*. Along the way, we will stop off and explore each of the Data Management domains.

This fictitious organisation is called *GoDelta*. Let's imagine that this company has been around for many years, previously under the name of *Finlay Bros*, and renamed during a rebranding exercise in the late 1990s – ahead of the 'Dot Com Boom'.

Their current product set allows everyday electronic products to be connected and controlled from the internet. Split into consumer and industrial divisions, their best-selling product is the *Delta Power Kit* – a 'smart' fuse box combined with connected power sockets that are controlled remotely using a phone app.

This app allows homeowners to, for example, turn on their oven before they get home, or control the lights in the house for security reasons while they are on holiday. The industrial version allows users to control equipment as part of their production line processes, and is advertised as offering significant power savings.

Like all organisations, *GoDelta* experienced issues because its data is in silos. Examples of the issues included preventing its management team from making evidence-based decisions, and restricting the Marketing function's ability to accurately target campaigns. In one specific case, this also caused the Customer Service team to overlook the fact that a customer, who had an issue with the 'home' version of a product, was also the CFO of one of their key industry customers.

GoDelta recognised it had a problem, and implemented a BI and Analytics capability to help break down the silos of data, and provide advanced reporting and predictive analytics to unlock the value of data across its various departments.

We're going to follow this project and learn how *GoDelta* crossed its own *Data Delta*, understanding issues that arose through the various Data Management domains, and how Data Governance was used to glue the features of each domain together.

From a Data Governance perspective, *GoDelta*'s journey began when a new Chief Marketing Officer joined the company. She came from a large organisation that described itself as a 'data-driven enterprise', and she quickly identified that *GoDelta* was facing many obstacles to growth because of its lack of maturity in Data Management.

Borrowing from her previous experience, she engaged a consultancy that specialised in providing Enterprise Information Management advice to help her prepare a business case, and promote the benefits of effective Data Management to her peers on the Board.

Initially, she secured some funds to carry out a current state maturity assessment (including a review of *GoDelta*'s strategic objectives) over the course of four weeks. The results of this were used to convince the Board to release additional funds to design a *target state* vision and develop a roadmap. Since then, the company embraced[60] the benefits of improving its Data Management capability. It acquired a comprehensive programme plan of staged initiatives, a target architecture, appointed a Programme Manager, and started a fledgling Data Governance Steering Group.

The key focus was on improved BI and Analytics, but the programme plan recognised the need to address a number of *other* Data Management domains to achieve this key goal. The Steering Group began to actively collaborate with its specialist consultants to establish Data Management Policies and Standards. These incorporated some key KPIs that the group actively used to monitor and direct developments going forwards.

In this way, Data Governance was used to shape the company's overall Data Management capability, and *GoDelta* recognised that this would continue to be the case long after the programme ended, as the new capabilities became part of the 'steady-state' operation.

Fortunately, *GoDelta* is already well on the way towards crossing its *Data Delta*. As we look at the various Data Management domains, we will revisit *GoDelta* to illustrate how the theory might apply to a 'real world' organisation.

---

[60] It would be more accurate to say that the company *largely* embraced this. There will always be pockets of resistance in any major change programme, and in 'real life', these need to be managed carefully and sensitively.

4.2 Implementation & Control – Enterprise Data Warehouse, Business Intelligence (BI) and Analytics

We thought we'd talk about BI and Analytics/Visualisation fairly early in our description of the *Data Delta*, because in our experience, this is often the most visible manifestation to an organisation that something is wrong.

We've already cited the frightening statistic that around three out of four BI projects fail to meet their objectives. Why? You can google the reasons easily enough, and if you do, two points will stand out.

Firstly, it's difficult to find anyone who designates their failure to having picked the wrong BI tool. The tools are all good nowadays – some of them very good indeed. But secondly, you will find a variety of reasons for even well-run BI project failure, and each and every one of them will – without doubt – be connected to some aspect of the *Data Delta*[61].

The existence of the *Data Delta*, and the failure of most BI projects, are fundamentally related. This is of huge importance, and is one of the clearest demonstrations that our definition of the *Data Delta* is correct and complete.

We can – and do – now use *Data Delta* theory to predict BI project failure, as in the earlier Airport example, in *Section 2 – Customer Case Studies*. Being able to predict future events is one of the key criteria for assessing the validity of any scientific theory, and the *Data Delta* concept achieves impressive results in this respect.

BI projects fail because of weaknesses in the areas of Data Management that sit above BI in our model of the *Data Delta*. Areas such as Data Governance and Ownership, Description, Data Quality, Access, Integration … the list goes on.

We can name individual BI projects that have failed because of failures in each of the Data Management domains. Conversely, and encouragingly, we can name BI projects that have *succeeded* because the organisation closed the gaps as it crossed the *Data Delta*. It's that simple. Ignore the *Data Delta*, and your BI project will fail as most do. Cross the *Data Delta,* and your BI project really should succeed.

Everyone that starts out on a BI initiative today has a vision of joining up the data from all the different parts of their organisation, perhaps 'mashing' it up with social

---

[61] 'Well-run' implies a properly defined and resourced project with realistic timescales. Obviously BI projects will fail like any other if they are poorly run, but the message here is that most well-run BI projects still fail.

media and other unstructured data, and presenting it to executives in the boardroom for 'self-service' analysis.

Your new BI tool certainly has the capability to facilitate those executive drill-downs, but as you head from the bottom of the *Data Delta* towards the top, you're most likely to hit the same stumbling blocks and dependencies as everyone else.

Do you want to populate your data warehouse? You'll need to have data integration thought through properly. Do you want to link customer transactions from different parts of the organisation? You'll need to have the advanced matching provided by a Master Data Management capability. Do you want to trace products from the supplier right through to delivery to the customer? You will have to make sure your reference data is managed effectively. Do you want any of this information to produce accurate results? You'll need a level of data quality that's fit for purpose. And so on.

Most organisations capture data for two reasons: operational and analytical. Operational data, such as name, address and purchases is essential to the smooth running of your organisation. If an address is missing, the customer will not receive their order.

Analytical data, on the other hand, zooms out from individual customers, and looks at the data as a whole. If one address is missing, the analytical data is unlikely to change much when looking at geographical customer regions. However, if everyone's address is entered using different formats, a regional analysis could be meaningless.

The 'Enterprise Data Warehouse, BI & Analytics' domain deals with management of data at this 'zoomed-out' level, providing a set of features that *should* be considered when embarking on implementing this kind of capability.

It's important to consider that most data is captured for operational reasons, with analytics coming along later as a useful by-product. Indeed, in many jurisdictions, data protection legislation only permits the collection of data for the purpose of providing goods or services; speculative data collection for less well-defined reasons is frequently not allowed.

Our fictitious organisation, *GoDelta*, decided to pull its data together from across all the silos to get a '360-degree view' of its customers. In layman terms, it wanted to see everything it could about customers, both at an individual level (such as when providing customer service), at a marketing level (providing tailored marketing to customer niches), and at an organisational level (to understand patterns and trends about where their R&D effort should be focused for the coming years).

Significantly, they wanted to answer questions such as whether their industrial customers discovered *GoDelta* products through home use first, or whether home users bought the home version of the product after seeing it being used successfully at work.

Answering these questions would provide direction for the R&D and marketing spend for some years to come.

At a technical level, a data warehouse is the ideal repository into which to pour data from across the organisation. Coupled with user-facing BI capabilities, it allows the data to be processed, stored and digested at all levels throughout the organisation.

Let's see what features a good Data Warehouse, BI and Analytics implementation exhibits.

4.2.1 Features

GoDelta's vision for a data warehouse was one of joining up customer transactions from across its internal systems, combining that data with social media and social networks (such as a customer's public *LinkedIn* profile), and providing that data in a self-service form to end users in the Customer Service, Marketing and Management teams. Going forward, they wanted to integrate the telemetry from their internet-connected products to better understand their customers' usage of their products.

In order to achieve this ambitious, yet common goal, they decided upon the following underlying principles:

- The data within the data warehouse should be made available across the organisation, subject to security and access requirements

- Data should be published from operational systems into the warehouse in near 'real time'

- Data lineage should be maintained with traceability back to the operational systems

- The data warehouse should act as the 'corporate memory' of the organisation

- Experts in the business should be used to provide a 'Virtual Centre of Excellence (VCoE)'[62]

- Integration of data into the data warehouse should be phased, allowing future systems' data to be added

The tools from the various Data Warehouse vendors offered many different feature sets and capabilities – many of which would be useful, and some that would not be at *all* useful.

Mobile phone apps to view a dashboard report? Fine. An email to the CEO showing the total customer spend for the past week? Great. This isn't the place to go into the specific features; there's enough marketing on the internet, and it's a fast-moving space.

What doesn't change, however, are the underlying principles. Let's have a look at why they're important.

4.2.2 What is the value/benefit?

The case for delivering enterprise-level BI solutions – by a combination of the right people, processes and technology – is overwhelming. Here are six of the reasons why you should implement an effective Enterprise Data Warehouse, and use world-class Analytical and BI tools to access it.

4.2.2.1 Data will be available across the organisation

Creating a data warehouse takes significant corporate effort, covering all aspects of people, process and technology. Integrating, standardising, and processing data into a data warehouse provides the most value in return for all that effort when data becomes available for everyone who has a use for it. This is why we're proponents of the Enterprise Data Warehouse (EDW). The name gives it away; it's a warehouse of data that's available for the entire organisation.

Time and again, we've seen organisations that have multiple data warehouses; the Finance and Sales and Marketing Departments each have their own, and Customer Services has another.

They each have their own custom feeds from operational systems; often the same systems are pumping data into multiple warehouses, and sometimes data is even transferred between these data warehouses!

---

[62] Virtual Centres of Excellence represent a formalisation of the 'institutional knowledge' of an organisation, rather than relying on individuals who know about particular technologies or processes to spread good practice eg 'If you've got a spreadsheet problem phone Sue in accounts, she's the Excel star', virtual teams can deliver a more formal and sustainable body of knowledge. Active participation in a virtual excellence team can be seen as a stepping stone in career advancement.

We would advocate bringing these data warehouses together into a single Enterprise Data Warehouse. Physically, you can separate sections of data into 'data marts'[63] for practical reasons of geography, security and functionality, but the principle stands; multiple operational systems should feed data into one EDW, and you should make that data available back to the *whole* organisation.

Of course, appropriate security must be a baked-in feature of any specific data warehouse or data mart tool, but we're talking about the functional capability here.

If someone has authority to access data that's stored in an operational system for reporting or analytical purposes, they should be able to look at the EDW/data mart for that data.

It's of little worth going the trouble of making data available across the organisation if no-one is aware that it exists, and this is where the Data Catalogue[64] domain (that we'll come to later) comes to the rescue. A well-maintained data catalogue can be used to determine what data your organisation has available.

As such, it should be the first place to visit before anyone attempts to generate a new report, produce a data extract, or establish a new data service or IT system. It could emerge that something similar is already available somewhere within the organisation.

4.2.2.2 Near real-time publishing

This next reason is straightforward to explain. Twenty years ago, it might have been acceptable to have a batch system where it took a week to process data from operational systems for analysis, but current technology allows changes to be detected, eg via 'Publish & Subscribe' interfaces, in near real time.

When your customers can comment on you in real time on social media, you certainly don't want to be annoying them with advertisements for things they bought from you last week. Near real-time publishing of data isn't always easy, and greatly depends on the operational systems providing data into the data warehouse.

Legacy systems that weren't built with integration in mind may find it more challenging to provide the data, and the same can be said for environments where systems are managed by external parties (as is common in local government contexts for example).

---

[63] Data Marts (DM) are a pragmatic solution to the realities of differing application vendors and physical geographies. It is all well and good to have the concept of one enterprise-wide warehouse, but the reality might be your organisation is Oracle-based in the US, SAP-based in Europe, and Infor-based in Asia. In this example, there might well be benefits from architecting three separate *physical* data marts that summed together at a *logical* level represent one EDW.

[64] Companies that implement a comprehensive Data Catalogue enable its employees to find the data they're seeking. They know where to look, and the Data Catalogue is a key dependency for the principle of making data available across the organisation.

But the reason for not providing near real-time data into the data warehouse is rarely technical. It's usually down to human factors.

4.2.2.3 Maintain data lineage

Central to what we are trying to achieve is gaining trust in information. Perhaps you have a report that states that sales were down in Scotland last week. Is it actually true, or is it that the results were so good, the Sales team then went out to celebrate, and didn't update their orders in time? Data lineage is the idea of being clear about 'Where does this data come from?'

In the example just given, there needed to be an indication that the UK totals shown exclude the Scotland results, as the Sales team missed the submission deadline.

One of the core principles of our *Data Delta* model is 'Data Ownership'. You should be able to look at a record (which is a collection of related data items), and determine *who owns which item*. The name and address? Yes, that's owned by the Customer Services champion. The email address? That's managed by the Sales and Marketing team. The shipping information? That's owned by the Fulfilment Department.

As data flows into the data warehouse, Data Ownership needs to flow with it. This is achieved by describing 'data lineage', utilising metadata stored in the Data Catalogue[65]. By understanding who owns the data, and for what purposes it has been captured, we can achieve compliance with regulatory requirements, and exploit the data to better effect.

4.2.2.4 Act as the corporate memory

The data warehouse should act as the corporate memory. By this, we mean that it should store – referenced against a time dimension – *all* the data that an organisation uses. When management makes a decision, backed up by evidence, the data warehouse and associated BI system should be able to provide a historical reference of that evidence.

This not only gives great support for compliance and audit requirements, but allows for the future development of trend analysis. It also helps from a 'lessons learned' perspective, by comparing the actual results of the decision to those predicted by the data – all of which can be used to improve future outcomes.

For example, a classic use of an effective data warehouse is to improve marketing decisions. Let's use our fictitious company, *GoDelta*, to illustrate this.

---

[65] This is a clear illustration of how one Data Management domain can be dependent on one or more other domains; EDW, BI & Analytics, as a domain, has dependencies on several *other* domains, including Metadata, and Data Catalogue (among others).

GoDelta's products seemed to be selling remarkably well amongst 25-30 year-old professionals. When they decided to market the same product set in a new geographic territory, the decision was taken to target their marketing at this same demographic. However, the marketing campaign didn't seem to have the desired effect, and although overall sales were satisfactory, the 25-30 year-old professionals in the new territory didn't appreciably purchase any more products than any other group.

Going back to the evidence, and comparing it against the current figures, allowed the company to identify that the spike in figures in that demographic was an anomaly. Further investigation showed that their product had been featured in a video by a well-known independent vlogger[66] popular with the 25-30s group. As a result of this discovery, *GoDelta* started a new marketing campaign in the territory by sponsoring *another* experienced vlogger to promote their product, this time with the desired effect.

4.2.2.5 Use your experts

This may sound like common sense, but the amount of corporate learning and re-learning that goes on is a source of constant amazement to us. Every department and system has its associated 'Fount of all Knowledge', who understands the ins and outs of the systems and data.

New insights can be gained by bringing these individuals together with those who understand how to use the analysis tools. This group of people – combining those that know about the systems and data with those that know how to analyse data – effectively forms the organisation's BI and Analytics 'Centre of Excellence'. You should consider making such a resource available within your own organisation. It represents a central pool of expertise for anyone with questions or ideas about how to use data. This also encourages innovation (ultimately, a positive thing for the 'bottom line'), and can even raise the desirability of your organisation to prospective employees.

An example from the world of Google is that of *CAPTCHA*[67] – the little box on websites where you type a set of characters to 'prove you're not a robot'. When Google scanned old books for the purpose of sharing them on the internet as part of their Google Books project[68], many individual words could not be converted into text (for whatever reason – such as being blurred or, perhaps, because of old-style font usage or paper damage).

By making this data available, and encouraging inventive uses of this data, someone had the great idea that they could present individual words to the millions of users signing

---

[66] Vlogger: video blogger.

[67] CAPTCHA's are those little pop-ups which seek to ascertain that we are a human completing an online form, not some form of computer 'Bot'. The word itself has a debated origin; is it an acronym or a backronym? What came first – the word or what it stands for? The idea comes from the concept devised by Alan Turing in 'Computing Machinery and Intelligence.' The word perhaps stands for 'Completely Automated Public Turing test to tell Computers and Humans Apart', or perhaps that was made up afterwards. Google's brand of CAPTCHA is called reCAPTCHA™. See: https://www.google.com/recaptcha/intro/index.html

[68] See https://books.google.com/intl/en/googlebooks/about/index.html

up to websites on a daily basis, and have real humans type in what those words were, thus fixing the missing bits that couldn't be recognised during the automated scanning process.

4.2.2.6 Phased on-boarding of data

Finally, the last underlying principle is to ensure that you start small and extend the warehouse in a controlled manner. With an elephant to eat, the best approach is one bite at a time.

When you cross the *Data Delta*, you're not going to do it in one giant step; you need to take lots of small steps. This applies to implementing a data warehouse.

A limited set of data related to 'customer' (or citizen or donor or service user – depending on your organisation type) is a perfect place to start, as these types of data (known as 'master data') typically comprise data from across your organisation. Bring in some data, show that reporting adds value, establish the Centre of Excellence, and … *iterate* – broaden out the breadth and scope of the data being targeted.

4.2.3 What does maturity look like?

As shown in our discussion on Data Governance, we find it helpful to refer to our guidelines for determining the level of maturity in terms of how the BI, Analytics and Data Warehouse capability is implemented:

Level 1 – Initial: There is no evidence of a coherent BI or Analytics strategy as there is significant variance in the way different business units handle information. Any reporting or dash-boarding in evidence tends to be closely coupled to specific software products and services.

Level 2 – Repeatable: BI/Analytics practices within specific departments or individual projects are successfully implemented, documented and repeated. There may even be local policies and standards, but there is no evidence that these are coordinated at a higher level, leading to inconsistent approaches or duplication of effort across the organisation.

Level 3 – Defined: Organisation-wide policies and standards are defined to provide strategic direction for Data Warehousing, BI and Analytics practice across all departments and functions. Departments build their local practices to deliver reporting based upon these standards.

Level 4 – Quantitatively Managed Data Warehousing, BI and Analytics practices are measured and controlled in accordance with organisation-wide standards, with all departments reporting compliance (or exception) back to the Data Governance function using KPIs and scorecards. This includes the provision of a centrally managed Data Warehousing, BI and Analytics capability for use by departments in delivering their reporting and analytics needs. This is supported by a BI Centre of Excellence.

Level 5 – Optimising Data Warehousing, BI and Analytics practices form a core part of the organisation's strategy, and are also considered as a material factor for every tactical project. Measurement and feedback from previous experiences are used to create better practices across the organisation. There is an active drive for improvement.

4.2.4 What is the impact involved in implementing the actions?

Successful provision of a Data Warehouse and Business Intelligence capability for your organisation relies upon good Data Governance. The governance features we've already described in *Section 4.1 – Data Governance* (such as the roles and responsibilities of your Data Governance Organisation, process change management, communication, and KPIs) are all important here. Let's see how a Data Warehouse and BI implementation leans on Data Governance.

4.2.4.1 Roles and Responsibilities

Perhaps one of the most important aspects of following our principles for Data Management is making sure everyone knows their job, and can perform it well. A RACI helps to define and communicate this to users and experts alike within your organisation.

The Data Governance Organisation should be responsible for the following:

- Performing a commissioning and strategic oversight role.
  This will involve requesting evaluations of specific technology solutions, and taking recommendations for the selection of tools and techniques for an enterprise-wide BI capability that's in line with the strategic aims of the organisation. Oversight will also be needed once the capability is established, to ensure that new projects and systems align with the standards of the BI toolset. For example, if a new system comes along that happens to offer its own data analytics capability, our recommendation would

be to evaluate whether those analytics could be rolled into the overall capability, rather than assume they will be implemented as stand-alone functionality. This may involve performing a physical data transfer, or somehow incorporating the capability in a virtual way so that it comes under the responsibility of the BI Centre of Excellence for developing and promoting skills and data usage.

- Promoting the BI Centre of Excellence within the organisation. This cannot be overstated, as the BI Centre of Excellence helps to drive the innovative and inventive use of data within the organisation.

- Ensuring that standards (and associated KPIs) are developed and rolled out across the organisation so that the different parts of the organisation are using the capability in similar ways, whatever the department. This relies upon the existence of standard definitions of terms in a Business Glossary, and on master and Reference data being managed centrally.

The Data Governance Organisation has a huge influence on the successful implementation of an enterprise-wide BI capability, as it is the only body with responsibility to represent the importance of the data asset across the whole organisation.

4.2.4.2 Process Change management

It's highly likely that in your organisation, like many others, there are existing systems with existing analytical capabilities, maybe even data warehouse functionality. Bringing these under the umbrella of a single enterprise-wide reporting and analytics capability, delivered through the BI Centre of Excellence is not without its challenges.

You will need to consider how this impacts on your existing processes and the people undertaking them, and also whether new processes will be required. This underlines the needs for a robust change management approach. As early as possible, and this *must* be embedded within the Data Governance Organisation.

4.2.4.3 KPIs and Monitoring

Defining Key Performance Indicators for the data warehouse capability is essential. Whether this be in terms of number of systems or datasets that are feeding data into the data warehouse, or the number of reports generated, or a mixture of both, the indicators you define can help to show the benefits of the initial implementation and help to show that the capability is delivering real value back into the business.

The implementation of an enterprise-wide data warehouse with BI capability usually generates some side effects, the most notable being that it brings data to the *forefront* of people's minds. As the most flexible and immediate way of generating view of data, it can also be the quickest route for realising if there are problems with the underlying data.

From this perspective, it is one of the reasons that we recommend establishing a BI capability early on, even if the data is of unknown quality. It can prove extremely valuable in exposing issues and monitoring progress on how they are being addressed (so long as the reports that *are* generated come with appropriate health warnings!).

Another side benefit is that it streamlines working practices. By removing duplication of effort, skills can be shared across business functions, and knowledge starts to flow across the organisation.

One important consideration persists in most organisations, though, and this relates to the allocation of budgets. There is often a reluctance to share employees between departments, such as, say, for the BI Centre of Excellence. Why should someone whose salary is part of the Finance Department's budget undertake work that benefits the Marketing team? In our view, this is one of the cultural factors that needs to be addressed and overcome.

It seems obvious to state that you're all working for the same organisation and, one would assume, all looking towards a shared positive outcome (such as increased sales, improved customer satisfaction, and more success in your field). At a personal level, being seen as an innovative leader is much more satisfying than being that person who always says 'No'.

There are many ways that budgetary restrictions can be overcome, whether it's a charging model across the various departments, allocating budget to the Data Governance Organisation so they can 'buy' expertise from across the organisation, or just pragmatic give-and-take. The exact details will depend upon the culture within your organisation, and this may represent a key challenge for your Data Governance Organisation (though it *is* an essential prerequisite as we described in *Section 4.1 – Data Governance*).

4.2.5 A tiny word of caution

No-one should be in any doubt of the importance of *advanced analytics* for commercial enterprises and government agencies, and this will only increase as the volume and variety of available data increases. We would be the very last people to want to *discourage* the effective use of high-quality data as the basis of making informed decisions.

However, we do wish to sound a note of caution – a point illustrated by the graphic below. The table plots cases of autism per 1,000 of the USA population against the cumulative total of movies featuring one particular film star: Jim Carrey[69].

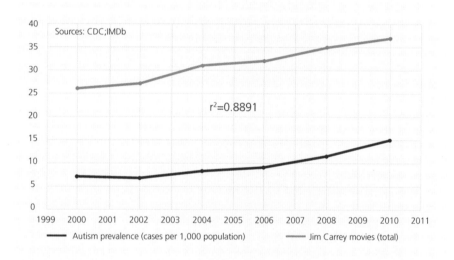

By using the standard regression analysis model found in modern BI tools such as *Tableau*[70], it is possible to arrive at a pseudo-analytical conclusion that the continued release of Jim Carrey movies is somehow impacting the rate of autism.

Common sense tells us that in this particular case, this result is clearly absurd; there cannot possibly be any causal relationship between these two variables. And that is the danger. There are lots of other cases where it isn't so obvious.

---

[69] This image is widely available over the internet (http://decisionmechanics.com/definite-proof-that-jim-carrey-causes-autism), and followed an intense debate over the causes of autism, in which Jim Carrey took part. We make no comment on the debate itself and what anyone said, didn't say, or meant to say. The diagram itself, however, represents a powerful image that proves our key point in this section.

[70] See http://www.tableau.com

This extreme Jim Carrey example is used to demonstrate a wider point. All statisticians know that a correlation between two variables can *never* establish causality. That statistical truism, however, flies in the face of popular understanding.

We constantly hear claims on TV made by everyone from politicians to sports pundits; the cause of inflation is X because X has risen at the same time as prices, or this team is better than before because their results have improved since they acquired player Y. These statements assigning causality are no more sound statistically than the idiocy of links between Jim Carrey movies and autism, but the flaws in the argument are much harder to spot. We don't intuitively 'know' the conclusion is wrong in the same way, and indeed the deduction might even 'feel' right.

Confirmation bias is the idea that we look more favourably on results that fit in with what we hope or believe to be true. It is difficult for non-statisticians to challenge results that appear to confirm their opinions.

Crossing the *Data Delta* is an absolute prerequisite for the successful application of analytics, but if you are making serious decisions based on statistics, don't rely on software tools alone, and make sure a suitably qualified Data Scientist has reviewed the results. People are every bit as important as process and technology. *Employ more qualified statisticians.*

4.2.6 What's next?

Let's get started! It's likely you will already have a data warehouse, or are thinking about establishing one. How does that become an enterprise-wide BI and analytics capability for sharing actionable information? By crossing the *Data Delta*, that's how.

Through the next sections, we'll work our way up through *Data Delta* model – visiting each of the Data Management domains, and showing how each unlocks the next level of capability, easing the way for the delivery of a successful BI and analytics implementation.

One thing to keep in mind is that, although we're demonstrating the power of crossing the *Data Delta* through the lens of BI, Analytics and an Enterprise Data Warehouse, there are benefits to be had for other implementation projects[71].

Here's a summary of the other Data Management domains from this perspective.

---

[71] Other examples include providing your business with a '360-degree view' of customers through delivery of a Customer Relationship Management (CRM) system, or providing the means to integrate data successfully from multiple organisations (such as in cases of mergers and acquisitions).

Document and Content Management: Lack of management of documents and the content within your organisation can weaken the advantage offered by your BI capability. Much of the information generated by BI and analytics tooling ends up inside reports and other documents. It is essential that these are managed appropriately with defined lifecycles.

Master Data Management (MDM): Master Data Management is like the master key that unlocks the capability to join up data from across multiple systems and silos within your organisation, and delivering that joined-up data into the data warehouse. Whether it's comparing citizens with service users, donors with recipients, or customers across various divisions, being able to get a complete view of how your customers interact with your organisation is tremendously powerful. We make no apologies for spending quite a bit of time explaining MDM. Where Data Governance is the most important 'people' part of the *Data Delta*, MDM is the most important 'solution' component. Of course, technology is not enough, and in our experience, where many MDM projects stumble is in making the project too 'technology'-focused. From a BI perspective, MDM is essential in terms of bringing together all the various pieces of data into a single 'golden view'[72] of master data (such as customers, citizens, products, assets, etc). But lest you think that is exactly what pulling data into a data warehouse is about, this is to diminish the task managed by MDM to match related records, to resolve duplicates and conflicts, and to determine which data items from which sources should be regarded as 'authoritative' when composing the 'golden view'. Many BI projects fail because it becomes too difficult to make sense of the data in the underlying data warehouse. MDM is a significant part of the solution to this problem.

Reference Data Management (RDM): Reference data is especially key to BI & analytics. This is the data that we think of as representing standard lists (such as countries, regions and customer types). As such, these lists play an important role in helping to categorise data in various ways eg this customer lives in Germany, they are a 'VIP', they are female, they have bought our Platinum Service etc. A key aspect of analytics is the ability to segment data, and highlight trends or make predictions *based* on these segments, and reference data is important in enabling this process.

Integration and Interoperability: Data that is captured by source systems needs consistent and well-defined mechanisms and controls to allow it flow across the organisation into the data warehouse. In this domain, we'll see how this breaks down the walls between the data silos within your organisation, by addressing the technical barriers to sharing.

---

[72] A 'golden view' is a well-established term in MDM circles for 'the best opinion you've got' – although there is rather more science to it than that. Whilst there is a lot of focus on obtaining a '360-degree view of customers', this rather nice marketing phrase overlooks the essential detail that some of the information you are holding might well be contradictory, and on occasion simply wrong. If when the customer first purchased your cable TV services they gave you one mobile number, but for the last three years every time they called your call centre they gave another, the 'golden view' would suggest that their current mobile phone is likely to be the one in your call centre records, not on the original purchase form.

Open Data: Alongside integration and interoperability, Open Data promotes the provision of raw data (or as 'raw as possible') to the public *for any use.* Where the integration and interoperability provides the technical means to get access to data, the Open Data principles provide the policy basis and mind-set to help departments become prepared to share their data.

Data Storage: All organisations need to store data and manage every aspect of the lifecycle. A Data Warehouse capability will have its own data storage requirements, but the ability of source systems to store data in a cost-effective, readily accessible manner, and provide data that is current requires careful management of the *entire* data lifecycle.

Security and Privacy: With all this talk of sharing data, it's important to remember that the default position is one of *security and privacy.* Publishing a list of all your customers is great, but you need to be certain that *only* those authorised to access that data can access it. A balance needs to be struck between unrestricted access to data, versus monitored or authorised access to data, as well as no access to data. In the Security and Privacy section, we'll take a look at some of the principles you should follow.

Quality: Data Quality is such an important requirement for data warehouse implementations that it often comes as a precursor initiative on its own. In this section, you'll see how data quality can make a difference across your organisation, why it's important to measure it, and why you should define what quality *looks like.* Even with the best data warehouse implementation in the world, without *known* data quality, you'll still wind up with arguments about the figures!

Data Architecture: Here we start to get into the realms of the technical, but defining data architecture at a strategic level is incredibly important to both ensuring that data is appropriately and consistently designed, and that the related processes and technologies provide adequate support for your organisation's requirements of data.

Metadata Management: Metadata is the data about your data. Managing metadata constitutes controlling how data is tracked, described, categorised, secured, validated, shared, used etc. Metadata is captured in assets such as your Data Models, Data Dictionary, Business Glossary, Data Catalogue and so forth. If you have these already, if they're up to date, and if you can access them during the design and requirements phase of your data warehouse delivery, then you're doing rather well. In most organisations however, the data about the data is very patchy indeed.

Modelling: Data Modelling is an essential part describing your data, and in this section, we'll share some principles that you should be following within your organisation. It helps if everyone is talking the same language about data, even for global multi-lingual organisations, and fortunately, this is easy to do. Standardisation, at this stage, pays dividends when you actually *need* to use your data for anything other than a very narrowly focused day-to-day activity.

Data Catalogue: With the Data Catalogue, we're back towards the pinnacle of the *Data Delta* model. Here you'll see how a well-maintained Data Catalogue represents the entry point to your data; it provides users with the pointers to understand who has what data within the organisation, what the allowable uses are, and what is the *meaning* of the data. The Data Catalogue is also the virtual store of metadata, models, definitions and semantic meaning – ultimately providing the ability to take the data from within your data warehouse and convert it into 'information'.

Each of the Data Management domains within the *Data Delta* are valuable in their own right, but when integrated with one another they provide the backbone that supports any initiative that seeks to make *use* of data. And don't forget, they're all kept together and given shape by Data Governance.

When all the other domains of the *Data Delta* are functioning properly, implementing a data warehouse is relatively straightforward; the technical folk know what the data looks like, where to find it, how to access it, and what it means, because the data is *controlled and maintained as an asset*.

4.3 Implementation & Control – Document and Content Management

Document and Content Management (DCM) is something of a Marmite domain![73] Some people are passionate about it; others detest it. We don't see it like that. Like almost every other domain, well implemented as part of a *Data Delta* solution, it's an incredibly powerful and valuable business toolset.

Done badly, it can give rise to a series of administrative obstacles that users find so insurmountable that they invest energy in circumvention. As an example, instead of complying with a company directive when filing email documents, some people might go to the trouble of sending company information via a private email account[74].

The precise definition of the distinction between 'documents' and other types of 'content' in DCM, can be difficult to specify exactly, and to be honest, we are not sure the distinction is a useful one. There are many good articles you can research if the distinction matters to you, but for most organisations, most of the time, the distinction is obvious, and there seems little business benefit to us in arguing over the exceptions.

DCM involves what most people refer to as 'unstructured data'. Technically, that implies it concerns the lifecycle of information held in some format that isn't a relational database. This includes most of the artefacts of everyday office life – letters, invoices, purchase orders, financial spreadsheets, emails, website content, blogs, data extracts, reports, contracts and agreements, images, audio and video files, and so on.

We think it's important to challenge 'unstructured' data as a term. There is a strong argument that DCM might best be described instead as relating to '*semi-structured*' data.

Let's again use our fictitious company, *GoDelta*, to illustrate this, and take the example of a complaint that was emailed to *GoDelta*'s Customer Services.

Clearly, this complaint was from a customer, and the customer's existing record was already held within a structured business application. The letter was most likely complaining about a product, a service, or a member of staff. Again, these data items all relate to information that is – or should be – stored in various structured databases.

In other words, a lot of the information relating to this complaint was already managed through structured systems.

But what about the letter itself? When it was received by *GoDelta*, it needed to find its way to the right person for processing. After actioning, it needed to be filed, and

---

[73] This might benefit from some explanation. Marmite is a food spread; it is entirely non-alcoholic, but the yeast which is its core ingredient is a by-product of the beer brewing process. It divides opinion in a quite remarkable way. People frequently express their opinions of this minor food product in terms of 'love' or 'hate'. The manufacturers of Marmite identified the polarity, and realised that they had no chance of converting the 'haters'. Their strategy instead was to revel in this division, and encourage the entire population to join one camp or the other. 'Marmite' has thus become short-hand for any product or idea that sharply divides an audience, where there is little, if any, middle ground.

[74] Indeed, at the time of writing, the fact that one of the candidates to be the next President of the United States used a private email server to bypass certain DCM restrictions is proving highly controversial.

eventually needed to be archived or destroyed. Clearly, Metadata Management was needed to support the lifecycle of this letter.

At various points in time, someone within the organisation may need to be able to locate the letter again. They most likely have cause to find it via its relationship to the customer, or the product/service it mentions, or even the staff member implicated by its content.

All those potential searches relate to the *structured* part of the correspondence. Yes, someone might conceivably want to locate the letter by carrying out a free-text search on some specific phrase contained within it, and it's great to have the capabilities to do that, but it's not going to be something you need to do every minute of every day.

So it's most important to manage the *semi-structured nature* of the correspondence. The unstructured content of the letter would doubtless have considerable value, too – that's why they wrote to *GoDelta* – so this will also need to be managed, just like any other data asset.

We focused on a single type of content here, but the arguments are generic. All content needs to be appropriately managed throughout its lifecycle to ensure that the information it contains *continues* to represent value to your stakeholders.

4.3.1 Features to consider

So what does good Document and Content Management look like, and why would an organisation like *GoDelta* need it?

Firstly, *GoDelta* needed to define what they knew about the documents and content they were dealing with. Typically, they were collecting information such as the 'document date', 'author', 'next review date', 'purpose' and 'version'. These headings are examples of metadata *relating to documents*.

The real benefits were introduced when *GoDelta* began to define document metadata that linked their documents to the *structured* data already under their control.

For example, when one of *GoDelta's* customers orders a product online, the version of the user manual shipped with the product is tagged against *that* customer's record. This allows the Customer Service team to email the customer if a new version of the manual is released.

Other useful information is captured at different stages.

GoDelta's Marketing department keeps a record of every promotional email sent to each customer. Conversely, when a customer emails Customer Service, the email is linked to the customer record. If the message is related to an order, then the email is linked to the appropriate order record for the customer.

By linking the various documents and other content with *structured* data, it becomes possible to undertake some inventive analytics at the product and order level. This includes sentiment analysis – has a customer had a good or bad customer service experience? Using real data that you have available will give a far stronger insight than any customer survey, however well designed.

Is there a problem with a specific product? Are common problems being found? Once again, these issues can be addressed by looking at the *patterns* in the data.

We talk a lot about sharing data throughout this book, and we'll devote a lot more to the security and privacy aspects in the coming pages, but clearly, the sharing and use of data should only take place within a defined security and access framework. This may sound obvious, but there are some instances which highlight important principles.

Examples include the CCTV footage used inside stores to track customer movements and prevent theft, or monitoring of employee activities (recording computer keystrokes, for example) to detect fraud.

Each of these will result in data, and there will be both valid and invalid uses of that data, and indeed legal and illegal uses of data. Information about how data can be used and its associated security details represent additional types of metadata. The metadata describes what types of information we want to capture about our data, including our documents and content, whatever the format.

4.3.2 What does maturity look like?

Here is some guidance on possible maturity-level definitions for the DCM domain:

Level 1 – Initial: There is no evidence of a coherent DCM strategy as there is significant variance in the way different departments and functions approach it.

Level 2 – Repeatable: DCM practices within specific departments or individual projects are successfully implemented, documented and repeated. There may even be local policies and standards within parts of the organisation, but there is no evidence that these are coordinated at a higher level, leading to inconsistent approaches or duplication of effort throughout the organisation.

Level 3 – Defined: Organisation-wide policies and standards are defined to provide strategic direction for Document and Content Management practices across all business units. Departments build their practices based upon these standards. There is central management of documents and content, including the ability to share and exchange documents across the organisation, and managed workflows are defined for producing and managing content. There is central management of a controlled vocabulary for certain categories of content (eg instruction manuals).

Level 4 – Quantitatively Managed: DCM practices are measured and controlled in accordance with organisation-wide standards, with all departments showing compliance through the use of KPIs and metrics. Monitoring is applied to workflows controlling the exchange of documents and content across the organisation.

Level 5 – Optimising: DCM practices form a core part of the organisation's data strategy, and these practices are considered as a material factor for every tactical project. Measurement and feedback from previous experiences are used to create better practices. There is an active drive for improvement. Customers (or citizens, donors, etc) are able to participate in document workflow, such as providing feedback for user manuals, website content, etc. Content is proactively managed by using data to anticipate the needs of the audience (both internal and external).

4.3.3 Value

At the time of writing this book, an interesting example emerged, which demonstrated what can happen when content is not adequately managed. This instance related to the UK's Department for Education (DfE).

It was reported that a live examination paper was accidentally published on the Department's public-facing website as a practice paper[75], but this was only discovered when, during a trial run of the exam some months later, a student informed his teacher that he already knew the questions. This resulted in the UK Government being forced to withdraw the entire exam for the year.

With more stringent controls – involving policy, processes and some appropriately applied metadata – this particular disaster could have been averted. It would have been apparent much earlier that this document represented a 'live' exam paper rather than a practice paper. Metadata controls could have prevented this from ever becoming available to the public.

In this case, the mistake had the unfortunate consequence of adding fuel to an already highly-charged political situation (many teachers and parents are against these examinations).

Another example from a very different sector. A few years ago, one of the world's most successful car manufacturers asked us to help them manage a particular problem related to Document and Content Management. Their problem should be familiar to any manufacturer of a complex product, where they need to support significant aftersales service and repairs. This means maintaining and distributing an accurate, well-structured and up-to-date set of the servicing instructions for each and every model variant they produce.

In the case of this global organisation – operating in many countries, and producing many models and variants – tens of thousands of servicing manuals needed to be provided, *each in multiple languages*.

The car manufacturer was having difficulty managing all of this content, and their translation bills were skyrocketing. One of the biggest causes was the lack of a standard way, across the board, of expressing similar ideas.

Here's an example from an instruction manual where these phrases are all used within a single document:

- align the parts
- make sure the parts align
- the parts should be aligned

These phrases are all effectively saying the same thing, but they all have to be translated independently, and that process has an associated cost. On the other hand, modern

[75] http://www.bbc.co.uk/news/education-36108449

translation services are able to recognise repeated phrases and re-use the same translation in each instance.

In the case of our automotive customer, we wanted to help them remove unnecessary variations, and to do this, we implemented a 'controlled vocabulary'. This had benefits, not only in terms of reducing the time and cost of translation, but also in reducing the effort to review documents. It also ensured that terms, descriptions and standard pieces of text were used *consistently* across the company.

In the 'parts' example above, the use of a controlled vocabulary during document authoring would have realised a 66% saving on translation costs. In our real-world case, our master content system exploited a combination of best practice Data Management approaches (Document and Content Management, Metadata Management, Master Data Management, and Interoperability via XML messaging) and saved *tens of millions of Euros* in translation costs in the first year alone. This approach unlocked *measurable value* from data.

The following two examples illustrate how the nature of the organisation can influence different ways of using Document and Content Management. One relates to the construction industry, and the other to law enforcement.

A Construction Industry case study

In the early 2000s, one of the UK's leading construction companies lost two High Court cases in quick succession. The reason, in both instances, was that 'side letters' [76] were produced in court by the plaintiff (a client of the construction company) to verify their claims, letters of which the construction company management team were unaware.

These were documents written by their staff that amended contract terms with the client, but which were not recorded in the corporate systems. The members of staff who had written the side letters had moved on, and the side letters had been *forgotten* by the construction company. However, they were not forgotten by the clients.

The cost to the construction company of these two cases ran into tens of millions of pounds. Something had to be done, and the Board decided on a radical approach. There would be no more 'side letters', because there would be no more 'hard copy' letters at all. The organisation would go paperless; the 'office of the future' [77] would finally arrive. All outgoing written communication – proposals, contracts, documents, emails, etc – would automatically be stored electronically. All incoming communication would be treated in the same way. And if someone sent something to them on paper, it was to be scanned in a post room, and the electronic version – not the original – forwarded to the recipient.

---

[76] A side letter is a separate official document, usually in the form of a letter that alters established contract terms. A typical example might be an agreed variation on standard payment terms. Since side letters are deemed by courts, certainly in the UK, to have the *same standing* as a formal contract, and they can potentially have enormous implications for both parties.

[77] The phrase 'the paperless office' goes back to "The Office of the Future", Business Week (30 June 1975)

There would be no paper correspondence in the organisation, and no electronic communication that wasn't managed in this way.

The programme to achieve this was a considerable success for a variety of factors.

Firstly, this was a Board-level initiative. People often talk about the importance of 'executive sponsorship' without being clear what is meant (the section on Data Governance above sets out our interpretation of this concept).

The role of Directors is to make things happen; this involves leadership, prioritisation and resource-allocation. The IT function had a significant role to play as one of the key enablers in this programme, but *had* it been an IT initiative (led by the IT Director), it would most likely have failed. That will be true in *your* organisation too, unless you find a senior 'business' executive sponsor to make your Data Management programme successful.

Secondly, there were other reasons for the success of the construction company. They had a well-defined objective, and remained aligned with it, not allowing themselves to get side-tracked. They were fairly ruthless in deferring 'bells and whistles' to a future phase.

They approached the programme with seriousness and integrity, and this formal approach to project management allowed them to focus on deliverables *without* getting drowned in detail. Finally, they employed some particularly talented staff. With realistic expectations on timelines, they chose a world-class solution, and completed an outstanding text-book implementation.

At the time of writing this book, they also have achieved their secondary objective of never having lost another court case because of a 'side letter'. And it's now ten *years* since that implementation took place.

The nature and character of the organisation concerned meant that this particular implementation was strongly *process-based*. Its operation was reflected in well-defined business processes, and was based around projects. The taxonomy of construction projects happens also to be well-defined, so matching terminology to key reference data was a relatively straightforward task.

DCM and Policing

For obvious reasons, we cannot divulge many details about our work with police and security services, though as a general point, in those scenarios, we are seeing no exception to the principles of how the *Data Delta* needs to be crossed. It would not be appropriate to give specific case studies in this sector, though there are some important general points that can be discussed in the public.

There are, for example, differences in emphasis in relation to the construction case-study above. Most of the documentation involved in a major criminal case is less neatly structured. An example is a witness statement. The details within a witness statement relate to one or more of four types of information: people, objects, locations or events (POLE). Hopefully you will find this acronym easier to remember after our earlier footnoted anecdote *in Section 2 – Customer Case Studies*!

POLE attributes need to be linked to reference and master data. Here's what the North Yorkshire Police have to say about the importance of making those links correctly:

> *It cannot be emphasised enough that the individuals responsible for recording need to understand the potential consequences of inaccurate linking. The sharing of information with other agencies and forces such as through the Police National Database (PND) is based on the type of involvement an entity plays within an occurrence. Investigators and specialist departments, such as disclosure, rely on involvement types to make risk-based decisions.*
>
> *Within policing and the security services, the three 'Vs' of data – the data volumes, the variety of data formats, and the high velocity of data flow – have pushed the boundaries of Document and Content Management systems. The process element is not as clearly defined as in the construction world, whereas the need to identify patterns and retrieve information is significantly beyond most commercial and other governmental activities. Specialist search engines have been developed to help manage this type of content, and to identify patterns more readily.*

The key point, in all examples, is that Document and Content Management must be seen as part of an overall Data Management roadmap. Only in this way can the data that these systems contain be turned into useful and valuable information for the organisation.

4.3.4 Impact

We talk a lot about data and information. Data represents the raw facts, and information is created when those facts are given meaning and context. But information should also evolve to become knowledge. This happens when information is enriched with the expertise, experience and insights of an individual or group of people. This is clearly something that has value, and which we would want to retain and exploit.

Knowledge, like data and information, is captured within documents and other types of content. Many readers will have heard or used the term *knowledge base*, which obviously constitutes 'a repository of knowledge'. For an organisation, this represents a valuable resource, but it will require some organised thinking and effort to ensure this is an asset, rather than adding to the burden of data ownership.

The *Data Delta* principles need to come to the fore here, ensuring that *all* types of content are owned, understood and described, secured, used and shared.

How might this translate into the daily routine?

If an old product is taken out of the market place, you need to make sure that *all* related and affected content is updated to reflect this. For example, everyone has experienced the frustration of broken links off web pages just at the very point you think you have found the product for which you have been looking.

Or another example, if customers are saying great things about a certain feature of your product, you might want to capture this, and share it with your Product Development teams.

The point is to think through all the *common* events related to your operation, and consider how your content plays its part.

Raise awareness about the value of content. Establish appropriate processes, supported by the capture of well-defined metadata. Educate people to use the processes, to tag content, to take ownership and generally, to think of creative ways to use and increase the value of this primary asset.

4.3.5 Next Steps

It's important that your organisation establishes and mandates a workflow for authoring, reviewing, publishing, and maintaining content. The actual workflow employed in each case should consider the type and sensitivity of the various documents and other content, whether it be materials for your website, marketing copy, internal newsletters, strategy documents, shareholder reports or *any* type of semi-structured content.

This doesn't need to be onerous or overly bureaucratic, and once the policy is established, use of appropriate tools and processes can be applied to keep everything under control.

Content is rarely created without a reason, and collecting appropriate metadata at key points in its lifecycle allows you to build a picture of the content's *'lineage'*, and ensure it is being used appropriately.

Ensuring that documents and content are reviewed at appropriate times is essential to make certain the information is still relevant and current. This needs to occur not only during the creation process, but also subsequently at intervals eg quarterly, annually etc.

This will also help to maintain compliance from a *Data Protection standpoint*, whereby Personally Identifiable Information (PII) should not be retained beyond its useful life, such as keeping data after the *purpose for which it was collected* has expired.

This will involve allocating accountability and responsibility for all content. You might choose to establish calendar functionality – perhaps as part of a workflow tool – to ensure that the periodic reviews take place.

We all know how frustrating it can be to find a document on a website that is clearly out of date. Regular review cycles, supported by KPIs and monitoring, can help to keep your content fresh and accurate. A great, up-to-date website creates the right first impression.

4.4 Implementation & Control – Master Data Management (MDM)

If Data Governance is the glue that binds the *Data Delta* domains together, then Master Data Management (MDM) *could* be viewed as the engine that powers high-value solutions.

The purpose of MDM is to facilitate the generation of a *single version of truth* for your organisation's most important data, whether that relates to customers, citizens, products, assets or any other key set of data. We need to analyse that simple definition and look at the core elements in considerable detail. We would, in particular, recommend that you *don't* skip this section.

There are many important points introduced, not least that in all probability, your standard procurement approach for defining your needs in this critical area *may not work*[78]!

And although we are, in this section, going to focus on MDM, it is important to restate the key points we made above. A successful MDM implementation can only take place within the broader context of crossing the *Data Delta*. Indeed, it is not an extreme position to argue that the key criteria for any successful MDM implementation rest on governance, data description, data quality and indeed security[79].

None of these are MDM topics per se, and that is the importance of the broader *Data Delta* concept.

We've mentioned Master Data Management throughout this book, but now's the time to roll up our sleeves and explain what it really means. We're going to get just a little technical in places, but only so that we can explain the concepts. This isn't an in-depth technical analysis of the topic. That on its own would fill an entire book, and there are many excellent ones available[80].

And this leads up immediately to a key point. The breadth and depth of the MDM challenge (and as we shall see later, the RDM challenge) is so large that the vast majority of organisations require significant external support to manage an implementation successfully. You need to have done this perhaps

---

[78] This may seem a strong assertion, but in our experience it has been true for many organisations looking at customer/citizen MDM solutions. If you are about to buy one of these, even if you get nothing else out of this book, *please* read the relevant section below carefully.

[79] It is worth pointing out that it is often MDM (along with enterprise BI) which first exposes data outside of silos, where specific applications manage security. One of the justifications for silos is the ease with which purpose-built applications can manage security inside their tight constraints. You may well need an additional enterprise security level to manage your information in a *Data Delta* world.

[80] We would certainly recommend this tome for anyone who needed to get 'under the bonnet' of MDM and understand the issues from a genuinely technical perspective. https://www.redbooks.ibm.com/Redbooks.nsf/ibmpressisbn/9780132366250

half a dozen times to get good at it, so there's little realistic prospect of end-user IT departments maintaining this level of skills and experience. Get help. Lots of it.

In terms of an easy-to-understand definition, MDM *enables you to join up information relating to the **same thing** (a particular customer, supplier, product, etc) from across your organisation, so that you can get a single view of their interactions and transactions, even if the details are scattered amongst a number of silos.*

Basically, if you want a 360-degree view of all your customer or citizen data, for example, then realistically MDM is the only technology platform that can help deliver this. As we will go on to explain, in certain forms of MDM, the centralised control of authoring this master view becomes the all-important requirement (eg maintaining products in the financial services industry).

This is powerful stuff. One of the hardest things for an organisation to manage is data that changes 'naturally' outside of its control, and this is what happens for information related to customers all the time. They move house, change phone number, get married and divorced (often changing their names as they do so), or change their marketing preferences on a whim (often not realising they're dealing with different parts of the same organisation). MDM is the black box that helps you actually *manage* these changes to restore and maintain control.

Let's look at a practical example of customer master data that resides in the Enterprise Data Warehouse, and we'll use our fictitious company *GoDelta* to underline the value.

GoDelta loaded customers and transactions from two parts of the organisation: orders from home users – imported from their online store, and orders from their industrial customers – which are managed in SalesForce.com[81].

The Sales team devoted a lot of time to building a picture of their larger industrial customers – understanding the decision makers and other key stakeholders responsible for authorising six-figure purchases of their automation equipment – and this was all stored as useful data in *GoDelta*'s SalesForce system. They also imported customer data from their Support Desk system, as shown in the following diagram.

---

[81] We are trying to keep *GoDelta* realistic – organisations rarely have 'single vendor' application footprints. Despite the fact that *GoDelta* uses a major ERP, they also use Salesforce.com as its CRM. Salesforce.com is a market-leading product, and many sales staff already have experience of working with it. These are powerful arguments for adoption, but create another silo of customer data. *GoDelta* is now committed to using the Data Management techniques of the Entity Method to break down its data silos.

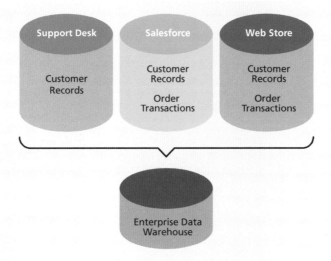

Figure 1: GoDelta's data sources feeding into the Data Warehouse

The diagram below represents what the data looked like once it was imported into CRM (for the sake of this example, the customer records contain names and phone numbers only; in a real implementation, additional fields would be included, such as address, email, and so on).

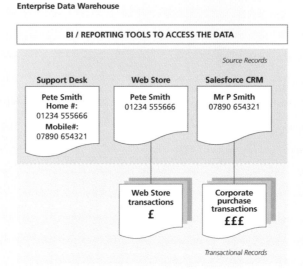

Figure 2: Logical structure using example data within a Data Warehouse

This is typical of the data within a data warehouse. Customer records from different source systems exist, and are associated with their transactions. But *only* with *their* transactions.

Notice that the diagram currently has no link between data from the Support Desk, data from the Web Store, or data from the Salesforce CRM system.

With enough knowledge of the data, it may be possible to link it with other available data to provide a more complete picture of our customer. This increases the value of the information that becomes available to people using *GoDelta's* BI tools.

For example, *GoDelta's* Support Desk record has both the home telephone and mobile numbers for the customer as well as details of their name. They could use this data to match against what they are already holding in the data warehouse, and identify that the Web Store orders from 'Peter Smith', and the Salesforce orders from 'Mr P Smith' were placed by same person, and that 'Pete Smith' is a high-value customer.

This would be useful information for *GoDelta's* Support Desk, and potentially, for those elsewhere in the organisation that are involved in providing both the home and the industrial product to this customer.

It's important not to put too much emphasis on the technical wizardry of MDM matching here; MDM solutions are about people, process and technology. Central to resolving GoDelta's challenges will be the governance process by which data stewards action and resolve data issues, especially those that arise from data matching.

One key function of MDM is to formalise this matching capability, and make the result of these matches available throughout the business operation in a consistent, validated, and traceable way. If you think about the footprint trail of data that a customer leaves behind them – each of which may provide opportunities for matching – very quickly, these patterns can become complex.

This next diagram shows an expanded logical structure for the data warehouse with master data added.

Enterprise Data Warehouse

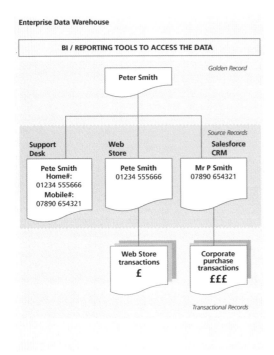

Figure 3: Logical structure of Data Warehouse including master data

Now it becomes straightforward for BI tools to gain access to a full and connected view of Pete Smith's transactions.

At this point, let's take a step back from the data warehouse example, and think about what formalisation of these matching capabilities means. We have not modified any data here. We have simply added another layer that provides an index or link between existing data.

Logically, the next phase is to *share* this knowledge back to the source systems. If a customer updates their mobile number when on a call to the support desk, the MDM system can facilitate automatically propagating that number back into Salesforce too.

Suddenly, it becomes possible not only to *view* data from across the organisation, but also to keep that data synchronised and consistent across the organisation.

Matching based on this type of similar data is not an exact science. Notice that we haven't used any unique reference numbers here. As is often the case, none of the systems in our example shared a common set of reference numbers. If they do, MDM still has a significant role in assisting with data quality issues eg one person has two account numbers. MDM includes the ability to understand and manage the risk associated with matching data across systems, with or without specific reference keys.

In our example, the risk involved in an incorrect match of Pete Smith and Mr P Smith is relatively low (if we made a false link here, the worst that could happen is that Pete Smith is erroneously given a higher status than he deserves).

But imagine if those transactions related to evidence pointing to a crime. Matching 'Mr P Smith wanted for a serious crime', and 'Pete Smith who had a speeding ticket' is a different order of risk altogether.

It will depend upon your key use-cases, but most major MDM solutions allow you to understand and determine the level of *false positives* (matches that are made, but shouldn't be), and *false negatives* (records that aren't matched, but should be) that are appropriate for your organisation.

This is a clear situation where MDM is providing a Data Management capability, but looks towards Data Governance for a decision on where to draw the line. It comes down to a fundamental question of 'what makes someone an individual?'

For example, a father and his son share the same initial and surname, and live at the same address. In the absence of any other data, should your systems consider that as a potential match? In the case of a marketing campaign, such a match has a relatively low impact. However, for decisions affecting people's credit history or health, the impact could be significant for both father and son. Where the line needs to be drawn depends upon *your* use-case, and no one else's.

This is made all the more complicated because in the real world, it is highly likely you have more than one use-case. If, for example, you are a local municipal authority dealing with residents in your area, you have a range of concerns from identifying fraudulent claims on your services, to identifying young people at risk through breakdowns in communication between departments. These different use-cases will make you want to draw lines in different places.

Within this context, the master data layer is quite commonly referred to as representing the 'single version of truth' or the 'golden view[82]'. That is only part of the story. We need to think about how the 'golden view' is maintained. In many types of MDM implementation, the 'golden *view*' is actually a physical 'golden *record*' that is then centrally authored. But whether a *view* or a physical *record*, it becomes the all-important '*single view of truth*'.

The concept of a 'golden view' is a sophisticated one. Areas of the business may well wish to see different views of the customer eg Finance want a trustworthy view, whereas Marketing want an accurate view with respect to a customer's privacy but are more relaxed with respect to certain aspects of data eg they don't necessarily require 100% accuracy in customer-age information.

For example, an extremely conservative matching philosophy could leave lots of 'probable' records unmatched, and therefore not be part of the 'golden view' for the right customer.

A level of Data Governance maturity is required here to draw out these views from across the organisation, and reconcile them into a logical 'golden view' which can be

---

[82] We did define 'golden view' in Section 4.2 when discussing BI. In case you missed it, the idea is that a golden view represents your best interpretation of potentially conflicting information, for example a misspelt surname in one of your systems would NOT be a part of your golden view.

implemented within budgetary constraints. Implementing an MDM 'golden record' speculatively and then expecting it to seamlessly deliver all views required without complex design analysis is unlikely to be successful.

That approach will almost always lead to unplanned and entirely avoidable iterations of rework or even worse, costly compromises in the production solution.

Now, we've never heard of anyone waking up in the morning and saying to themselves, 'What I need to make my organisation successful is an *MDM system*'. But lots of people will find themselves preoccupied in thinking, 'I need a single version of the truth – a trusted view I can rely upon' (or words to that effect).

Many times, this desire centres on information about customers and citizens, sometimes it is products. Different strokes for different folks, but *everyone* wants to get rid of ambiguity in their master data.

One leading industry analyst undertook research into why organisations were undertaking MDM. This is easy to find on the internet with google searches, but we are sceptical of the responses, since they involved asking people to order a pre-defined list of 'model answers'. We think the risk of confirmation bias in that sort of approach is too high.

When we ask our clients about their reasons for being interested in MDM, we get answers such as:

- Regulation – especially GDPR and Basel 239
- We simply don't know enough about who our customers are
- I want to sell more to our existing customers, but we don't even know what they have already
- We can't identify our top 100 customers

MDM is often seen as the 'silver bullet' to achieving customer or citizen 360-degree view solutions.

Together with BI, it stands as one of most common areas where organisations begin to be aware of the *Data Delta*. And just as in our earlier discussion on BI in *Section 4.2 – EDW, BI & Analytics*, success in this domain is very dependent on understanding the entire Data Management landscape.

We said in *Section 3 – Crossing the Data Delta* that central to success is bringing business users with you at *every step*. As well as making sure they have key involvement in Data

Governance, Data Description and Quality Management areas, we also made the overarching point that the IT side of the equation needs to be delivered incrementally in relatively short time periods.

There, we suggested a time slice of six months as a typically standard project period. If you plan a six-month project, and it slips to seven or eight months, you can still keep the business on side. But if you start off with a year-long plan, or even longer, then slippage to fourteen or sixteen months becomes too long to be managed.

Since MDM is so dependent on other aspects of the *Data Delta*, the overall task is almost certainly far too large to fit into a six-month time slice. This doesn't mean that you should be taking shortcuts, but you do need to break the problem down into a series of initiatives.

The point of the *Data Delta* model is to show how the various elements interrelate so you can do this effectively. Going about the task in this way will enable you to deliver incremental value frequently via a series of agile implementations.

At the risk of ruffling the feathers of a few vendors, let's also state that you may not need to take advantage of *all* the capabilities of their entire product set at the outset of your journey. That said, there is often a strong and genuine case, both from a procurement and technical perspective, to go ahead and purchase a more comprehensive solution than you might need for your early iterations. Certainly, you will want to avoid having to make more changes to an already complex IT environment than is strictly necessary.

And, from a procurement perspective, vendors will always provide a better deal for a larger purchase. The important thing is to establish your needs and your targets, and *develop a clear roadmap* that is right for you.

4.4.1 Features and styles of MDM

There's a great deal to say about MDM, so we'll start at the beginning, and try our best to be clear. If you already would class yourself as 'MDM-literate', please at least skim this material rather than skip it entirely. We do think we have some important points to make to you too.

In analysing MDM solutions, there are two key considerations that you need to address amongst dozens of other issues: what *type of data* are you mastering, and what *functionality* do you require?

Data

Our experience indicates that there are three types of master data that are the focus of an MDM implementation, which we will later review in detail.

- Customer/Citizen data – this accounts for about 75% of MDM implementations that we encounter, a rather higher figure than the overall market share

- Product data – this accounts for about 20% of MDM implementations that we see, which is correspondingly somewhat lower than the overall market share

- Other master data (assets, staff, routes, etc) – together accounting for the remaining implementations

Some implementations cut across these different types of data – usually as organisations see the returns from mastering one type of data. Such an implementation is described by different vendors as '*multi-dimensional*' or '*multi-domain*'. We will stick with *multi-dimensional*, to avoid confusion with the 14 Data Management *domains* that comprise the Data Delta.

Functionality

In terms of required functionality, this splits into several types for consideration.

- Read-only master data versus read/write master data
- Whether your master data view should be logical, physical or some combination of the two
- Consistency and completeness

Before we dive into the detail, it's worth reflecting on how organisations arrive at having multiple data silos.

Competition in the solution marketplace

For over twenty years, the large ERP[83] vendors have been making a concerted effort to dominate and 'own' your entire IT application space. From the many hundreds of organisations we've dealt with, we can't find a *single* one where the ERP vendor has succeeded in 100% ownership of the entire enterprise application space (though they've come close in a few instances).

---

[83] Enterprise Resource Planning – large vendors include Oracle and SAP, among others.

Like all large companies, these titans of IT have been challenged by smaller companies; companies that can move swiftly to capitalise on advances in technology to offer value for money with, say, their Cloud-based CRM systems or innovative BI and Analytics tools.

Over time, this leads to most end-user organisations having a diluted mix of solutions from a range of vendors and providers.

Internal evolution

Then there are the factors related to an organisation's history.

It is inevitable that a long-established organisation will undergo *several* internal reorganisations over the course of its lifetime. This might be the result of strategic planning, or perhaps related to changes in the external marketplace, in terms of Mergers and Acquisitions.

For example, after the 'Big Bang[84]', we saw banks expand to offer insurance and other financial services. Now, still in the wake of the global financial crisis of 2008, we are seeing many of those same organisations being forced to divest and demerge by statutory imperative ('too big to fail' being a real concern for many Western governments).

At any one time, an organisation can be operating both *with* data stored within a whole host of unrelated systems data, together with data it has *inherited* from previous companies.

When two organisations merge, they might need to deal with an overlap of records relating to the same individuals. For example, a bank and an insurance company might have had a set of common customers prior to their merger. Similarly, two 'high street' retail stores that merge to reduce overall costs might discover they were selling many of the same product lines acquired from the same vendors.

Whether through technological progress or the natural cycle of organisational evolution, it's inevitable that most organisations will have multiple data silos. The challenge is to identify a 'single version of truth', and to maintain it as your organisation ventures forward. The factors that cause multiple data silos aren't going to go away anytime soon. The challenge is how to use Data Management principles to get in control *and stay there*.

---

[84] The Big Bang in Financial Services occurred on 27 October 1986, when new rules were introduced by the London Stock Exchange to remove many of the previous differences in working practices between retail and merchant banking in the City of London. The London initiative appeared so successful that it led many other major markets around the world to follow suit. A majority of observers, however, now believe that the inadequate financial regulatory regime that followed Big Bang was at least in part a cause of the global financial crisis of 2007-2012.

4.4.1.1 Customer/Citizen Data

This topic is at the heart of most MDM solutions, and is often the key driver for organisations to decide to cross the *Data Delta*. So let's first define this strategic area of customer or citizen data a little more closely from an MDM perspective.

The correct way of looking at customer/citizen data is in terms of a 'party'. A party is any person or organisation with which your organisation has a relationship (there are others, for example, your suppliers).

We also need to consider the concept of hierarchies eg people in families, and organisations in groups. If you are a bank, you might want to know your loan exposure to a given individual, but you might also be interested in the 'family unit' as a whole. If you are in government, you might want to know what services you are providing to a given individual, but also to the family unit.

Of course, this raises a privacy and security matter that has both legal and practical ramifications.

For example, a leading global hotel chain introduced a customer MDM solution a few years back without considering the privacy implications. The nightmare actually happened on the very first morning in their Nairobi hotel (one of the authors was on site) when a novice receptionist, fresh from her training course, welcomed the couple standing in front of her, saying, 'Good morning, Mr and Mrs Brown! We're delighted to welcome you back to stay with us again'. Sadly, this *particular* Mrs Brown had never been to Kenya before, and Mr Brown had some explaining to do.

So, just because you might have a *need* to see hierarchical and relationship data, it does not follow – from either a legal perspective or a practical one – that you *should* be doing this. You need to think carefully through the privacy issues for your organisation.

And thinking through the issues carefully is absolutely what *hasn't* happened with almost every organisation's party data.

So it is worth pointing out that there can – and often should be – a difference between how data is modelled in an MDM solution, and how it is exposed to end users and applications.

For example, a local authority might, for very legitimate fraud detection reasons, implement the concept of family relationships inside its MDM design. That does not in the least imply that these sometimes private relationships should be available to anyone else other than staff involved in fraud detection.

In terms of thinking about party information in general terms, there are a number of identifiable characteristics. Firstly, there will be lots of records representing each customer, citizen or supplier, possibly thousands for some organisations, and tens of millions for others. And the data on them isn't all represented by nice clear codes – certainly not their name, and in many instances around the world, not their address information either.[85]

Unless you are already working inside a transactional MDM solution that forces consistent data, the key question we need to ask at the centre of any party-focused MDM solution is whether two records belong to the same party or not. If they do, there should be some way of linking the information together. There are lots of options here that we will discuss later. You might decide to physically merge the records or just create a link between them, but the most important thing is that if two records represent the same person, this can be determined.

So consider this example:

In your CRM system you have a record for 'Pete Smith at 123 Acacia Avenue'. In your ERP system, you have a record for 'P Smith at 123 Acacia Ave'. Are these the same party? The same person? Yes or no?

Hopefully, you answered with the word '*Probably*', and that is where *your world needs to change*.

The consequences of 'Probably' are truly profound, and as we will go on to show, impact everything related to party-focused MDM (including your procurement process).

For most people, there is a 'Eureka!' moment when these implications hit home. It is our earnest intention for you to have that moment while you are reading this book, well away from any sales cycle, or vendors competing to promote their cause.

Let's explore some typical confusions on personal data to develop the importance of 'Probably'. The following is based on a real example, though we are considering how the data might be represented in two *fictitious* enterprise systems: CRM and Salik[86].

---

[85] Dubai is an interesting example. Because of the relatively advanced state of e-Government and e-business, there is no driving requirement for home delivery postal mail. You can, if you wish, pay for a physical PO Box, but most people and organisations choose to communicate electronically. There is not, therefore, the business driver to have systematic postcodes for mail delivery. As an example, the official address of the *Ministry of Justice* is 'behind Ministry of Education, near Al Twar Center, Dubai, United Arab Emirates'. This is a very useful descriptive address to find the building, and doesn't need to be codified for postal mail.

[86] 'Salik' is Arabic for 'open' or 'clear', in the sense of driving on an 'open road', where the traffic is flowing freely. The road toll system in Dubai is known as the *Salik* system.

This is the data:

	CRM	**Salik**
Name	Peter Julian Smth	Peter Julian Smith
Nationality	Great Britain	United Kingdom
D/L no	1370766	1370676

These days, everyone will be familiar with standard 'search and select' pages; they are prevalent in many web pages on the internet. The search function might be to enable you to buy cars, or search for a customer or look for residents who have driving permits in a particular street. There are endless examples of applications that all work exactly the same way.

Suppose, that – in an MDM world – we want to find a citizen. Here is our simple and very familiar search page. In this example, we have entered values for Name and Driving Licence number.

There is nothing in the least remarkable about this. We have requested records that contain 'Pete Smith' and that have a driving licence '1370765'.

Here, however, is an example of the result page number returned by the MDM solution:

Now have a careful look at that page of results. Although it might look familiar, it's actually different from the *standard* results pages you see in most business applications.

This is because *none* of the records on this page match the selection criteria. Or rather, none match *exactly*.

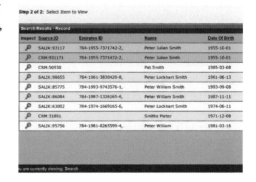

The top two records in green represent the closest match, but you'll see that one of them has two characters in the Driving Licence field inverted, and the other has the surname misspelt.

The MDM system is looking for records that are a *close* match.

There are several ways this result can be achieved, and we will try to be careful not to fall into the trap of using one vendor's terminology. The techniques that different vendors use are not all the same, but the key point we are making is whether or not the solution can achieve this type of 'close' match.

In terms of 'close' matching, some vendors have capabilities for 'fuzzy' searching, while others have 'probabilistic matching' technology. Under the bonnet, these are not the same, and indeed will give differing results on occasion to each other. You may well need to decide which is right for you.

However, for clarity in this section, we will use the phrase 'close matching' as a generic term to describe this type of 'fuzzy' or probabilistic matching, in contrast to traditional 'rules-based' matching.

If you are planning a transactional MDM model where data is maintained centrally in a golden record, and then pervasively distributed, obviously once you have that golden record this 'close matching' capability is less important. It would only be relevant with information sources outside your control eg people phoning in to a call centre.

However, if your legacy systems are such that a transactional model isn't a realistic proposition, and you are faced with data being maintained in different systems, this close-matching capability is essential when dealing with real world data quality issues.

It's based on some very smart advanced mathematics, but these are 'behind the scenes', and only your system implementer needs to understand what is really going on. Best of all, modern systems are capable of close-matching within response times that equate to those which use the traditional 'rules-based' approach.

A rules-based approach assumes that you can build a set of specific rules for finding a match. For example, you might have a rule stating that 'Avenue' and 'Ave' are to be treated the same, or 'Pete' and 'Peter' are the same, or even 'Smith' and 'Smth'.

However, in a rules-based world, you could never go as far as saying that the two driving licences numbers, '1370766' and '1370676' were the same. There are just too many potential variations to be considered if you did that.

So the key difference is that, using a traditional rules-based approach, you can address *some* types of data quality issues by catering for obvious 'near-miss' comparisons. But these are finite, limited and often impractical. Sure, you could match '*Smith*' and '*Smth*', but what about '*Jones*' and '*Jnes*'? Indeed, what about '*Smith*' and '*Smtih*'?

However, with matching techniques based on statistical frequency which will find close matches, you don't need to pre-define rules in anything *like* the same way[87]. The engine itself will cater for all those 'near-miss' variations.

Before we go on to consider how you might use this technology in the real world, there are two immediate and wide-ranging implications of this capability.

Firstly, the *data quality war becomes winnable.*

If you think the accuracy of your current master data isn't good enough in *Data Delta* terms[88], then MDM technology that allows for close-matching offers a way forward. If a computer system can successfully match across these sorts of data quality issues then, for some purposes at least, perhaps the poor quality isn't quite the enormous problem it seemed yesterday.

It is sadly worth noting though that there is a potential downside here. We've experienced organisations which have reneged on Data Governance and description responsibilities, and thrown all the responsibility – and blame – onto 'close-matching' technology.

These are examples of where organisations haven't embraced *Data Delta* concepts of the relationship between the 14 domains. You are only going to get the benefits of all this clever technology in the context of an holistic approach to the people, process and technology aspects of every domain within the *Data Delta*.

Secondly, we need a significant change in our language when thinking about *acquiring* close-matching technology. In a rules-based world, we were used to asking, 'Can your system find these records?'

It's a straightforward question, with only two possible answers. It can or it can't; there is no third option. That question doesn't work in a world where 'close' matches are possible. Any close-matching engine *can*, by definition, find any record. If you type in 'lop' and were looking for 'xylophone', the odds of you finding a match aren't zero. They are very small – tiny! – possibly 0.001, but *not* zero.

---

[87] Your matching engine will need to be trained or 'tuned' to produce good results on your specific datasets, but this is at a different level of data generalisation and is rarely about specific examples. For example, a list of UK citizen names will look quite different to the equivalent list in France or Brazil. By tuning the engine, the same matching engine will yield excellent results against all these different datasets. The process is analogous to tuning a Formula 1 car to race around different circuits. It's the same engine; it's just set up slightly differently by some expert engineers.

[88] It's okay – we know – we've seen everyone else's, and yours is the same!

To usefully describe the capabilities of matching engines, the key question changes from a binary one: 'Can your system find these records?' to a quantitative one: 'How well does your system score these records?' In terms of close matching, *scoring* the probability is everything.

There's no point in saying, 'Yes, I managed to match 1370766 and 1370676, but the probability was so low that we ranked the match as the 100,000[th] best result'.

This is important because it enables you to procure the *correct* MDM solution. There is every chance that before reading this, you would have approached your MDM procurement process – the writing of your RFP[89] – using traditional rules-based, binary language to describe the matching requirement. Instead, what you really need to procure is a system with a matching capability that meets your needs. Sadly, we are aware of many organisations which have purchased MDM solutions that were inadequate for their needs because *they asked the wrong questions in their RFP*.

Buying a Customer/Citizen MDM solution

Think through in detail about how you are going to procure the right MDM solution for your organisation. Our most important point is the need for this exercise to be undertaken within the context of a wider *Data Delta* initiative. Technology on its own will always fail.

However, if your requirements include moving beyond rules-based matching, once you learn that it's almost impossible to ask precise yes/no meaningful questions of the capability of a close-matching scoring mechanism, it's fairly obvious you need to put greater emphasis than usual on the practical, demonstration side of the procurement process.

An interesting question to explore is: how do you manage a test drive of a customer/citizen MDM solution to assess this? You need a plan that reflects both your available resources, and what is reasonable to ask a vendor to undertake in a pre-sale situation. It's unrealistic to issue an RFP to, say, five potential vendors, and ask them all to invest several weeks of effort in building a 'Proof of Concept' solution for you. Instead, we would recommend the following approach.

In the first instance, let the vendor do their standard demonstration, using their own data and system. Vendors will be very happy to comply. Don't be afraid, though, to ask for more examples during their presentation. If they show they can type in '*Smth*' and find '*Smith*', ask them about '*Smath*', '*Smit*', '*mith*' etc. Try to gauge whether you are genuinely being shown true close-matching . . . or just 'smoke and mirrors'. Use this to help you produce your shortlist of solutions.

Once you have the shortlist, it's a useful and perfectly fair test at this stage to ask your shortlisted vendors to load your own test data. You will need to be in a position to provide some data into their demonstration system[90]. This doesn't involve vendors doing months of work without reward, but means you can benefit from a meaningful session based on actual data examples with which you are familiar. This exercise should be good enough for you to arrive at a 'preferred vendor' status.

If you need to go further, then by all means consider a formal Proof of Concept with your chosen vendor where both parties will need to invest considerable effort and expense to finalise your procurement choice.

4.4.1.2 Product Data

Another major call for MDM solutions relates to *product data*. There are some striking differences between this and customer/citizen MDM.

For products, you will not have the uncertainty associated with matching name and address data, which is at the core of the party data challenge. You also, almost certainly, won't have as many products as you do customers/citizens, and that is usually by an order of magnitude.

There are, however, strong and pressing reasons why organisations need to better manage their product data.

- You might find yourself having lots of product data that is of poor quality. Perhaps it's related to a history of different management regimes and IT systems, or your different regional centres treat product data differently. Or your organisation has grown through acquisition, and has acquired data that was generated with very different people, processes and systems.

- Perhaps your products are complex – products and components *within* products – and you sometimes sell a finished package, and sometimes a single component. Automotive and manufacturing sectors rest on product solutions that understand bills-of-material, 'parts explosion', and the concept of supersessions[91]. When Entity was formed nearly 30 years ago, much of our work was focused on advanced parts systems for the automotive trade[92], together with the related challenges of

---

[90] Vendors should be able to bring a demonstration system into your organisation on a laptop, or connect to a Cloud-based system, or else provide it as a Virtual Machine (VM) for you to load onto a suitable platform.

[91] Supersessions relate to the idea that as for example cars are improved, there are implications of forward and backward component fitting different models. Can you, for example, put a vehicle sensor from a 2015 BMW 5 series into a 2016 model? And vice versa?

[92] In the early 1980s, the German car giant, BMW, withdrew its concession to their UK distributer, BMW UK, and started selling cars directly to the UK market. The IT department of BMW UK set themselves up as an independent software house, from which Entity emerged. Our chairman, Chris Finlay, started his career working on product management applications for BMW 40 years ago. We have been in this space for a very long time, and have learned a lot along the way.

branch networks – which stocks were best held centrally, which at branches.

- This image relates to the footnote discussing vehicle sensors and shows the complexity of the parts explosion involved. Within this single picture there are over 100 parts within parts:

- Product complexity may be tied to externally varying conditions so that, at the time of making a sale, you don't know *exactly* how much profit you are going to make out of your product.

If you answered 'all of the above' to that little list of product challenges, you may well be working in Financial Services[93] or a related industry.

Banking and Financial Services products can be particularly complex to manage, which is why there are purpose-built tools to help.

If, for example, you have sold a product to a customer that contains a fixed-price element – perhaps a mortgage product with the first five years on a fixed rate – then your profitability from that product sale is not clear at the *time* of sale.

You, as the bank, might need to consider buying alternative products by way of a 'hedge'[94] so that you can contain the downside of your accumulated risk on your product sales.

We have a lot of experience of implementing MDM solutions in banks. It's an area where some key Data Management principles are often put to the most extreme test. The first instinct of banking professionals is to want to do *everything*, and to want to do it properly. We have nothing but respect for an organisation that wishes to address every element of its *Data Delta* challenge. Sadly, our experience is that going down the 'mega-project' path of doing everything at once *always* ends in tears.

Sometimes, the realisation that the project is too big comes early on, when the full cost of doing everything is calculated and underlined neatly in an executive report. In other cases, it comes down to the timetable. For financial institutions that have succeeded in

---

[93] There are other industries that come close, but possibly only Financial Services can answer 'Yes' to every single element. A gambling company such as the bookmaker, *Paddy Power*, might come close, and there are aspects of property development with properties sold for a fixed price 'off plan' before the construction costs are finalised, which also result in particularly complex product management challenges.

[94] 'Hedging' simply represents the process of off-setting a risk, and so minimising the potential extremes of pain or gain. This is exactly the same technique used by bookmakers who become concerned that they are 'exposed' on a particular outcome of a sporting event. They can offset their exposure with another bookmaker, effectively by betting the other way, so that although their maximum potential profit is reduced, more importantly, so is their maximum potential loss.

crossing the *Data Delta,* these two scenarios have lead naturally to another conversation; one where *agile* thinking needs to come to the fore.

Sadly, a costly programme does sometimes get underway, only to collapse later – at huge expense. This can happen after years of limping on, failing to meet deadlines, and with the budget spiralling out of control. These are dark days, and the reaction can often be: 'Let's stop and do nothing'. Avoiding such a nightmare scenario is the reason we argue for designing the optimal *Data Delta* route so passionately at the outset.

As with any data initiative, we urge the organisation to begin with a clear view of their objectives. For example, in a bank, the business case is often clear. These might be regulatory requirements, risk mitigation, digital transformation, customer up-sell, efficiency, etc (though it's usually some combination of all of these elements).

Banks sell a multitude of products to their customers, and are always alert to mining cross-sell and up-sell opportunities. There are many products with only subtle variations to distinguish them from each other, such as a loan that's offered on better terms to gold or platinum cardholders. In such cases, the bank will clearly want management information on related products.

Then, there are those products that represent a high risk to the provider eg a fixed-rate mortgage. When selling that product, the bank made an estimation of future trends of the value of money – an estimate that is never going to be perfect. How much money the bank will make – or possibly even lose – from such products, is a key concern, and a bank needs to be able to *analyse* the impact of rate changes across a range of products quickly and simply.

In MDM terms, mastering product data is about having access to current information about products and their hierarchies, and critically, how this information is *authored* going forward. 'Authoring' will take you straight into workflows, and critical to the success of any authoring system is how effectively and practically the workflow engine works.

In this age, the larger challenges tend not to be overly technical; these can be readily solved by a combination of good products and talented staff. The real challenges are *process* based.

Process design for automated workflows always has to focus on two cases: standard, and the exceptional.

The arrival of a pervasive mobile internet is great in theory, but staff will continue to go on holidays and take leave, and may not always remember to change their 'out-of-office' settings in order to divert workflows.

In some cases, product master design also needs to include managing rich media product information such as images, videos and audio. All this information should form the basis of your product catalogue.

The information behind your catalogue may need to be drawn from many sources of data. You should expect there to be conflicts between these sources, all of which need to be managed as part of the solution or its implementation.

Almost without exception, the data quality challenges for a product-based MDM solution are every bit as daunting as those for a customer/citizen solution. There is, for example, a considerable market in off-shore low labour-cost companies, whose only function is to manually 'clean' product files and apply standard coding systems. These tend to be sector-based; the oil and gas industry has its own set of unique product challenges, as does the food and beverage industry.

Applying Data Management principles to gain and *maintain* control of your product data is unlikely to be a low-cost undertaking. It's important to start with an understanding of what it is you want to do, and why you want to do it. As with every element of crossing the *Data Delta,* you will need to build a sound cost-benefit case.

4.4.1.3 Other Master Data

Depending on your core business, there are many potential areas where the value of data can be improved by introducing Master Data Management concepts. We've helped a railway to master its track assets, a shipping line to master its routes, and a retailer to manage its stores.

However, we are careful not to lose sight of the maxim: 'If you have a hammer in your hand, everything looks like a nail[95]'. Don't forget that with an approach such as the Entity Method, you aren't stuck solely with the MDM hammer. By introducing effective Data Management – consistent data definitions, centrally-managed reference data, data quality remediation, etc – you might well find that the need to *master* some of your data can drop down the list of priorities.

---

[95]All the management theory books attribute this concept of – if you only have one tool, you will over use-it – either to Andrew Maslow in *The Psychology of Science* (1966), or Abraham Kaplan in *The Conduct of Inquiry: Methodology for Behavioural Science* (1964). Earlier references to Mark Twain are now discredited.

4.4.1.4 Multi-dimensional MDM

All of this leads nicely to 'multi-dimensional MDM', where we consider mastering several – possibly interrelated – elements of master data.

We'd like to start by asking whether you are sure that this is what you need right now.

The most frequently quoted use case we hear in this respect is: 'I don't know what products my customers have'[96]. Clearly this is big problem, and one that many organisations face.

The consequences are serious. Poor customer service is inevitable, and you will find it much more difficult to sell more product to your existing customers if this is your situation. If you don't know what they've already got, how can you target the *right* new products to the *right* customers? If you are facing this problem, then you certainly need to get across the *Data Delta*.

But don't fall into the trap of jumping to the end game. The single most common cause of not knowing what products your customers have is that you actually don't know your customers. Let's say you have a CRM system, ERP, and possibly some kind of bespoke operational system. This means that you could have, at least, three different records of the same customer, with each showing they have different products.

Looking at any one of these records in isolation will not give you a complete picture of what products this customer has purchased. However, this could all be fixed by implementing party-based MDM for managing your customer records.

But let's assume that multi-dimensional MDM is for you. What does it offer? The real point is that it has all the specialised capabilities for managing any type of master data, be that party (including individuals and organisations), products, assets (or any kind of 'thing', however complex), locations (and routes between them), and events.

Clearly, that is an enormous functionality breadth, and not every vendor will necessarily score highly in every aspect. This should encourage you to think of MDM in terms of a journey with a roadmap. This allows you to acquire and implement the right solution to tackle your primary concerns first, and possibly defray the cost of other aspects of the solution until later.

[96] Or, in a government context: 'I don't know which of our services our citizens use'.

The following picture illustrates a possible target state. It represents a highly simplified view of *possible* systems inside a bank, but for the sake of argument, this example uses only two dimensions of master data: a customer (party) master and a product master. We are *not* recommending this model (it would actually be a little unusual) but we are using it to illustrate that different styles of MDM *can* coexist, providing different features as your organisation requires.

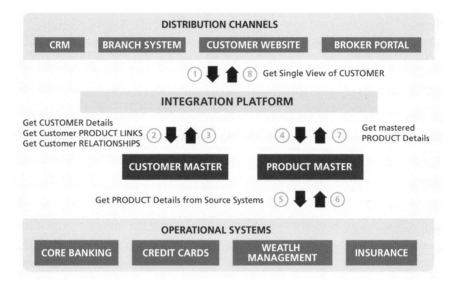

The 'Distribution Channels' are a Customer Relationship Management (CRM) system, a number of remote local systems within the various branches of this bank, the main customer websites, and a number of remote systems belonging to third-party agents who sell this bank's products (this might include insurance brokers, for example).

None of these distribution channel systems actually hold information about customers, but instead rely on the 'Customer Master' system. Similarly, they don't hold any product details either, but communicate with the 'Product Master' for the product catalogue.

The 'Integration Platform' is a technical component that allows all of these various systems to communicate without being directly linked to each other.

The 'Customer Master' is a party-focused MDM system that holds all the physical records relating to customers – their personal details, a list of the products they have bought (NB this is only a link to the product records, and contains no actual details about the products themselves), and also any relationships to other customers within the same bank.

This particular bank has decided to make its customer master a physical repository so that it can collect together all manner of information about each customer. It is interested not only in personal details and product purchases, but also, details on the demographic profile and lifestyle of each person. This includes their preferred methods of communication, their willingness to receive marketing information, any feedback relating to customer satisfaction (such as surveys they may have completed), credit history etc. As such, the 'Customer Master' acts as the central repository for any information related to a customer.

The 'Product Master' also represents a central repository, but it does this in a different way to the 'Customer Master' in this example. The technique used here is illustrative only. A bank, or other organisation, might, for example, choose this path if it were using legacy applications for product maintenance that it didn't want to amend at this time. So rather than centralising Product Maintenance, which would be a more common approach for many banks, this bank decided to leave its source systems *untouched* for the time being, but build a 'virtual' master aggregating the content of the legacy systems.

Notice the additional links (arrows 5 and 6) reaching down to the 'Operational Systems' in the diagram. These systems each manage their own sets of products and, rather than holding a physical copy of these, the 'Product Master' represents what is known as a 'virtual master'.

The bank wants to have a single product catalogue, so it implemented a product-focused MDM system to intermediate between the various 'Operational Systems', resolve any conflicts between them, and present a single view of its products to the 'Customer Master' and to the 'Distribution Channels'.

This is not purely a transactional model, because, unlike the Customer Master, the Product Master does not hold all the physical details of each product in this instance, but relies on the Operational Systems to supply aspects of this information. Some organisations choose to implement their party masters this way too, at least in the first instance. We will explain more in the next section, but some vendors refer to this model as *co-existence*; others as *hybrid*.

The arrows on the diagram show how this multi-dimensional MDM configuration allows the various 'Distribution Channels' to get both a complete view of the bank's product catalogue, and also of its customers[97]. This also means that those systems need to inform the Customer Master about any new or updated information about a customer.

Here's how the components work together when retrieving all the information about a customer:

- Any one of those Distribution Systems can request details of a customer (1), which leads to;

- Retrieving their personal details, relationships with other customers and product links from the Customer Master (2 and 3), and the product links lead in turn to;

- Requesting product details from the Product Master (4 and 7) which;

- Retrieve the product information from the Operational Systems (5 and 6), before the whole batch of information about the customer is …

- Returned to whichever one of the Distribution Systems (8) made the call.

This example shows how this bank made use of different MDM capabilities to keep control of their master data. They did that according to the type of data they mastered. It's unlikely they would tackle both of these things at the same time. They might have implemented the Customer Master first, and created links between that Master and the Operational Systems to handle retrieving product information, or they may have started with the Product Master.

These are the types of considerations you will need to think about, and it's the reason we highlight the need for a clear roadmap.

4.4.2 MDM Implementation Styles

There are several different ways of implementing MDM, and it's important to have an appreciation of these because not all the available products support all of the styles.

---

[97] For simplicity, we are ignoring the security aspects of this. Clearly, there needs to be some control to constrain who can see what information based on their level of authorisation.

Some people choose to start with one style and move to others later, and this comes back to the importance of a *roadmap* to plan out your journey.

What are the major styles and why does it matter?

Firstly, let's explain the issues, and then go on to the jargon. To do this, we'll revert to our example of having three enterprise systems, each containing customer or citizen data.

Imagine that you are going to implement Master Data Management to deliver a 'single version of truth' about your customers or citizens.

There are three core topics to be considered in terms of implementation style, but they rest on a profound understanding of a huge range of related requirements eg trust rules, the need for batch or real-time updates, the requirements for prospects or purchasing customers only, whether you have single views of the master within different domains eg brand view/enterprise view etc.

A key point to convey is the complexity of this subject. We are trying to 'keep it simple' by identifying the essential matters, but a successful MDM implementation will need to look much deeper. Having said that, the three core topics are:

1) Should this view exist as a physical database, effectively a fourth data source relating to customers – one that contains the master data? Or do we instead hold a set of pointers to the original records in the other three systems, which represent a 'virtual' view, to the master 'truth' data in the three core systems?

2) How do you maintain the 'single version of truth'? Do you implement new functionality to maintain the customer data centrally, or do you allow people to carry on maintaining records in the core business systems?

3) Having created a 'single version of truth', do you write this back to the source systems (this can be configured as an automatic process), or do you allow those systems to continue with potentially incorrect data?

In reviewing these questions, it is essential to 'stay agile' and not make decisions at the outset which preclude future directions. It is common to consider an MDM journey, rather than a single 'end state' implementation, for all the reasons we explained in *Section 3 – Crossing the Data Delta*.

You may have different answers to each of these questions at different stages of your journey.

In trying to work towards answers to those questions at each stage in your journey, we'll use some diagrams to help in the explanation, and introduce some standard industry jargon.

1) Consolidated and Registry Styles

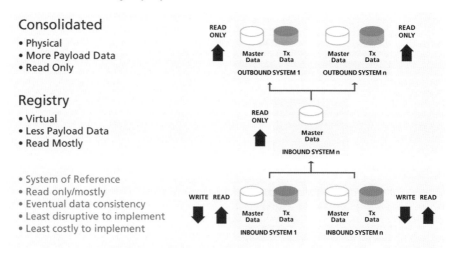

Consolidated
- Physical
- More Payload Data
- Read Only

Registry
- Virtual
- Less Payload Data
- Read Mostly

- System of Reference
- Read only/mostly
- Eventual data consistency
- Least disruptive to implement
- Least costly to implement

Consolidated and Registry styles have essentially the same information flow, and can be shown using the same diagram.

The principle is that the master data (shown in the *centre* of the diagram) is maintained using data from the source systems (towards the *bottom* of the diagram). From the perspective of the source systems, this a 'non-intrusive' operation, because the Master Data system only reads the data from the source systems and doesn't change their copy in any way, although it can be enriched and standardised. Changing data in the source systems is the *only* way to affect the master data in this model.

The 'golden view' of master data – the single version of truth – can either be maintained as a physical record (Consolidated style), or as a virtual view (Registry style).

This model allows data to be pushed out to other systems – such as a data warehouse –

as shown in the top part of the diagram. This means that BI and management reporting can derive immediate benefits from having a 'golden view', even though data anomalies persist in the source systems (these could be addressed manually or simply left alone).

2) Co-existence Style

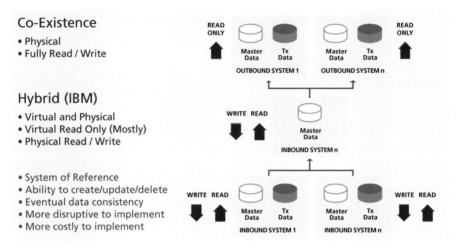

This model is similar to the previous one, but here the 'golden view' *can* be maintained both centrally (within the Master Data system) as well as from the source systems. This is generally known as the Co-existence style, but IBM terms this as Hybrid. Coexistence also relies on data updates in MDM being distributed back to source systems.

3) Transactional Style

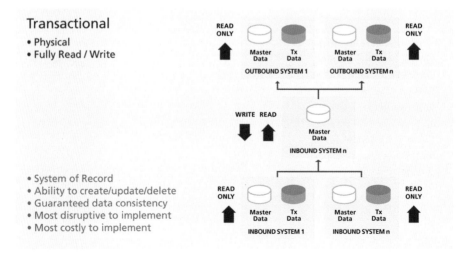

In the Transactional Style, all maintenance capability for master data is removed from the various source systems, and is replaced with a central maintenance capability. Given that data can only be maintained in one place, data consistency is guaranteed.

Let's explore the options in more detail to help you answer the key question: 'Which is the right style for me?'

There are several advantages of using a Registry-style approach. There is minimal work required to standardise the data before it can be loaded eg Foreign Keys do not need to be resolved, and so relatively little data cleansing is required. Close matching can make use of values across *all* member records – not just the 'golden view'. If required, multiple 'golden views' can be made available for different audiences or purposes. This last advantage can be useful, for example, to provide a low-cost and secure way of exposing your 'golden view' – both internally, but also to your customers or citizens, allowing them access to the information you hold about them.

The drawbacks of the Consolidated and Registry styles are that they typically support *read-only* use of the 'golden view'.

Furthermore, in the case of Registry Style, there is a lower consistency of master data because the MDM system holds a smaller and simpler data model. Performance of read-and-extract services may be slower than for physical implementations. This can be addressed using appropriate technology, but that clearly has a cost.

Turning attention to the Co-existence and Transactional styles, the benefits are that the models support all read-write use cases for the 'golden view'. Because of the greater breadth of data held within its data model, there is a higher consistency in the master data. Performance of read-and-extract services will be faster than for the Virtual style (assuming equivalence of the hardware environment).

Although there are significant benefits to these models, there are drawbacks too. There is more work involved in standardising and transferring data from source systems into the physical data model of the MDM system. Close matching is less effective here, because it can only make use of the values actually located *inside* the 'golden view' and not the member records, because it does not match across attributes.

Only one 'golden view' for each data entity is supported – this is physically persisted within the system – so exposing different views for different audiences becomes more complex to achieve.

In addition, the Transactional style requires high levels of customisation, and usually involves integrating the maintenance functions of existing systems with the MDM system (otherwise there can be a significant business impact in forcing users to maintain master data directly on the MDM system).

There is a great deal to consider in order to make the right choice. Here are three different ways in which organisations use MDM.

Collaboration is best supported by the Co-existence and Transactional styles. Here, master data is maintained centrally. Typical uses include product authoring or perhaps, customer on-boarding in a complex organisation, such as a bank. Cross-departmental Data Governance is an absolute prerequisite, supported by an effective workflow capability. The governance aspect needs to understand concepts of 'state' – such as whether activities related to product creation are at draft/review/approved or final status.

Operational use is supported by all the MDM styles. It rests on having effective interface services to support business processes through a Service Orientated Architecture (SOA). Using this makes it possible to achieve high-performance (real-time or near real-time) updating. This usage model relies on the concept of 'service orchestration', where changes are applied in a pre-determined sequence to minimise conflicts (such as two users updating the same record).

Analytical use represents the simplest approach, and is also supported by all the MDM styles. Its primary objective it to support Business Intelligence and analytics uses with an EDW. It's typically batch-based, though the batches can be processed in near 'real time'. The key idea is to add 'intelligence' to the data warehouse by providing meaningful information to its 'Star Schema'. For example, the MDM system can make the data warehouse aware that customer data is mastered through the 'golden view' (rather than, say, the CRM system), but also that records with, for example, a driving licence of '1370766' and '1370676' both belong to citizen 123456.

As you'll appreciate, the various styles of MDM are important to understand. No one said crossing the *Data Delta* was going to be easy. The consequences of making the wrong decision can actually widen the *Data Delta* rather than closing it.

For example, a major Middle Eastern bank fell between the cracks of *all* recommended implementation styles, and ended up with its MDM solution becoming nothing more than one more inaccurate data source to deal with. This required a full re-implementation to fix the issues, and deliver the value it was looking for. Clearly, there's more to this than simply *buying* the right solution!

4.4.3 What does maturity look like?

So, as for the previous Data Management domains, let's now pause to reflect on our guidelines for determining the level of maturity in terms of how Master Data Management is implemented inside an organisation:

Level 1 – Initial: There is no evidence of a consistent strategy to identify, manage, reduce, or understand replicated copies of master data, even within single business functions or departments.

Level 2 – Repeatable: There is evidence that some departments are identifying master data, and are attempting to reduce or understand replicated copies of master data. For example, there is evidence of some consolidation across different systems, or MDM tools are being evaluated/purchased – though primarily for targeted projects.

Level 3 – Defined: There is a centrally-governed MDM programme supported by policies and standards, and the organisation is in the process of implementing the strategy to understand replicated data so that instead, mastered data is used as the 'golden view' for new applications, existing systems and management reporting. For example, there is evidence of comprehensive modelling of master data, and/or MDM tools are being used as part of a strategic BI/MIS programme.

Level 4 – Quantitatively Managed: The organisation has implemented MDM, and is using metrics to monitor and evaluate the success of data mastering. All new applications and management reports use the mastered 'golden source', and legacy systems are being migrated to do so.

Level 5 – Optimising: Legacy applications are migrated to use 'golden source' master data repositories, using data feeds to propagate master data across the organisation. The organisation is striving towards eliminating data replication. Master data is managed and maintained within dedicated repositories rather than business applications.

4.4.4 Value of MDM

Essentially, MDM is complex. A simple ideal like 'a single view of truth' rapidly gives rise to fundamental questions. Are you talking about a view of that, or do you want to maintain it centrally? How is cross-departmental authoring going to be managed? But it's really worth pursuing, because once you have a single version of truth for your master data, you can get some real and measurable business benefits with relatively little additional work.

Let's return to the example we used of the multiple records relating to Peter Smith:

	CRM	*Salik*
Name	Peter Julian Smth	Peter Julian Smith
Nationality	Great Britain	United Kingdom
D/L no	1370766	1370676

Consider how this information might appear firstly in an enquiry page:

Note that the information down the right-hand side of the page is *blank*. The enquiry function cannot link the two records, and therefore finds no information about tolls, fines or vehicles.

However, simply by changing the same enquiry function to use the 'golden view' or 'golden record' – the single version of truth – the following page would be returned:

All we did was make a tiny change to the enquiry program to be driven by the 'golden view', and much more useful results were automatically returned.

Some straightforward changes can yield immediate benefits in Business Intelligence and other information systems, even from a simple read-only-style

MDM implementation – where the 'golden view' is not propagated back to the source systems.

Our experience suggests that there will be many unforeseen benefits of moving your organisation to have a single version of truth. Some benefits can be seen in advance, whereas others will emerge only once your key users start using the single version in their day-to-day lives.

Here's an example, taken from one of the world's largest telecommunication providers.

This particular organisation had master data spanning across seven enterprise systems – referred to as the 'Seven Sisters'. Prior to their MDM initiative, they had 110 *million* master customer records across the seven systems. A clue that this total was somewhat overstated was that the adult population of the country involved was no more than 40 million.

Dealing with a national-size population, this data was surprisingly fast moving; house moves, marriages and divorces, children leaving home and going to work, and so on. The data therefore had to be de-duplicated by a specialist bureau each week. The bureau marked up 'probable duplicates', which were then sent back to the telco for processing by a team employed specifically for this task. The cost of that team was running at 1.6m USD per month.

A plan was hatched with the objective of reducing the size of the remedial team. The plan involved introducing MDM technology, and bringing the de-duplication function in-house. The process was considered business-critical, and so a formal parallel run was instigated to 'A-B test' the old and the new methods. The organisation was reasonably satisfied with the results of the external bureau; it simply took too long to do, and there was an external cost.

The parallel run proved much more challenging than anticipated, because it proved to be exceptionally difficult to make the results of the new MDM approach *as bad* as the bureau approach, which were naturally the results that everyone had accepted for years.

The new in-house MDM approach was based on probabilistic matching, whereas the old bureau approach rested on deterministic rules. They used very sophisticated rules, developed, tried and tested, over perhaps twenty years, but deterministic nonetheless.

The parallel run was eventually achieved by 'strapping down' the capabilities of the probabilistic matching engine so that it produced similar results. Then, over a series of phased releases, the 'straps' were taken off, and dramatic improvements in data quality were rapidly introduced.

The measurable benefit delivered in this instance was a 75% reduction in cost of the clear-up team. That represented a saving of almost exactly 1.2m USD per month. No one at the outset expected these results, but they were achieved and changed the subsequent project phases.

As a footnote to this story, the organisation achieved one other significant benefit by introducing this technology. Given that the volume of data was so huge, the telco and the bureau had accepted a rather basic method of transferring the data each week for the de-duplication process.

A bureau employee would travel to the company each week with their laptop. This would then be plugged into the telco's systems while the data was physically copied across, and then the bureau employee caught a train, and carried the laptop back to their office where it was loaded onto *their* mainframe.

The data wasn't even encrypted; it was *en clair*[98]. One wonders just how many violations of fundamental security standards were involved in that bi-weekly exercise. What's more, the data was carried back the same way!

The point is that these organisations – and countless others like them – have achieved benefits just by creating their 'golden view' and adapting business processes around it. Many people make an assumption that once you have a 'golden view', the next step should immediately be to write it *back* to all your source systems.

Perhaps in time you might need to do this, especially if you work for a bank, but many organisations choose not to – both out of cost concerns, and out of practicality. Let's explore that a little.

Suppose one of your source systems is Oracle (or SAP, or even something else entirely) and you discover in your 'golden view' that an account code was set up incorrectly. The code happens to be used in four other systems, but let's imagine that the Oracle code had the letter 'O' typed instead of the number '0' in the middle (a simple human error). Once the data is matched as part of the 'golden view', the MDM solution 'knows' that the Oracle system is wrong. A little bit of web services black magic, and you could push a change message back to your Oracle system.

So the correction arrives at the Oracle system. Now we hit a problem. By design, Oracle makes it impossible to change an account number. The reasons are obvious from a basic

---

[98] The French term 'En clair' is used in classical cryptography to describe a version of the text that is not coded. A more modern phrase would be 'cleartext'.

understanding of double entry bookkeeping. It would completely negate Oracle being your 'system of record' if you could change an account number once monies were posted to it.

To cite a real-life case, we know of a major bank which felt that their core banking system was too fragile to withstand the risk of adding another interface. They decided to apply any changes identified by the MDM system, only by manual processes using existing functionality.

But there are other reasons why you might choose to *not* write back, even if it's technically possible, and the source systems are robust. Let's return to this now familiar real-world example:

The data on the card on the right is clearly incorrect (which, by the way, was most likely caused by an error in the reference data for countries). So what are you going to do with the card if you choose to fix the data and propagate the 'golden view' back to the source system concerned? If it were just this one cardholder, you might be tempted to fix the data and re-issue the card. That's fine in relation to the surname error, but what about the nationality? There are over 250,000 UK citizens with driving licences in the UAE, and the chances are that *every one of them is wrong*, especially if this was caused by a simple reference data error.

The costs and logistics of issuing 250,000 new cards seems prohibitive. Conversely, it can't be right to change the underlying data but leave the cards in error. The whole purpose of the card is to represent the data of the issuing authority. When you have data and physical cards out of sync, you're on a slippery slope.

In this case, the only sensible option seems to be to 'live with' the situation until the card needs to be re-issued, at which point it can be fixed. The 'golden view' is correct, so all reporting and analysis can be correct. The data anomaly just becomes a minor point that doesn't need to be fixed today.

There are many examples of this, but our general message in terms of MDM functionality is to think through the business implications very carefully before embarking on writing the 'golden view' data back to source systems. We definitely are *not* saying *never* do that, but equally, we are absolutely saying don't *always* do it.

Think first: the costs and potential risks are high, and there might be other ways to achieve the same benefit.

4.4.5 MDM Summary

We have covered a lot of ground, but this is still no more than an overview of the full scope of MDM-related considerations. MDM experts will undoubtedly smile at some of the simplifications we have had to make to take a largely non-technical audience this far. But our key messages are that taking control of your master data represents one of the most powerful steps involved in crossing the *Data Delta.*

However, MDM, in turn, relies on many other aspects of the *Data Delta.* Try to implement MDM without addressing governance, data description, data quality, data security etc and sadly you will fail. We have seen too many organisations try to go down that road. Please don't add to the MDM failure statistics by making the same mistake.

Finally here, the analogy that MDM is the 'engine' that powers Data Management holds very strongly. Engines are wondrous things, but very few of us have ever purchased one; we usually buy an entire car.

As drivers, we know a great deal about what it is we want the engine to do, but that is very different from knowing how an engine works, how it interrelates with other components of the car, and therefore, what engine will best meet our needs.

Just like buying a car, we recommend you take advice from experts who understand the entire picture, but you should *also* seek to take MDM and its implementers out for a test drive.

4.5 Implementation & Control – Reference Data Management (RDM)

Many informed observers believe, with considerable justification, that Reference Data Management (RDM) is *the* litmus issue as to whether an organisation has truly grasped the consequences of the *Data Delta*. RDM can be seen right up there alongside Data Governance, where the consequences of the gap are perhaps easier to understand.

The business cases for both Data Governance and MDM are well rehearsed. Improving your organisational information by making your data *better* through Data Governance is an established road.

The attraction of an MDM solution delivering a single view of truth for customers and citizens, products and services is immense. These are easy arguments to win.

The case for RDM is slightly more subtle, and not helped by the fact that some of the major vendors have historically simply proffered MDM tools, MDM thinking, and MDM approaches in this space. There have been fewer marketing bucks banging the RDM drum.

RDM also has such a humble beginning. Standard coding systems. Lists. Just how difficult can that be? So if it's so easy to get right, how is it, for example, that one of our clients, a leading insurance provider, had at least *seven* different copies of brand codes?

'So what?' is the obvious comeback.

Here are six arguments to think about. There are in fact many more reasons to *improve* your RDM that are specific to individual business sectors eg banking, NGOs, governments, pharma, retail etc, but these points represent a considerable consistent case for RDM investment:

1. You are diminishing your analytics capability today. In a real world example, we've *already* used several times in this book, confusing the UK and GB is an unacceptable error. You are bound to draw the wrong conclusions from your BI and Analytics engines if you are analysing data against invalid and inconsistent headings. Bad data drives incorrect information, which leads to false assumptions and inaccurate actions.

2. You are missing out on one of the most important and clearly defined 'next steps' of the internet, which is here already in embryonic forms and will dominate the next generation of internet development for years to come. There is much more

about the 'semantic web' in *Section 5 – The Future*, and how it relates both to Big Data analytics and the Internet of Things (IoT). Even today at the beginning of this exciting new development, there are massive benefits to moving towards internationally recognised coding conventions.

3. Compliance is becoming more and more of an issue for a wider range of organisations. For example, fines for non-compliance with GDPR at 4% of turnover are punitive. As we've already highlighted, GDPR is *not* just relevant to organisations within the EU, but all organisations that *trade* inside it. You'd better get your reference data sorted so you have clear boundaries on compliance.

4. If internationalism is important to your business, RDM offers the lowest-cost entry point that delivers genuine value. It may well be too expensive to translate everything to do with your organisation into major world languages eg English, Mandarin, Arabic, Portuguese, Spanish, Hindi or Russian. Standardising your RDM data across language is, however, achievable at realistic costs, with huge potential.

5. Uncoordinated management of reference data is a massive inhibitor to efficient and timely change management. Weeks can be lost due to data integration issues resulting from misaligned reference datasets. Often a good deal of a company's intelligence, and therefore competitive advantage, will be embedded in its reference data. The ability of an organisation to exploit its competitive advantage is directly correlated to the agility with which it can manage its own reference data. RDM also greatly simplifies the process for integrating new systems, for instance in the case of acquisitions, or rationalisation of like-functioned components within an organisation.

6. You are wasting money by *not* introducing RDM – not just the cost of maintaining a list seven times when you only need to maintain it once, but all the costs of reconciling between the different versions. The cost of all that wasted time when figures for different interpretations of a sales region just don't agree.

The case for investing in RDM is massive. So what exactly *is* reference data?

Where Master Data Management looks after data that changes in a relatively uncontrolled manner (such as information about people, organisations and products), RDM applies controls to data that is inherently more stable.

Reference data relates to the classifications, groupings, lists and hierarchies that allow you to categorise your data in a structured way. While an individual reference data record has value, it's the managed set of reference data records, and their relation to each other, that provides greatest value for your other types of data.

A simple example could be a gender flag ('M' or 'F'). This is easy to manage, one would think, but is it being used in the same way across your organisation? Let's say you create a report that looks at gender bias when comparing social marketing engagement vs product sales. As it happens, your Marketing department is capturing 'M', 'F' or 'Other' through their social media interactions, and your website captures 'M' or 'F'. But how does the 'Other' get handled in your report?

It's this question, on a much larger scale, with hundreds or possibly thousands of reference datasets, that is addressed by RDM. Through good Data Governance, and appropriate toolsets, the answer is manageable, and standardised across your organisation.

RDM is also a key gateway to the future. Well-defined reference data will be one of the easiest ways to add value to your data by linking your reference data dynamically to other information sources on the internet. For example, imagine that you are considering a global price change, but you want to know the impact of national sales taxes on your end-customer purchase prices. There's no need for you to try to maintain this data, which changes frequently in any case, if you can link to it through your sales country reference data.

Bringing an RDM system online should go hand-in-hand with the governance *overseeing* it. The Data Governance function of the organisation can assign reference data domains to subject matter experts (SMEs) in the organisation best placed to manage them. A RACI-type pattern can be used to ensure that change management for reference data undergoes appropriate consultation, impact assessment and sign-off throughout the organisation.

Since reference data is, by its nature, widely distributed and shared, any large scale organisation should invest in appropriate RDM tooling to mechanise the governance, mapping and maintenance of reference data.

Note that the introduction of RDM needn't be hugely disruptive to existing systems. An RDM system can be brought online, and begin populating reference data repositories from 'underneath', which is a simple change to the maintenance functionality. While previously, a given reference dataset may have been maintained using a clunky or IT-intensive process, the values can now be populated directly from the RDM system.

In an agile way, more and more reference datasets can fall under RDM on a *priority* basis, with the highest priority reference datasets being those which are business critical, volatile, widely distributed, complex or a combination of these. This agile approach requires relatively modest upfront investment so that an RDM solution first be proven within an organisation's operational capability, while immediately bringing some of the more problematic reference datasets for an organisation under rigorous and efficient management.

4.5.1 Features to consider

The definition of some types of reference data might be directly within your organisation's control (items such as cost codes, branch lists, the chart of accounts[99], etc). Other types will be out of your direct control (such as supplier product categories, regulatory classifiers or ISO country lists, etc), though, even in these cases, you do still have control as to when you apply values from these controlled reference data lists.

There are four key characteristics you should be aware of in order to make sense of managing reference data. However, just as with MDM styles, this is just scratching the surface. A more comprehensive treatment than we have space for here would consider complex issues such as data latency, volatility, and distribution styles:

Version Control

- Controls that define which versions of reference data are current, which are future, and which are archived. For each system and analytical environment.

Map & Transform

- Defined standards to translate between the same logical reference data that have physically different records between systems and versions.

Deployment

- Provides processes to allow systems and analytical environments to receive current versions of reference data and mappings.

Aggregation Policy

- Standards to ensure that where there is an implied hierarchy within the data, the same method of aggregating fine grained data up to a coarser grained level is applied consistently.

Figure 5: Key features for effective Reference Data Management

[99] Though we have happened upon examples where even this isn't true.

Note: Throughout this section, we'll use the term 'list' in relation to reference data. Although lists are a common form of reference data, it is often also hierarchical, comprising lists and sub-lists – many levels deep – that are tightly related. For example:

Product group
    Product category
        Product type

We're using the term 'list' in shorthand form, but we also mean these hierarchies too.

One final thing to remember before we get stuck in. Reference data isn't just about single values in a list; there may be a complex data model for each data item. For example, 'Country' reference data may just be a list of country names, but *behind* each name, there may be additional definitions, such as information on the demographic makeup of the country's population, locations, geographical features, and so forth. Whether this is part of your reference data all depends on how it needs to be used.

The key characteristic for managing reference data successfully is that you are kept informed of any change to the data, or have the means to discover changes through a process, such as regularly checking a published ISO list.

This is different from master data, where the data will often change long before you become aware, such as in the case of a person moving house. Sometimes the boundaries between Reference and Master Data can be unclear[100].

4.5.1.1 Version Management

Within any organisation, operational systems come with their own built-in reference data, whether this is a pick list of name prefixes (Mr, Mrs, Dr, etc) or data that is *specific* to the business domain.

Often you have no control over these lists. They simply come as part of the system, and are edited by the users in response to changes. Has the R&D department created a new type of widget? A new product category could be created. Have some employees started working from home? Why not create a new employee type? Are some employees being issued with smartwatches? That can be added to the asset management database as a new *'wearable'* category.

This kind of ad hoc change to reference data happens fairly frequently in most organi-sations. Ideally, we would want to control this altogether, so that it can happen centrally through a request process. The request might be: 'May I add a new *'wearable'* category to

---

[100] Whether you manage data as Reference or Master Data depends upon your intended usage of the data and level of control. If your organisation is responsible for compiling lists of countries and associated data (possibly with multiple external sources each contributing information in an ad hoc fashion that you need to make sense of), then your country data should probably be managed as Master rather than Reference Data. It's useful to note that there is a large overlap between MDM tools and RDM tools; they have overlapping goals and functionality.

my system?' And, two weeks later, after careful consideration by committee, the request is approved.

This is something that most organisations would consider overly bureaucratic and cumbersome. As a result, there is typically no management of reference data at all. There needs to be a middle ground. Essentially, RDM must be a *central priority* of the Data Governance function, and an organisation-wide communication strategy that focuses on RACI involvement and responsibilities *must* be introduced.

We advocate a method of version management and notification. Naturally, all reference data within an organisation will exist along a spectrum. At one extreme is data that can be totally controlled by a central function, with changes deployed to the rest of the organisation on a schedule. At the opposite extreme, we need to be thinking about managing the ad hoc changes that occur. And this is where version management comes into play.

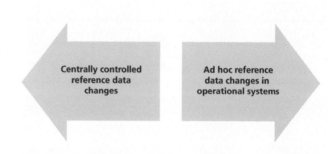

Figure 6: At an organisational level, all control of reference data changes resides along a spectrum

All reference datasets should have a main or 'canonical' version – the version of a reference dataset that the organisation considers to be current and accurate. Working copies of the reference data may be held in multiple operational systems across the organisation, and also, perhaps, in the data warehouse.

These working reference data lists may or may not reflect what the canonical version prescribes. Any given list is likely to be duplicated in a number of places, and each copy may have 'local' variations that differ from the canonical version. The introduction of an RDM tool provides an ideal repository for the 'canonical' versions of your reference data.

Changes to the canonical lists need to be versioned, and this is where the control comes into play. Changes to the canonical version itself can be *requested* and considered eg "Can we add a *wearable* category?" Or a change could be simply be *made* within an operational system, with a subsequent notification eg "We have added a *'wearable'* category".

Either way, the current version of the canonical list isn't changed. Instead, a new canonical version is created that contains the change (or, more typically, multiple changes). The diagram below shows this flow.

Changes and notifications may be automated using appropriate technology or managed through business process. Both approaches will need some kind of manual review and human interaction to provide the appropriate versioning, mapping, transformation and deployment.

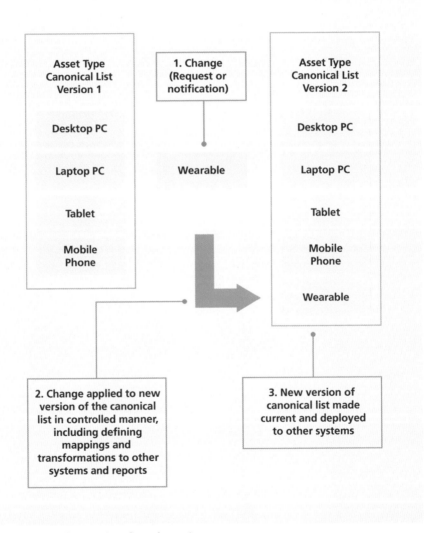

Figure 7: Key steps when managing reference data versions

It's important to remember that although these steps look simple, the whole process can sometimes take days or weeks in a large organisation. This is why it's important to have a standard process that is managed through the Data Governance function.

When you are dealing with multiple requests and notifications from different business units regarding changes in reference data, the ability to organise these changes into versions allows you to identify and manage conflicts *before* they have a large impact. This is an extremely useful capability when taking data from *multiple* systems into a data warehouse.

By way of an example, imagine you work for a technology retailer that has expanded into selling consumer gadgets related to the Internet of Things (IoT). You already have a range of smartwatches in the *'wearable'* category, but now your Marketing department wants to categorise a company-branded baseball cap as a *'wearable'* asset too. Your baseball cap has Bluetooth connectivity and in-ear headphones, enabling it to receive audio from a suitable device, but does this really put it in the same category as your smartwatches?

The answer, of course, is "It depends", and this is probably a question for the appropriate Data Owner within your business to resolve, and they may need to consult with various interested parties before coming to a conclusion.

Along with the actual change to the reference data itself, the *mappings* are also defined between versions of reference data and the systems that use them. This is important for managing compatibility across everything when some systems are still using a previous version of the reference data.

Mapping and Transformations

Once you have your master list of references defined and versioned, you can begin to provide mappings and transformations.

Let's look at mapping first.

Mapping is the direct one-to-one association between records, often known as aliases or synonyms. The data item *'wearable'* could map to a cost code of *'0923a'* in the Accounts system, and *'WRBL'* in the CRM system.

This is where RDM tooling helps. In the same way that Master Data Management tooling is able to combine multiple versions of a record into a single 'golden view', RDM tools can take a *single* reference data value, and provide different mappings that make sense for specific operational and analytical systems.

Mapping is also useful for providing a central store of multilingual translations. While the data item is *'wearable'* in the canonical list, there could be translations for all other languages that your organisation needs to support.

This means that when the item appears on a report or in an operational system in Germany, they are referring to the *same* underlying concept.

The following diagram illustrates some possible mappings from a canonical list to other systems.

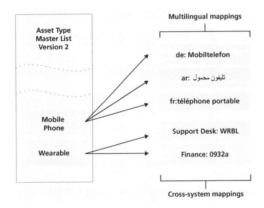

Figure 8: *Mapping a canonical reference data list to other systems and languages*

Transformation, on the other hand, is more complex. This provides a mechanism for handling one-to-many mappings. For example, if *'wearable'* mapped to the CRM system record *'portable devices'* – which also contained 'tablets', 'laptops' and 'mobile phones' – this allows a one-way mapping only.

The CRM system could create reports based on *'portable devices'*, but would not be able to call out specific *'wearable'* devices. That might be fine if you're reporting only on the CRM system, but if you want to cross-check the Finance system against issues relating to *'wearable devices'*, the mapping won't work.

In order to make sense of this data, more rules need to be built, and they're likely to allow for additional data and be specific for each system.

Typically, these rules are built into ETL (Extract, Transform, Load) and Data Quality tooling, so that when data is lifted from the CRM system – which serves its purpose perfectly well without knowing directly about *'wearable'* items – into the data warehouse, the data can be further interrogated to understand more about it. The example in this case becomes a bit more complex.

To illustrate this, let's assume that the model number or asset tag of a device is also recorded in the CRM system. Also, in this example, the organisation has a business rule stating that the identifiers for *'wearable devices'* always conform to a similar pattern, but one that's different from identifiers for 'tablets' and 'laptops'.

A rule identifying that pattern allows the basic *'portable device'* category to be expanded or enriched to become *'portable device – wearable'* for example. With this extra information in the data warehouse, it now becomes possible to provide cross-system reporting from both Finance *and* the CRM system.

As you can imagine, identifying these patterns in the data – and building the associated rules – takes time and effort. This is where much of the hard work comes in when dealing with changes between different versions of reference data.

Priority will need to be given to the various systems and reports according to your specific business environment – some changes will be straightforward; others will prove more challenging. However, understanding that a change is required, and planning appropriately for it, is much easier to deal with than finding out when the Finance Director is complaining to you that the figures didn't add up in the most recent management report. Again.

4.5.1.2 Testing and Deployment

Once you've created a new version of a canonical reference data list (and the associated mappings and transformations), you need to think about deploying it to the systems that *use* that reference data. There are two aspects to this – analytical and operational – which both need to be tested.

We'll deal with the analytical usage first.

With analytical usage of managed reference data, you have the capability of working with the data in your data warehouse in a standardised way, even though it may have originated from multiple systems (each holding their data in different ways).

As an example, our fictitious organisation, *GoDelta*, wanted to create a unified report showing the trend of 'usage over time' for product categories that are in the following stages: 'R&D', 'Production', and 'End-of-life support'.

Even though the product category definitions varied across the different departments, such as '*wearable*' in R&D, and 'Fax Machines' in end-of-life support (with some overlap), the reference data containing the product category list provided the appropriate mapping and transformations to join up this data across those different datasets, *and* provided the report in different languages.

In order to provide this data to the reporting environment, the reference data needs to be deployed to the data warehouse. A straightforward load of the reference data and mappings will suffice, using transformations to provide additional enrichment using data from the specific systems.

By managing reference data deployments in a planned way, you can provide change logs to stakeholders so that they are prepared for when *more* data appears in their reports. This is where the testing aspect comes in.

Depending on the volume and amount of change between versions, different reports may need to allow a period of time for testing of the new data. This might involve a simple test deployment of data followed by running a report, or it could require mirroring an entire data warehouse environment to allow end-to-end testing of the data and reports.

We have seen both. When planning an analytical environment, it's important to ensure you allocate enough resources for controlled testing of the data, in the same way you would allow for testing of software or hardware changes.

For many organisations, analytical usage of managed reference data provides the main return on their investment in RDM. In this scenario, source systems change their reference data as necessary for operational reasons, and provide update notifications (or, if you're lucky, advance requests for changes) to the canonical reference data list.

These changes are versioned, mapped and transformed, and deployed to an analytical testing environment, and ultimately a live analytical environment. From here, the managed reference data allows effective and standardised reporting.

This brings us to the second use of RDM; that of operational usage.

It's possible to take managed reference data further. With appropriate mappings and transformations in place, you have the option to push the new version of managed reference data back *out* to the systems that use it, effectively ensuring that each of the systems is using the same version of the reference data.

Achieving this is clearly more involved, especially in an automated fashion, as it will depend entirely upon the ability of your systems to receive reference data from an external source. Normal system analysis, planning and management of a software project will be required for each system.

Getting more technical still, the common architectural pattern for deploying reference data to operational systems is known as a 'Publish/Subscribe' model. The new version of reference data is 'published', and those systems that *can* make use of it, 'subscribe' to those changes, and make updates appropriately. This pattern makes it possible to bring new systems on board over time, since no changes are required to the data being published. It's only a new subscriber that is added.

The 'Publish/Subscribe' model is also achievable entirely through business process – rather than using technology – by letting people know when there is new data available, and ensuring the updates are entered into the operational system.

This can be fragile without strong infrastructure, and you'll need to ensure checks and balances are in place to ensure that the data is appropriately deployed to each operational system.

That being said, 'pub/sub' is here today and work wells in most common use cases.

A more advanced technical pattern is a live-lookup of reference data, where the operational system will look directly into the RDM system to get its reference data. This is often difficult to achieve, primarily due to the cost of providing a high-performance infrastructure, and modifying the operational system to get its reference data from the central system. You need to assess the right approach for *your* organisation.

4.5.1.3 Aggregation Policy

While this final consideration is primarily for *analytical* uses of reference data, the principle applies for reporting on individual operational systems as much as for a multi-system data warehouse environment.

When you aggregate, group, or otherwise derive calculated data from finer-grained raw data, you need to ensure that the same rules are applied consistently across the organisation.

A simple example might be the monthly sales figures per year. Does this mean 'calendar' or 'financial' year? It's perfectly possible to use either, but you need to ensure that there is standardisation across the organisation.

In most organisations, a jargon develops, but the meanings are often different across the different parts of an organisation, and this may not be obvious to everyone *within* the organisation. We'll deal with this need for standardisation in more depth when we talk about the principle of describing data in the Data Modelling, Data Architecture and Data Catalogue sections.

Let's look at a relatively complex aggregation scenario. *GoDelta* tracks 'employee utilisation' against projects, with subcategories within the projects, such as product development, marketing and sales.

These hours are aggregated to track the time spent on different aspects of a project, which is used to inform future planning. But the reference data for the timesheet system included not only projects, but also some non-project tasks, such as holiday, sick leave and administrative activities.

GoDelta's project planners were only using the time booked against specific projects to get their totals, and were ignoring this non-project time.

Time and again, they found that their estimates for how much time someone *should* be allocated to a project failed to fit with the *actual elapsed time* that someone was allocated to a project. This was because people were allocated to a project even when they weren't booking time against it, such as when they were on holiday.

When they compared their *actual utilisation per employee* to the HR department's productivity reports, they found large discrepancies. Further investigation revealed that this could be explained by those non-project time categories. They decided to change their reporting approach to allocate the non-project time categories proportionally across *all* the projects, which – as a result – improved their estimates.

In this case, although the same data was being used, the different application of it within departments resulted in data being aggregated in a different way, which omitted or misinterpreted the results. By ensuring a *consistent* policy on the meaning of the reference data and how it should be used, disagreements between reported figures could be resolved before they occurred.

4.5.1.4 Sustainability

An effective RDM solution should provide a standard low cost-of-ownership mechanism for adding new lists and system-to-system mappings.

The list management capability insulates an organisation from the need to identify all reference data list domains at the start of RDM work. Agile thinking is important across the entire *Data Delta*. RDM is no exception.

4.5.2 What does maturity look like?

Now that you understand the key features and activities that characterise effective RDM, let's review the maturity-level definitions for this data management domain.

Level 1 – Initial: There is no evidence of RDM across the organisation. Operational systems contain reference data that is managed purely for the operational use of that system. Any analytical system has ad hoc reference data mappings created in a reactive fashion to cope with reference data changes.

Level 2 – Repeatable: Specific operational systems' reference data is managed in a planned manner, with mappings and transformations taken into account as part of reference data changes to cope with any impact on specific analytical systems.

Level 3 – Defined: There is central management of reference data, typically in a Data Warehousing environment, and changes to reference data from operational systems are notified to this central set of reference data. Mappings and transformations are made to cope with changes to operational data.

Level 4 – Quantitatively Managed: Reference data changes are managed through versioning, with changes and change notifications being identified and monitored in order to group changes into specific deployable versions of reference data and associated mappings and transformations.

Level 5 – Optimising: Reference data changes are actively planned and tested prior to the changes being made, in order to understand the impact on operational and analytical systems. This allows time to assess impact analysis, so that resource can be allocated in relation to the perceived value of the change.

There is quite a leap between the lowest and highest levels of maturity, so let's look at the value you can realise by achieving the higher levels.

4.5.3 Value/Benefit

The prime benefit of RDM is predictability. By removing the element of surprise from analytical reporting and operational environments – caused by reference data changes in another system – the effort to deal with those changes can be planned and resourced.

Reference data will always need changing in response to business requirements and external influences, but the knowledge that it *will* change can be used to great effect by planning and managing the change appropriately.

It's important to remember that there needs to be a value judgement against the imposed levels of control and process. Taken in isolation, the management of reference data appears to be extremely onerous compared to the returns it offers.

But when you consider the management of reference data as part of a joined-up information management strategy – combining the effort with Data Governance and other data management initiatives – there is huge commonality in terms of standardisation, notification and decision-making processes. The benefit in reducing duplication of effort across the organisation and being able to react to changing business environment starts to become clear and achievable.

It is not so widely recognised that, when he conceived of the World Wide Web, Tim Berners-Lee proposed an extension of its use (called 'Linked Data'[101]) whereby machines, as well as people, could follow connections between pieces of information (webs of meaning) and use this to 'understand' information. This idea is gradually gaining ground 'out there', especially as more and more data is being released as 'Open Data' by governments, private enterprises and others. For example, there is a version of Wikipedia called DBPedia that is developed in a form that can be used by machines to infer meaning.

A top tip: you heard it here first! If organisations were to bring their reference data under control centrally, *and then* attach semantic links to each value in the reference data lists, they would be able to exploit the enhanced 'meanings' and associations available in the 'www.' community 'out there'.

For example, while it is one thing to recognise that a person lives in a city called York (a city in the north of the UK), it is quite another to be able to ask questions of your data about *information that is not contained within your data*. How about, 'Give me a list of all my customers who live in the north of England from cities that have a population greater than 600,000'.

---

[101] See http://5stardata.info - Tim Berners-Lee 5* Open Data

By tagging a person's record with a piece of reference data denoting their town/city of residence (eg York), and then associating that piece of reference data with other related information 'out there' (eg a definition of York that contains many other pieces of information, including 'the current population of York'), it becomes possible to ask a whole array of questions that can be answered based on information available on the Internet that can be exploited by machines. The beauty of *this* is: you can use this information without having to 'import' it into your organisation. Today, you might be asking a question relating to the population of cities; tomorrow, you might be asking a question about the way a city is governed.

Our view is that RDM is extremely valuable in a world that is waking up to the power of analytics. Management of reference data is a key aspect of allowing all parts of an organisation to attach meaning to their data, and to ensure that the meaning is consistent (both to those inside and outside its walls). This becomes increasingly important in the IoT, where machines will also need to be able to discern the 'meaning' of data.

4.5.4 Impact

For many organisations, introducing RDM and the associated governance can involve a structural shift in mindset where Reference Data Management moves from a reactive, often IT-intensive, process to a road-mapped, business-managed and business-owned process. In this way, reference data values and their mappings are planned in advance and RDM publishes the reference data throughout the system as a simple, established business-as-usual (BAU) process.

There is no doubt that such a shift is overwhelmingly positive. However, mindset shifts are more difficult to achieve in practice than process shifts or changes in technology. The effort and planning needed to transition effectively to *formal* RDM should not be underestimated.

In particular, a Big Bang, waterfall approach is almost always ill-advised, and the success of the transition will be more dependent on the maturity of the organisation's Data Governance function than the RDM technology.

We advise organisations to establish the correct process for agreeing the definition for a reference dataset with the key SMEs involved. This involves ensuring that appropriate consultation takes place with both business and technical stakeholders to identify and plan for impacts and also design the system-to-system mappings for the agreed values.

In some areas of the system eg CRM, a more granular set of values may be required, which are then rolled up into a coarser set for analytics purposes.

The governance process should ensure all of this 'leg work' is done on paper and not discovered through system defects which crash the schedule. Also, don't be too academic or purist with respect to reference data. If there are three or four flavours of a reference dataset across the system, but those values are effectively static and have not caused any operational impact, then it may not be economical to bring them under management.

Like any other *Data Delta* initiative, there should be business case justification for bringing reference datasets under management. No one is looking for Utopia – there isn't value in managing every list in your organisation.

With respect to the RDM technology, where it reduces impact is in mechanically publishing the values and mappings throughout the system, with analytic and transaction components *both* unaware that the values are being input from a centralised source.

As we have already seen, an RDM system can reduce operational impact by introducing a common stewardship interface for maintaining reference data with customised workflow to support different approval processes along with granular security. It can then be plugged into the databases around the architecture to seamlessly publish reference data values.

Once the RDM central source is connected to a particular operational database, it becomes relatively low cost to bring more of that database's reference datasets under management. However, overall the collective positive impact of an RDM technical solution is less pronounced than the strong Data Governance surrounding it.

It is as simple as this. If the appropriate reference Data Governance is in place, an organisation can attain a measurable increase in agility in actioning its reference data-contingent changes, even with a fairly modest investment in an RDM solution. On the other hand, if the governance of reference data is a technology solution only, the implementation is unlikely to achieve its objectives.

Even worse, it will also be a blow to the momentum of the organisation in its journey across the *Data Delta*, having invested in an RDM platform, and then not achieved success.

4.5.5 Next Steps

So how do you actually get started?

As part of crossing the *Data Delta*, you'll be building a catalogue of the data used throughout your organisation. This catalogue will provide information such as who owns or is responsible for the data. On the back of this, you can start to ask for notifications when reference data is changed. The combination of the cataloguing exercise – which we'll talk about much more in the Data Catalogue section – and in receiving notifications will provide three insights that you can use in an RDM pilot.

- Understand where there is commonality of reference data lists between systems, even if the actual data values might be different. An example of this is multiple systems having a list of product categories.

- Measure the approximate volume of reference data changes over a defined timespan. Patterns will begin to emerge so that, for example, name prefixes ('Mr', 'Mrs', 'Dr', etc) will change infrequently, while product categories might vary more frequently.

- Where there is commonality between the reference data used across systems, you will gain some view about which actual systems change their reference data more frequently. You can use this information to better understand why the frequency of change is different, given that the underlying reference data is notionally the same across the organisation.

Armed with these insights, you're well placed to embark on an RDM pilot. Our recommendation is that you identify reference datasets that have a reasonable amount of change and divergence between systems.

This gives you the opportunity to gain experience, and to rationalise your processes, mappings and transformations. You can then use this managed reference data in an analytical capacity to reveal new insights about the data across the multiple systems.

4.6 Usage & Sharing - Integration and Interoperability

Despite the best endeavours of the major software vendors, almost every major organisation in the world has acquired business applications from more than one supplier. The breadth of need, the availability of leading-edge applications, coupled with the decline in the organisational power of central IT departments, means that today's application landscape is undoubtedly more diverse than at any time in the past.

This is the natural consequence of the velocity of innovation within the IT industry. Looking to the Business Intelligence (BI) tools market as an example, for a long time, the traditional enterprise application vendors (such as IBM, Oracle and SAP) seemed to be closing up the market – launching incrementally *improved* versions of their product set every couple of years.

But then came an explosion of newcomers led by *Tableau* and *QlikView*, and the game changed. It didn't take long for customers to recognise that this new generation of tools was a generational shift ahead of previous offerings. *Tableau*, in particular, is relatively easy to deploy, and end-user departments were able to install and make use of the product themselves, sometimes without their central IT departments ever becoming aware that a major new software solution had become part of their enterprise.

Doubtless, the traditional vendors will catch up, either through accelerating their own product development or through acquisition of niche players. They all have the resources to pursue either strategy. But this 'leapfrogging' of innovation by new companies looks as if it will be part of the BI landscape for the foreseeable future which, after all, is how the business world is supposed to work.

This means that the challenges of integration and interoperability are here to stay. Those of you who read *Section 2 – Customer Case Studies* in detail might remember the example from a leading airport where we described their current 'point-to-point'[102] integration approach as 'spaghetti'. This section sets out the case that the most important thing to remember in terms of an Integration strategy is the recognition that there is a *better* type of pasta!

We ought to get one difficulty out of the way first.

There is no recognised definition of the terms 'integration' and 'interoperability' around which we can build a consensus. Alternative vendors have slightly different meanings which they have selected in order to suit their product set. So let's not try to separate the terms, but just acknowledge that between them, they cover all means of linking data in different systems together, either through the *movement* of data (in some form of batch

---

[102] By 'point-to-point', we mean that integration needs are addressed individually, with a unique path built between the source and object systems for each requirement. Although effective in the short term, this approach ultimately leads to a tangle of paths that presents a massive maintenance headache, and indeed increasing ongoing cost.

or real-time mode) or by *providing access* to data across applications, without it physically being moved. These are all represented in the diagram below.

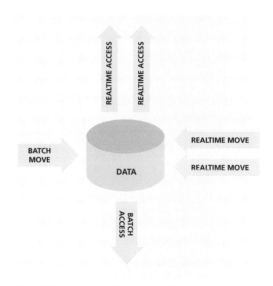

Figure 9: Data Integration for Access and Movement

Resolving this series of topics in a way that works for *your* organisation is central to crossing the *Data Delta*. We've already discussed how a flaw in their integration strategy led to one organisation having a significant failure with their BI programme, which ended with a six-figure settlement.

It's worth noting that a large percentage of *Data Delta* issues end up being expressed in terms of a 'BI failure', since that is often where the data consequences are exposed to the end-user. Usually though, the problems with BI represent the *symptom*, not the cause.

But BI isn't the only place where an integration failure can manifest itself.

One major solutions vendor found itself being attacked by its competitors because – as they pointed out – under the covers, one of its solutions was in fact two products.

The problem was not the products themselves; one was a specialist industry-vertical solution, and the other, a world-class set of financial ledgers. The problem related to how they were linked together, which was not that well. Their customer base was not happy, and it was a weakness their rivals were very effective in exploiting. As sales fell, it was clear that something had to be done but, instead of looking at the problem from a *Data Delta* perspective, there was a knee-jerk move towards the 'opposite extreme'.

Their approach went something like this: 'Let's build a *real-time* link between the two products, so that we can prove the system in a demo situation and absolve ourselves of criticism'. This was a profoundly flawed approach, steeped in emotion, not logic.

The organisation decided to invest heavily in product integration, and certainly got to the point where the solution could be demonstrated effectively, but all they really achieved was to replace one set of integration issues with another. They failed to win over their installed customer base and, consequently, the charges of their rivals held fast.

What was *actually* needed here was a clear understanding of the objectives. They needed to address the problems their customers were experiencing, and the context in which these problems were occurring.

The actual business requirement was a need to interface a set of financial ledgers. Financial ledgers around the world are interfaced in 'batch' mode. There was no real business justification for any 'real time' integration, with all the incumbent expense and technical challenges that involved.

A well-designed batch interface would have cost considerably less money, could have been developed in a fraction of the time, and would have delivered the robustness required by the customers. And once the customers were content, the accusations of their commercial rivals would have fallen away.

What then is the best approach towards an integration and interoperability strategy?

The general advice is to begin with a clear understanding of what you need to achieve from a business standpoint. If your objectives related to being more responsive and agile, then you need to move away from using point-to-point data exchanges between systems.

If you currently employ point-to-point solutions and it works, we are not suggesting that you should throw it away on Day One, but you might want to consider including the replacement of this approach on your roadmap.

Point-to-point links between applications encourage a 'spaghetti'-style situation, where every possible connection is represented by a different strand of slippery spaghetti. The result is a tangle of interfaces that is exceptionally difficult to maintain, especially when the original developers and support staff move on.

In preference to point-to-point connections, you should implement a layered integration approach at the enterprise level. So, in pasta terms, we are talking about *lasagne*, rather than spaghetti. Separate layers of integration capability will enable applications to re-use shared services, making it far easier to maintain and upgrade than difficult-to-manipulate spaghetti.

Differing layers of the 'lasagne' provide the capability to exchange data more readily, in industry-recognised formats (such as XML[103] or JSON[104]) and, just as importantly, apply common business rules to data.

Rather than allow each system to decide what data quality it will accept, you can build the appropriate business rules into the integration layer (eg checking that a customer/citizen identification code is in a valid format), thus ensuring that poor quality data is *not* propagated across systems.

There are many advantages to a layered 'lasagne' approach. For example, as improvements are introduced, they will benefit multiple systems so that you receive a better return on your investment. This approach also makes it far easier to build test environments.

4.6.1 Features to consider

The following diagram represents the type of layers that combine into a data integration and interoperability 'lasagne':

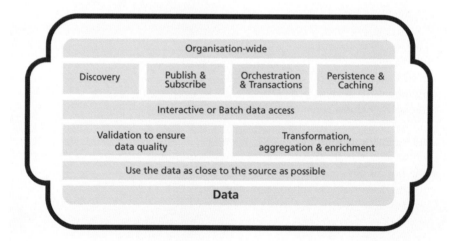

Figure 10: Layers of data integration

---

[103] https://www.w3.org/XML
[104] http://www.json.org

Each of the layers describes a feature or principle that's important for a successful data integration strategy. Cutting in from the top, let's examine what each layer delivers to the overall dish.

4.6.1.1 Organisation-wide

A coherent Data Integration and Interoperability strategy should cover the whole organisation. If your aim is to treat the data which is valuable to the whole organisation *as an asset*, you should ensure the investment in making that data useful and available is as targeted as possible. Central to this is the idea of not repeating effort[105].

Technologies such as an *Enterprise Service Bus* (ESB) allow multiple systems to share data in a self-service fashion across the organisation. This provides a central location for your data services to deliver their payload. It's much like an actual bus in the real world, with data being the passenger that's picked up from one application stop and delivered to another – without the two stops ever knowing about the other.

4.6.1.2 Discovery

There should be a means for discovering the data services available for accessing the data shared across the organisation. In a large, multi-national organisation, there are likely to be hundreds – if not thousands – of data-sharing services that *could* be useful to other parts of the organisation.

In many instances, these services provide the same data, but are only made available for specific projects. We'll revisit the notion of data discovery, and of advertising the availability of datasets and services, in our discussion about the Data Catalogue, but it's important to keep in mind that a Data Integration and Interoperability policy can *only* be effective if potential consumers of the data know it's there.

4.6.1.3 Publish and Subscribe

The Publish and Subscribe model is an architectural 'pattern' that enables a Service-Orientated Architecture (SOA) approach. This idea has been around for many years, and is designed to create services that are based around a model of the real world.

Throughout most of the world, for example, when you visit the supermarket or restaurant, you do not need to haggle over how you will compensate each of them for the goods they provide (it's unlikely that they'll be interested in bartering chickens or in your offers of lawn mowing). Instead, you and your service providers use a recognised

---

[105] There's a concept known to computer coders as 'keeping oneself DRY', where DRY stands for 'Don't Repeat Yourself'.

standard: money. In certain places you might haggle over how much money is involved, but broadly speaking, most of the world transacts using some form of money.

This standard allows the supermarket and restaurant to make their services available, and have the service consumers access their offering in a standard fashion as and when they need them.

They all have 'service-level agreements' (SLAs), such as early closing on weekends, and may sometimes experience problems – the supermarket is out of stock of your favourite beans – but, the boundaries that define the common standard are well-defined and known.

Applying these ideas to your data, and the services that deliver it, allows consuming systems to be built faster and more easily. The usual negotiations that are necessary to agree the terms of exchange for each point-to-point arrangement between systems *are no longer required*, as everyone works to the same standard.

The Publish and Subscribe approach is ideal for distributing data to lots of interested parties. This could equate to a group of grocer's customers registering their interest in a new type of vegetable (kale, anyone?), which they each receive when the grocer subsequently notifies them he has it in stock.

4.6.1.4 Transaction Orchestration

Turning here to our fictitious company as an example, consider a situation where *GoDelta* had taken an order for a product, and had registered a request in their ERP system to have the product shipped. Subsequently, the customer cancelled their order and their payment is reversed, but the *request to cancel the shipping failed*.

These steps represent a series of dependent activities that must all either succeed together, or else fail together. *GoDelta* needed to be able to detect that the shipping cancellation had failed, and use this event to prevent the order from being cancelled (and the payment from being refunded).

All of this should appear to the customer (or the person acting on behalf of the customer) as a single transaction.

If all of the steps succeed, then the customer receives confirmation. If any of the steps fail, then the customer is informed of the problem (possibly being advised to try later, or else contact Customer Support).

- In the case of placing an order: if the payment is taken but the shipping request fails, the customer will be unhappy, and will complain.

- In the case of cancelling an order: if the payment is refunded, but the shipping cancellation fails, the customer will still receive the goods, but *GoDelta* would be out of pocket.

Controlling this type of situation is what is meant by 'orchestration'. The idea is that each of the separate activities above would be represented by a distinct data service (place order, make payment, request shipping, cancel order, refund payment, cancel shipping).

Services are strung together ('orchestrated') in a logical order so that all of the related services either succeed together or otherwise, if any one of the services fails, anything that has already changed along the way needs to be handled in a sensible way.

Why is this important? Once you're in a position to make data services available for use across the organisation (well done!), it's critical that any changes made through those services maintain the overall 'consistency' and 'integrity' of your data.

The point is to keep all related data in step, wherever the various parts of that data happen to be stored. In the example above, data related to placing an order might variously be located in *GoDelta's* Finance system (for payments), in the CRM system (for customer records), and in the ERP system (for shipping and fulfilment).

Orchestration provides the means of *binding services together* into automated workflows, to ensure that *all* the data changes relating to a business transaction (eg a customer order or a cancellation) happen as they should.

4.6.1.5 Persistence and Caching

We have discussed data services, and we have mentioned some of the operational systems (Finance, CRM, ERP, etc) that sit behind these services. The data services are effectively providing a standard interface to and from the operational systems.

It's possible for an operational system to become overloaded by the requests it receives via data services. However, many of these requests are an unnecessary waste of processing time and effort, because they relate to information that has already been provided recently and has not changed since that time.

A 'persistence layer' allows such information to be stored or 'cached' after the first request. Subsequently, the services can check to see if the information is stored in the cache and, if so, use it rather than bothering the operational system to provide the same information again. This alleviates unnecessary requests to the operational systems.

Like many of the capabilities we are discussing in this section, this is usually provided by an ESB – the same component that hosts the data services themselves.

4.6.1.6 Interactive or Batch Data Access

Every organisation has data access requirements, and they typically live along a spectrum of accessing one record at a time, and very frequently, to accessing millions of records at a time – hopefully, less frequently.

When you make your data available for sharing, you need to provide your users with an indication of the type of access they should expect.

Without this, they might inadvertently attempt to access millions of records several hundreds of times per second. In some cases, these apparently extreme requests might be viable, but these cases require special handling – the territory of high-performance computing and 'Big Data' solutions – which come at a price.

In general terms, *large volumes of data* should be handled by processes designed to work with data 'batches', and *interactive services* should focus on fewer records.

4.6.1.7 Validation to Ensure Data Quality

A 'service-oriented' approach implies an element of standardisation, and this makes it easier to control and improve data quality. This is because all the data passing through those centralised data services can be subjected to data validation rules, which allows errors to be detected, handled and reported.

This will ensure that any systems subscribing to your data services will only receive data that is of known and measured quality (something we'll revisit in the Data Quality section).

The integration architecture is an important component in improving data quality, and can reduce the need to invest in stand-alone data quality tools. This idea of weaving best practice into the fabric of your operation is a central theme when it comes to crossing the *Data Delta*, and often the value derived is greater than the sum of its parts.

4.6.1.8 Transformation, Aggregation and Enrichment

It's often the case that we need to merge pieces of data together, or perhaps perform operations and calculations on data to provide additional information.

The lines between transformation, aggregation and enrichment are not easy to draw, but they all represent adding some value to the source data. This allows data that is stored in one form to be presented to consumers in a different, more useful form.

An example could be identifying customer records, retrieving their order records, and calculating their total spend or their top ten purchases per year. This information could be presented by a data service as a complete package.

Such enrichment operations might be provided as a data service if the resulting information could prove useful to other areas across your organisation. Remember, one of the key objectives is to share information and reduce re-work.

4.6.1.9 Proximity

The final layer in the 'lasagne' represents the principle of using data as close to the source as possible. This relates to the concepts of 'lineage' and the trust we are able to place in the data we choose to use.

Lineage is the capability of being able to track the provenance of data throughout its lifecycle. Where did the data originally come from? Who has changed it along the way? What changes did they make?

Clearly, the more that data is passed around and transformed, the less we will be inclined to trust it, especially if no-one is able to say what has happened to it along the way. This accounts for an alarmingly high proportion of the data we see within many organisations.

A centralised integration platform supports this principle by providing services that interface directly to the operational 'systems of record'. This data can then be aggregated, enriched, re-validated, and 'packaged' for ready consumption by other systems or services.

This is significantly preferable to allowing data to be passed around, *possibly via email*, and to be subjected to all manner of transformations, only to be passed on for others to use. We have seen many organisations base key decisions on data that has lived a quite nomadic style of life!

4.6.2 What does maturity look like?

Data integration and interoperability are a crucial component for any organisation intent on allowing data to be shared. Let's see what the various levels of maturity might look like:

Level 1 – *Initial:* Where data is shared, there is little or no use of common data definitions and services, within or between departments and their systems. A significant amount of data sharing across the organisation happens manually, typically by email, spreadsheets and data files, facilitated through personal connections.

Level 2 – *Repeatable:* Formal cross-department agreements are in place to facilitate ad hoc data sharing. A significant amount of data sharing happens in a point-to-point manner. Data is typically shared based on the requirements of specific projects, and no recognised data definition standards are used.

Level 3 – *Defined:* Policies and standards are defined to provide strategic direction for Data Integration and Interoperability practice across the organisation. Basic collaboration across departments happens in a controlled manner. Data definitions tend to be related to the needs of specific projects. There is use of recognised standards, such as XML and XSDs, SOAP or JSON

Level 4 – *Quantitatively Managed:* Data Integration and Interoperability practices are measured, monitored (against KPIs) and controlled across the organisation. Common data definitions and reference code lists are published to allow standardisation and are used when sharing data. Advanced service-oriented interoperability is the norm.

Level 5 – *Optimising:* Sharing data via common definitions, services and protocols is core to the organisation's operation. Core processes and internal organisational structures are aligned for better exchange of data through, across, and outside the organisation. Appropriate use of metadata, reference data and master data ensures that data maintains its meaning when transported. Standard technical protocols are adopted to make it easy to share data. Processes are automated.

4.6.3 Value/Benefit

- A centralised integration platform brings about a number of benefits that allow greater operational resilience across the organisation by restricting the number of 'touch points' and data hand-offs.

- Standards can be applied, and Data Governance compliance measured more efficiently, as there are fewer points to monitor.

- The solution can simplify the delivery of projects by providing standard reusable data service components (which themselves are able to include a provision for addressing data validation and quality concerns).

- Diagnosis and remediation of problems is more efficient as the integration design has fewer components between participating systems.

- Service level and operation level agreements are simpler to establish and manage, through a single point of management and measurement.

- Data exchange between departments and third parties is easier to implement, as all data passes through a centralised service platform.

- Data quality can be monitored directly to identify inconsistencies in data used by different parts of the organisation.

4.6.4 Impact

Most organisations will already have a large number of systems and processes that communicate in a point-to-point manner. They might also have an ESB and tools for transforming and moving data from place to place – such as Extract-Transform-Load (ETL) systems.

- There is a need to establish a policy around the use of data services and methods of integration and interoperability. This should be supported by standards, including a description of any common data formats.

- Organisations need a clear roadmap for phasing out point-to-point connections in favour of a service-oriented approach. Departments should be discouraged from sharing data via uncontrolled methods (such as email), and from transforming and sharing data in ways that threaten to weaken its reliability.

- The Data Catalogue should be updated to include data services available for re-use, but also to ensure that any existing entries reflect service updates or services that have been taken out of use.

4.6.5 Next Steps

The implementation of integration and interoperability is primarily a technical concern. However, the business needs to be aware of the benefits available from this Data Management domain.

As with any activity related to crossing the *Data Delta*, this domain needs to be addressed with the overall objectives of the organisation in mind. What is the primary data that is – or needs to be – shared? How is this currently achieved? What capability improvements could be advanced to unlock more value?

Current capabilities should be evaluated, and future targets mapped against a roadmap of improvements.

Don't forget to consider how to improve the way that reference data, master data and transactional data are made available. They represent key components in your *Data Delta* journey.

You are likely to end up with a picture that looks something like this:

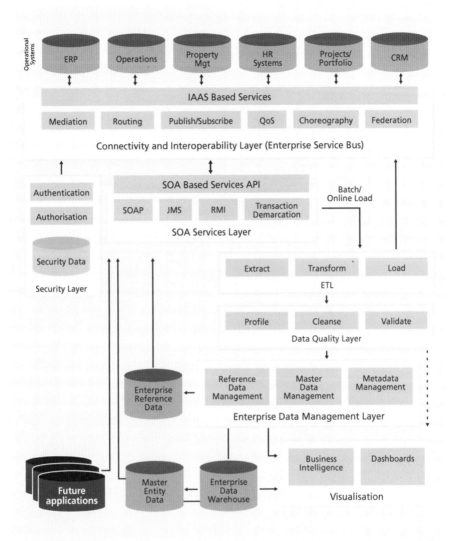

You can draw this diagram in many ways, but it's important to be able to get it on a single PowerPoint slide – for ready consumption by the non-technical executives you seek to persuade.

By all means, move the boxes around, and redraw the picture so that it's of relevance to your organisation, but don't be tempted to include any more detail, or you will lose your audience.

Use this type of diagram (possibly referring to the CRM and ERP systems) to explain the key principle of eliminating point-to-point communication in favour of a more layered technology (which is enabled by the ESB).

Above all, remember the secret to this entire topic is in your choice of pasta – *choose lasagne, not spaghetti*!

4.7 Usage & Sharing – Open Data

"[Open data is] going to help launch more start-ups. It's going to help launch more businesses ... It's going to help more entrepreneurs come up with products and services that we haven't even imagined yet." (President Barack Obama[104])

Open Data is a worldwide movement that is seeing increasingly more corporate and government data being made available for free use by anyone, in any way they choose. Note that this explicitly excludes data that is confidential from a commercial perspective, and also any 'personally identifiable information' (PII).

The availability of such data has led directly to new start-up enterprises in the open market, as well as innovations by established organisations. Open Data has provided opportunities in many areas, including science and medicine, city planning, marketing, financial trading, political and humanitarian campaigning, creative arts, transport and navigation, etc.

Our fictitious company, *GoDelta*, recognised that its domestic and commercial *Delta Power Kit* products represented a unique opportunity to provide information about the use of power in the form of Open Data. *GoDelta* recognises that the issues surrounding 'sustainability' and the consumption of power were becoming increasingly important to people at every level of society, and saw that it had a role in helping people to be more aware of how they and others use power. The connectivity provided by its products already allowed this data to be collected.

GoDelta established an Open Data initiative to consider how best to engage with its customers so that they would be comfortable with *GoDelta* using their data in this way.

This data would not contain any personally identifiable data, but *GoDelta* decided not to publish data mined from the devices of its customers without their permission. Instead, the company used this initiative as an opportunity to communicate with its customers and strengthen its relationship with them, emphasising the value that this use of Open Data would offer. It would allow their customers to benchmark their energy usage against comparable households or industry peers, as well as establishing *GoDelta's* position in the wider community. In return for its efforts as a publisher of Open Data, *GoDelta* hoped – and expected – to attract more attention throughout many forms of traditional and social media, and thereby more potential customers.

---

[106] President Obama made this remark when on his *Middle Class Jobs and Opportunity Tour* in Austin, Texas [9 May 2013] when visiting Applied Materials, a prominent local business. Applied Materials make materials for engineering solutions, which are used to produce virtually every new chip and advanced display in the world.

In terms of its own use of Open Data, *GoDelta's* Marketing function was already benefiting from the information published by an organisation that had the lofty intention of providing a 'URL for every company in the world'[107]. Though they start with the URL for a company's website, this organisation also pulled in related data from a number of other databases.

Like *GoDelta*, your own approach to Open Data needs to consider both the publishing aspect – what data you should publish – and your organisation as a potential consumer of Open Data.

4.7.1 Features to consider

There are many advocates for Open Data, and their number seems to swell almost daily. Much of the impetus has been generated by the public sector, but don't make the mistake of thinking that private companies have nothing to gain by publishing Open Data.

A particularly forward-thinking proponent is the United Nations. Here is a summary of their position:

> *Opening up government data is fundamentally about more efficient use of public resources and improving service delivery for citizens. The effects of Open Data utilisation are potentially far reaching for sustainable development with a positive impact on innovation, transparency, accountability, participatory governance and economic growth. Open Government Data (OGD) can help countries improve development programmes and track progress, prevent corruption and improve aid effectiveness. The benefits of Open Data and improved access to public information gain greater visibility and relevance today in the context of the 2030 Agenda for Sustainable Development.[108]*

We have identified five key features of an Open Data policy:

4.7.1.1 Open by Default

The principle of 'Open by Default' is an intention that is reflected in the policy statements of organisations across the world. One example comes from another government source – the Australian state of New South Wales (NSW)[109]. Their

---

[107] There really is such an organisation. Check out OpenCorporates.com.

[108] Taken from https://publicadministration.un.org/en/ogd. The UN e-government survey that identifies the top e-governments in the world represents fascinating reading. For those who don't want to know any of the detail other than who is 'top of the table', the answer is South Korea, who have been focusing on Data Management for decades. However, whilst congratulations to South Korea are most definitely appropriate, a detailed reading of the survey indicates what a disappointing standard the world is at. South Korea may be first, but the competition isn't great. No government has yet managed to undertake a credible journey across the *Data Delta*, though we would say that the UAE (with the Abu Dhabi Government's Data Management Programme leading the way) has the best plans. Of course, we would say this, since we at Entity helped to develop Abu Dhabi's Data Management Strategy, but it's true anyway!

[109] NSW Government, (2016). NSW Government Open Data Policy. See https://www.finance.nsw.gov.au/ict/resources/nsw-government-open-data-policy [Accessed 25 June, 2016]

policy defines the concept of 'high-value datasets', and highlights the importance of prioritising the release of such information.

High-value datasets are defined as exhibiting one or more of the following attributes:

- Responds to a need and/or demand identified through public or stakeholder engagement, or supports positive social outcomes

- Has the potential to enhance services or service delivery

- Furthers the core mission of the agency

- Increases agency accountability and responsiveness

- Increases government transparency

- Will create economic opportunity, generate efficiencies, or reduce costs

- Will support evidence-based policy-making or research

Data should be regarded as 'open by default' inside an organisation as a matter of policy.

This means that data is only withheld from publication on an exceptional basis; albeit that those exceptions are wide in scope (most likely related to security, commercial sensitivity, confidentiality, privacy, or data quality concerns).

It is important to be very clear in stating your organisation's intentions. Open Data can only be of value if those that use it feel they can trust that the data source will not change – or disappear – unexpectedly.

With this in mind:

- Define your Open Data position publicly in a statement of intent, such as an announcement, strategy or policy, so your plans for providing and developing your Open Data are clear.

- Publish data via a portal, so that all the data that has been released can be found easily in one place. A portal may be a central website from which data can be downloaded, or a website that lists all Open Data stored at various different locations. Each portal should include a registry file that lists all the data and metadata used on the portal, as well as providing appropriate Application Programming Interfaces (APIs) for developers. Where it will not be immediately possible to publish all data on a portal, the location of data should be communicated clearly and not moved without notice.

4.7.1.2 Quality and quantity

The principle of 'Open by Default' leads to an obvious concern that Open Data exposes the quality of data held by organisations; organisations that are, at the same time, desirous of presenting themselves in a positive light. However, the NSW Government expresses the sentiment of many other Open Data advocates:

> Data should be made available with a statement regarding its quality, as this will allow potential users to determine whether the data is suitable for their requirements. Data quality issues should not unduly delay the publishing of datasets.[110]

What should such a data quality statement include? NSW points to the approach outlined by the Australian Bureau of Statistics' *Data Quality Framework*[111]. This measures the quality of data against seven measurement dimensions: internal environment, relevance, timeliness, accuracy, coherence, interoperability and accessibility. These are *all* characteristics that you will be in a position to quantify and describe once you cross the *Data Delta*.

We recommend following these three practices in line with the principle of 'Quality and Quantity':

a) Use robust and consistent metadata – this represents the fields or 'elements' that describe the actual data. As a starter-for-ten[112], the G8 Open Data initiative has established a repository on GitHub[113] that tracks metadata items used within various datasets published via portals of its member nations.

b) Ensure data is fully described, as appropriate, to help users to understand the data fully. This may include:

- A Data Dictionary that provides explanations about the data fields used;

- Documentation to show how the different data entities interrelate; and,

- A User Guide that describes the purpose of the collection, the target audience, the characteristics of the sample, and the method of data collection.

---

[110] Ibid.

[111] Abs.gov.au, (2009). The ABS Data Quality Framework. [Online]. See http://www.abs.gov.au/websitedbs/D3310114.nsf/home/Quality:+The+ABS+Data+Quality+Framework [Accessed 25 June 2016].

[112] For non-UK readers, this became a catch phrase from one of the earliest UK TV quiz shows, University Challenge. Getting a 'starter' question right scored ten points, and won the right to try to answer some harder supplementary questions on the same topic.

[113] GitHub, (2013). Available at: https://github.com/nsinai/G8_Metadata_Mapping/blob/master/index.md [Accessed 25 June 2016].

c) Listen to feedback from data users to improve the breadth, quality and accessibility of your data. This could be via public 'User Group' meetings, a feedback mechanism on your data portal, or other appropriate communication channels.

4.7.1.3 Usable by All

It would be counterproductive to publish data only to find that no one uses it, and publishers have a responsibility to ensure their data is *usable by all.*

Make your data available in convenient open formats so that files can be easily retrieved, downloaded, indexed, and searched by all commonly-used web search applications.

Open formats (such as non-proprietary CSV files), are those where the specification for the format is available to anyone for free, thereby allowing the data contained in a file to be opened by different software programs.

4.7.1.4 Release Data so as to Improve Governance

A key aspect of achieving the highest level of maturity in Data Management is about continuous improvement, and this, in turn, implies that you set up a feedback mechanism – receiving and acting on information received from users of your data.

With this in mind:

- Consider how you can develop links with external organisations and individuals to allow them to provide feedback about the kind of data they would like to see released

- Be open about the data standards used

- Document and talk about your experiences of working with Open Data (both as a publisher and a consumer, as appropriate) so that others can benefit and engage with your narrative

4.7.1.5 Release Data to Encourage Innovation

What better way to demonstrate your value as an organisation than to point to the successes you have enabled others to achieve?

These pointers will help in this regard:

- Support the release of data using open licences so that minimal restrictions or financial obligations are placed on the re-use of the information (whether used commercially or for non-commercial purposes)

- Ensure that data (and related metadata, including licenses) is *machine-readable* by providing data that's well-structured (many consider that the maturity of Open Data should be measured using Tim Berners-Lee's 5-star Open Data[114] scheme)

- Release data via APIs, where appropriate, to ensure easy access to the most regularly updated and accessed data

- Encourage innovative uses of the data, perhaps by promoting challenges or events (such as *hackathons*[115]), offering prizes or providing mentoring for users of your data

When making datasets available for sharing, it's important to specify a licence that explicitly states whether or not re-use is permitted and any restrictions that apply. Even when no restrictions are to be applied, and the data is completely open for re-use, there should be an explicit licence to this effect.

This is particularly significant to consumers who combine datasets from different sources to create new ones, and whose own ability to publish, in turn, will be constrained by the most restrictive licence they inherit. For this reason, try to use the least restrictive licence possible.

Licensing is also important because in many jurisdictions, intellectual property rights will exist to prevent third parties re-using data without explicit permission. Determining 'default' rights may require applying multiple pieces of legislation and making subjective decisions about which legislation applies to the particular circumstances (based on the source and nature of the data being shared). If an explicit licence has not been stated, there is therefore a risk that potential users of a dataset will be discouraged from a lack confidence about whether the 'default' position *allows* use of the data.

---

[114] 5stardata.info, (2012). See 5stardata.info/ [Accessed 25 June 2016].

[115] A *hackathon* is an organised event where enthusiasts such as computer programmers and other techie types come together for a few hours or days to work intensively on developing their ideas. The goal is to emerge with better ideas or even some working software.

4.7.2 What does maturity look like?

Level 1 – Initial: There is no evidence of a coherent Open Data strategy. Instead, departments build walls around their data to prevent access. Where data is published, it may only be in a human-readable format (such as images or PDF reports).

Level 2 – Repeatable: The organisation has experimented with Open Data internally or externally, but there is no evidence that these experiments have been coordinated outside specific departments or projects.

Level 3 – Defined: Organisation-wide policies and standards are defined to provide strategic direction for Open Data, driven by defined goals for both internal and external data sharing. Open Data is being published according to a centrally-governed strategy and via a centrally-managed portal.

Level 4 – Quantitatively Managed: Open Data practices are measured and controlled in accordance with organisation-wide standards, with data sharing initiatives reporting KPIs back to the Data Governance Steering Group. Open Data publishing is measured against the 5-star Open Data[116] scheme.

Level 5 – Optimising: Open Data practices form a core part of the organisation's data strategy, and are considered as a material factor for every tactical project. Measurement and feedback from previous experiences are used to create better practices across the organisation. There is an active drive to make more data publicly available, at high levels of quality, and reaches 4 or 5 stars against the 5-star Open Data[117] scheme.

4.7.3 Value/Benefits

From the perspective of the value of Open Data to organisations as consumers, there are a number of potential benefits, both for enhancing your existing product or service provision, and also for repackaging the data and making the output available for sale in some form.

This could include a smartphone app that is powered, either wholly or in part by Open Data, or a more direct offering such as a subscription service, whereby customers pay to make use of your data.

Some organisations, particularly though not exclusively in the public sector, have recognised that they can benefit by *making data open* for others to develop applications (especially mobile apps). There are cases where governments that initially set out to provide apps for their citizens have retrenched and cut back their own development

---

[116] Ibid.
[117] Ibid.

activities because they recognised that the apps developed by third parties (individuals or private enterprises) were better and proving more popular with users.

From a government perspective, this can lead to a triple payback of saving internal development costs, stimulating the economy, and leading to increased satisfaction amongst citizens.

Given the right conditions, this same model can translate into the private sector too eg financial investment houses or insurance providers might choose to provide certain types of market or quote information for third parties to integrate into apps (or disseminate in other ways), which in turn, could lead to increased business for the original provider of the data.

Open Data is an effective way for organisations to demonstrate value and to create an ongoing relationship with potential customers.

4.7.4 Impact

From an Open Data governance perspective, your Data Governance function will need to oversee a number of activities:

- Establish or review your organisation's policy and standards for Open Data in line with the features we have been describing here. This should lead to an assessment of any existing practices relating to Open Data to ensure they are appropriate for use within your organisation.

- Evaluate all the ways that Open Data is published (if at all) and propose a suitable migration plan to transfer everything to a central Open Data portal.

- Define service-level and operational-level agreements to support your provision of Open Data services.

- Make sure as many people as possible inside your operation are aware of Open Data, related policy and standards, and the commitments to publish data via the centralised Open Data platform.

- Evaluate and classify all data sources to determine their potential suitability as Open Data. A similar evaluation should become part of any data-related project so that any new data sources, or changes to existing data sources, are evaluated from an Open Data perspective.

- Monitor and report – against appropriate KPIs – the service level and operational-level commitments, and act to address any issues relating to Open Data. The operational-level considerations need to extend to include appropriate capacity planning from an infrastructure perspective.

- Develop the appropriate processes – automated, where possible – to publish all data identified as 'open'.

- Endeavour to apply an explicit licence, to make it clear how each dataset can be used, even when no restrictions apply.

- Ensure that entries for all Open Data are maintained within your Data Catalogue.

4.7.5 Next Steps

Your organisation should be seriously considering its policy about Open Data. The Digital Age will be characterised by sharing data in both directions, and you should be prepared to participate in this.

We believe there are significant benefits that accrue from Open Data, whether you are in the public or private sector. The world outside your corporate walls is clearly a complex one. However, world governments and high-profile corporations *argue strongly* that the most effective model for future success is based on transparency and sharing.

Focus on establishing your Open Data policy, on developing a roadmap for the data you can share now or intend to release later, on measuring and improving data quality, on related security issues, and on exploiting the Open Data provided by other organisations.

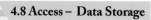

4.8 Access – Data Storage

The development of Data Storage technology, along with advances in computing processing power, was one of the great success stories of the twentieth century. It has continued unabated into the new millennium.

Gordon Moore's Law[118] tells us we should expect computing power to double every couple of years. If only everything in life could get twice as good, and at a similar rate!

The continued reduction in the unit cost of data storage has quite literally changed how we think about the topic. It wasn't that long ago that organisations thought in terms of what data they could afford to store, and for how long. Unless you work for Google, most of us no longer think like that. If we as an organisation need some data, there is no question about whether we can afford to store it.

At the same time, our definition of data has expanded beyond recognition. Within one generation, we've evolved from structured database tables, through static images, to streaming data, audio and video. And we are doing it in colour, not black and white!

In some senses, this shift in our expectations may have turned into complacency. When capacity and costs were a real constraint, we used to *have* to think carefully about our data archiving strategy – which we developed in accordance with the usefulness of data – and how its value declined through its lifecycle. Since then, it's as if someone, somewhere in IT, said, 'Don't bother with that anymore – I've got some spare old servers with loads of capacity.'

Given the seemingly unlimited availability of storage capacity, there is a tendency to overlook archiving. In fact, archiving should never *only* have been concerned with cost and capacity. It represents the natural conclusion of the data lifecycle – that point where the true cost of ownership outweighs the value of data, because it has so little value to your organisation.

True cost of ownership goes significantly beyond a mere consideration of data storage costs. Think, for example, of the costs related to ensuring data quality. They remain consistently high.

To lose the concept of 'needing to archive' is to lose the discipline of assessing the value of data throughout its life, and this is the antithesis of everything we have been extolling in this book.

[118] See http://www.mooreslaw.org/

New worlds of storage availability have opened up before us, but we shouldn't discard the discipline of tracking the value of data. In the past, this was necessary to release storage and reduce cost. It is still necessary today, but for reasons related to reducing risk, complying with regulatory requirements and, more generally, to be aware of the inherent value in our data.

Respect for the value of data will ensure it is appropriately safeguarded, but will also lead towards unlocking and making better use of that value.

We've seen major changes to storage design with the advent of virtualisation and Cloud technologies. A key area where this presents new opportunities is that of Business Continuity and Disaster Recovery (BCDR) – a key *Data Delta* concern. Once you subscribe to the notion of data as a valuable asset, the question turns to how your organisation would survive a disaster that *threatened your data asset*.

4.8.1 Features to consider

There are three main aspects to consider about data storage or the 'management of data at rest'.

4.8.1.1 Data capacity

Data capacity management is about ensuring you have the right amount of storage and processing power to exploit your data – with enough room for growth in the future.

As part of building your Data Catalogue, you'll gain an understanding of the amount of data that exists in the various parts of your organisation. This is captured as metadata. Tracking changes that occur to this metadata over time allows you to produce real-world evidence in support of planning your capacity requirements. This results in plans that take into account all aspects of the data lifecycle and of data recovery.

Technologies such as virtualisation and Cloud computing allow you to provide both the storage and processing capacity your organisation needs now, but also for any unused capacity to be targeted dynamically where it is most needed. Increasing utilisation in this way ensures you're getting the best value for money from your hardware, but does require careful monitoring.

If you're running at 20% capacity, you have plenty of room to cater for unexpected spikes in usage, but for most of the time, 80% of your available capacity is being wasted. If you're running at 80% capacity, you're making much more efficient use of your resources, but you need to be on the ball in terms of looking out for those spikes in capacity.

Taking the right approach can save significant costs.

We advocate engaging a specialist firm to undertake a study on your behalf to ascertain the current utilisation levels of your existing hardware. This will allow you to make some informed decisions about whether a move towards more virtualisation could *save you money*.

In any case, you need to ensure that your infrastructure is adequately monitored, and is following a plan so that your future capacity requirements are covered, and that a nasty surprise isn't suddenly revealed sometime in the future.

4.8.1.2 Data lifecycle

We have mentioned the concept of a data lifecycle several times now. This is also something that you'll need to consider when managing your data 'at rest'.

Data will pass through several states on its journey through the organisation and, from a data storage perspective, these states each attract a number of characteristics which need consideration. These come under the following headings: Capture, Retention, Maintenance, Use, Retirement, and Disposal.

Let's examine these through the eyes of our fictitious company.

GoDelta first receives or 'captures' data within the organisation in a number of ways, including data entered into an online system by 'end customers' or staff, and data files provided by third parties. Outside the operational systems, lots of additional content is generated in the form of documents, spreadsheets, mailed correspondence (much of which is scanned by the post room), emails, publications (both online and offline), and marketing collateral (including posts on social media and specialist sites).

As it began to look into the possibilities of sentiment analysis and social media profiling, the company started to experiment with extracting information from Twitter posts.

All this information has 'value' to the organisation to a lesser or greater degree, but to realise that value, *GoDelta* needed to make sure that, whatever its form, the data remained available *when needed* to those who needed it. It also needed to be comprehensible (clear and concise), trusted (accurate and relevant), and appropriately secured.

Though some of these concerns related to other Data Management domains, the captured information needed a home to reside in, and this home needed to be capable of satisfying characteristics that related to availability and security.

Information should only be retained for as long as it's needed. *GoDelta* implemented a programme that would eventually see *all* captured data being registered within its Data Catalogue, along with metadata that describes its purpose and various other 'housekeeping' attributes, such as the date of capture.

The company's Data Governance Steering Group developed a *Data Retention and Disposal* policy that specified, for the many and various types of data and content, how long the data should be kept, and how to make decisions about its retirement or disposal. This implies a need for processes to manage data retention (also included in the policy), and *GoDelta* will be considering these processes as well. They determined that Data Owners would be appointed to be accountable for ensuring that the processes were carried out effectively.

One aspect of making data appropriately available relates to ensuring that data can be maintained when required throughout its lifecycle.

While this does not apply directly to some types of content (documents that are printed offline, for example), it should be possible to keep the metadata descriptions that relate to all content up to date. *GoDelta's* plan was that this capability would be provided by its Data Catalogue tool.

A key theme of our message is that all data should be used consistently and in line with the purpose(s) for which it was initially captured. Consistency of use has aspects that cut across many of the Data Management domains, but the key points relate to having clear and concisely-defined descriptions of data, and then ensuring that all uses align to these descriptions.

Something that is often missed is the need to ensure that *anyone and everyone* acting on behalf of the organisation – including, but not restricted to contractors, consultants and temporary staff – is made aware of its policies on Data Management, and their responsibilities to use data as directed by these policies.

There should always be a justifiable reason for disclosing information to third parties and, again, this should be done in line with Data Management policies and standards.

All data that is deemed to be approaching the end of its useful life should be considered for retirement (to a secure offline or near-line archive) or disposal. All 'live' data and content carries inherent risks and ownership costs. Retirement and disposal need to be considered in terms of minimising risks and costs, but also to ensure that any requirements relating to confidentiality, privacy or conditions of use, are observed.

Laws relating to data use vary throughout the world. In the UK, at the time of writing this book, the following represent valid reasons for keeping data in a 'retired' state as opposed to disposing of it entirely.

- Legal data retention: Certain laws (such as the UK tax regulations) may require you to keep the records for a specific period of time.

- You may need to keep certain data to be in a position to respond to information access requests by customers or citizens. For example, retaining a history of customers' names and addresses would allow you to respond to this type of query: "Did I have an account with you when I lived at '23 Acacia Avenue, YourTown', and did you mis-sell Personal Protection Insurance[119] to me?"

There are many technical solutions available that automate the task of archiving data, such as taking periodic snapshots for either an entire system or a specific storage device. Some options even allow scheduled procedures for archiving data that 'comes of age' and needs to be retired. In some cases, it is also possible to configure a read-only front-end user interface for searching and viewing the data. It is worthwhile considering this type of automated tool to help in implementing your archiving policy.

Data disposal requires special consideration at the policy level, and the policy needs to take account of regulatory and business requirements. Many legal jurisdictions allow individuals to request that you *delete* any data you hold about them.

The key is to be in the position of identifying what data *you do have* that relates to an individual, and once you have successfully crossed the *Data Delta*, you will be in this position.

Irrespective of the legal requirements, it's good practice to weed out the data that no longer represents any value, but continues to carry risk and incur cost.

Don't wait until whenever that next data migration might occur before attending to stale data; this should be a planned activity rather than a by-product of some other task. This will have the dual benefit of being able to show compliance with regulations, while allowing you to predict your data storage requirements more accurately over the longer term.

---

[119] In the UK (at least), PPI mis-selling is an ongoing scandal. It has spawned a huge number of spam phone calls and emails offering to help claim back compensation from financial institutions. The PPI compensation claim industry largely exists because people can't actually remember what they were sold 10+ years ago, and who sold it to them.

4.8.1.3 Disaster recovery

The third aspect of data storage relates to disaster recovery, which is part of a larger discipline known as Business Continuity and Disaster Recovery – BCDR[120].

We often hear frustrations expressed by people within the business about running out of storage space on shared drives and file servers: "Why these restrictions? Why does it take so long to get more space? I can buy a terabyte hard-drive at my local store for next to nothing."

Resilience and recovery are good examples of why quotas need to be controlled. When the resource in question is part of an operational system on which the business relies, simply adding more capacity is not enough. Any additional space also needs to be covered by physical and strategic data recovery mechanisms.

There's good coverage at the physical level, with technical standards such as RAID having been around for many years.

The strategic level relates to the ability of recovering from a disaster, and requires appropriate planning. The plan should consider how your organisation would be affected by a catastrophic disaster that rendered one or more components of your data landscape inoperable.

The plan also needs to ensure that your recovery capability has the capacity to store a number of versions of the data supporting your operational systems, analytical systems, and archives. The risks of a disaster occurring should be assessed, and the mitigations and responses documented. Your plan needs to include periodic rehearsals of your disaster recovery measures.

These provisions are like an insurance policy. You hope you never have to use it, but once you have it, you'll have the peace of mind that comes with knowing you're covered.

---

[120] It's impossible to do justice to BCDR in this type of book. Readers are encouraged to refer to ISO22301 – Business Continuity Management (http://www.bsigroup.com/en-GB/iso-22301-business-continuity) and also the UAE's Business Continuity Management Standards (http://www.ncema.gov.ae/dassets/download/b6f229f6/AE_SCNS_NCEMA_7001_2015_ENGLISH.pdf.aspx - undoubtedly the most aesthetically appealing BCDR book of its kind!). The entirety of the Entity Method is about unlocking and protecting the value of data by crossing the *Data Delta*, and your BCDR provision is a key component of this.

Case Study

Let's look at a real example of disaster recovery that's been well documented.

You know that you are looking at a genuine disaster for your organisation when the news reports of the fire in the building next door include the words 'Richter Scale' to describe the explosion.

In this particular case, the Richter rating was 2.4, and was described as the largest explosion in the UK since WWII. Thankfully, despite the enormity of the conflagration, there were no fatalities. It took place next to a large office complex, but over the course of a weekend.

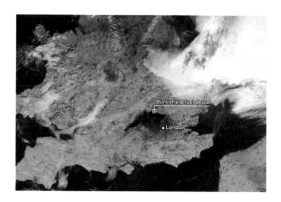

The story took place at the Buncefield Oil Storage Facility in Hemel Hempstead in the UK. A massive fire, early on a Sunday morning, engulfed the oil depot itself, as well as surrounding office blocks, one of which was occupied by Northgate Computing.

Northgate was, at the time, one of the major data processing agencies for the UK Government. One of its responsibilities included running the payroll for the UK's National Health Service (NHS); the *fifth-largest*[121] employer in the world (at the time of writing the NHS employs around 1.7 million people).

Northgate had a full disaster-recovery provision in place, and this immediately swung into effect. The fire took place on 11 December 2005 – with the all-important Christmas payroll runs due for imminent processing. Time was clearly of the essence. As well as a contractual liability, in terms of meeting their contract conditions, there was a very human realisation that Christmas could be ruined for over a million households.

The well-rehearsed routines were triggered, and a fully-replicated IT capability was made available, with the latest data restored from offsite storage. The payrolls were run on time, everyone got paid and, presumably, had a fantastic Christmas (well, everyone except the insurance companies). Was that the end of it?

Not quite.

---

[121] Fifth-largest as opposed to third within popular understanding in the UK, and still a huge employer by global standards. Numbers one and two are the Chinese and American armies respectively, but three belongs to Walmart and at four is McDonald's. The British Health services is in fifth place in front of a series of gargantuan Chinese and Indian institutions.

The customer-facing systems were afforded the highest priority as part of the contractual position. However, the priority for each of the other systems had been decided a long time ago, and had not been ordered to reflect the changing nature of the business. So, the Finance system was next in line to be restored, but the company's email system was towards the bottom of the list. When the procedures were planned, email simply hadn't been considered that important.

These days, most companies could probably operate for quite a few days without a finance system. Customer receipts would continue to flow in, and if you aren't making supplier payments as quickly as you should be, well, for once you have a great excuse.

But try running a modern business without email for three or four days. It can't be done.

Email has replaced mail and fax as the primary method of written communication, both externally and internally. Indeed, many processes rely on it, and falling back on telephone conversations just isn't the same.

The lesson here is that organisations – in the widest sense of the word – need to become involved in planning for recovery after a disruptive incident, and the procedures need to be reviewed and updated frequently. No one can predict what developments lie over the horizon, and as these become part of the operation, they need to be factored into the recovery provision.

A final word on Buncefield. Spare a thought for the Northgate employee who purchased their pride-and-joy Porsche car the week before the fire. As they were going away on Annual Leave for a fortnight's diving holiday in the Mediterranean – and didn't relish the idea of leaving the car outside their house – they decided instead to leave it inside the secure compound at their offices, which came with its own security guard. It was bound to be much safer there. Or so they thought...

4.8.2 What does maturity look like?

These are some suggested definitions maturity levels for Data Storage:

Level 1 – Initial: There is no evidence of a consistent Data Storage strategy. No data lifecycle exists, and data is kept, deleted or archived on an ad hoc basis. Backups exist but are untested.

Level 2 – Repeatable: Data Storage practices for specific systems or within specific departments are successfully implemented, documented and repeated. However, there is no evidence that these are coordinated at a higher level, leading to inconsistent approaches or duplication of effort across the organisation. Data backups are maintained with specific systems undergoing test restores in an ad hoc fashion, or within specific departments.

Level 3 – Defined: Organisation-wide policies and standards are defined to provide strategic direction for Data Storage practice across all systems and departments. New and existing systems are beginning to follow data lifecycle standards to evaluate short, medium and long-term storage requirements. Back-up standards are maintained across the organisation for the purposes of operational restore and disaster recovery.

Level 4 – Quantitatively Managed: Practices are measured and controlled in accordance with organisation-wide standards, with KPIs being reported back to the Data Governance Steering Group. Centralised data storage plans are available with departments using resources from centrally provisioned data storage, whether physically located in a data centre, or delivered virtually through numerous providers. The organisation has a comprehensive Business Continuity and Disaster Recovery provision.

Level 5 – Optimising: Data storage and data lifecycle management is delivered as a service across the organisation, with proactive monitoring and planning in evidence for current and future data systems. The Organisation's Business Continuity and Disaster Recovery provision is reviewed regularly.

4.8.3 Value/Benefit

A robust approach towards data storage, information lifecycle management and disaster planning mitigates against service outages – either as a consequence of demand exceeding the available capacity, or a catastrophic incident. Continuity of service is a key factor in enabling the organisation to meet its objectives, and to maintain stakeholder satisfaction.

A move towards virtualised processing and storage resources has several benefits.

- There is likely to be a significant cost saving as utilisation can be managed more effectively and maintenance is more centrally focused.

- Preparation for disaster recovery is easier when all the resources to be included in the backup are in one place.

- For a similar reason, this also makes it simpler to establish a layered integration architecture with central data services (see the section on Integration and Interoperability).

- From a governance perspective, centralisation makes for more effective security, performance and compliance monitoring.

4.8.4 Impact

Creating and implementing a joined-up organisational Data Storage strategy is necessarily a gradual process. This is likely to require a significant period of time to change, especially if individual departments have previously been responsible for their own data storage arrangements.

During the design phase of IT projects, the non-functional requirements around volume, performance, capacity and throughput should be sized with virtualised environments in mind (for both current and future requirements).

Existing non-legacy systems should be moved to a virtualised and managed environment.

If it has been a while since the last review, the BCDR arrangements should be considered and updated as appropriate.

4.8.5 Next Steps

The Data Governance function should have data storage high on its agenda in terms of defining the overall strategy for Storage Capacity, Data Lifecycle Management, and BCDR.

This strategy should become part of the 'common practice' implemented across the organisation. System upgrades and new systems – whether bespoke or off-the-rack – should demonstrate alignment with the strategy.

If your existing systems are not protected by adequate backup and restore provisions, you really need to stop reading at this point, and task some people to address this! If you're unsure, find the accountable person and ask them.

And, even if you're comfortable that everything is being backed up appropriately, you should always remember to check when the restore routine was last tested.

4.9 Access – Information Security and Privacy

Information Security management is needed to protect your organisation's information while balancing its compliance obligations, any specific risks that apply to its data assets, and the business requirements that underpin the operation and its use of data.

The privacy aspect relates to protecting personally identifiable information (PII) from undesired exposure or inappropriate use, and being able to provide evidence of its use.

Management of security and privacy concerns need to be applied in proportion to the size of the threat presented by the loss, misuse, unauthorised access to, or modification of each type of data.

All information requires some level of protection, but certain information requires particular attention because of its sensitivity and related risks. Determining the security controls to apply is based on classifying all data from the perspective of sensitivity.

4.9.1 Features

Organisations around the world invest lots of time and effort in creating and implementing their own security standards. One study[122] in 2013 noted that, globally, there are over a *thousand* security publications, and that this makes for a "complex standards landscape".

While there are many generic references to IT security practices, many 'information security' documents exist in the context of specific information domains (such as Big Data, information sharing, Data Warehousing and Analytics).

However, taken together, these resources do tend towards some common themes, suggesting that information security has a core 'best practice'.

The Australian Government[123] outlines seven core principles underpinning a central information security policy:

1) Security policy and planning

2) Information security and third-party access

3) Information asset classification and control

4) Operational security management

---

[122] PWC, (2013). *UK Cyber Security Standards Research Report*. Department for Business, Innovations and Skills.

[123] Protectivesecurity.gov.au, (2013). *Information Security Management Core Policy*. [Online]. Available at: http://www.protectivesecurity.gov.au/informationsecurity/Pages/default.aspx [Accessed 12 May 2014].

5) Information access controls

6) Information system development and maintenance

7) Compliance with legislative and regulatory measures

Looking at the details behind these principles – don't worry, we're not doing that here – makes it clear that the application of information security principles cannot exist in a vacuum. A wider approach to Data Management and Data Governance is required to provide a context for applying appropriate security controls. The Entity Method is designed to address this wider context.

When it comes to implementing an Information Security policy, the good news is that there is a comprehensive and proven set of standards – the ISO 27000 family[124] – and these have been widely adopted by organisations around the globe as the basis for their information security provision. If you don't already have a set of Information Security standards, you would be well advised to start here.

HMG's Infosec Standard No.1[125] is aligned with ISO 27001:2005, and outlines a six-step process for assessing information security risk.

1) Catalogue the landscape – producing a diagrammatic model if necessary

2) Define the focuses of interest

3) Define the threat sources

4) Define the threat actors

5) Identify the risks and estimate risk levels

6) Prioritise and present the risks

Armed with a risk assessment, you will be well-positioned to begin addressing the risks appropriately. The effort required in implementing all the appropriate counter-measures should not be underestimated. This is likely to require a programme in its own right.

All this is good so far, but …

---

[124] http://www.27000.org

[125] http://www.cesg.gov.uk/publications/Documents/is1_risk_assessment.pdf – note that this standard is no longer supported by the CESG – the security arm of the UK's General Communications HQ (GCHQ), but a risk-based approach is still widely regarded as an effective basis for planning information security. The latest standard is ISO 27001:2013. We favour the previous version of the standard with regard to risk assessment because the latter is too loosely defined.

Although ISO 27001:2013 contains a control related to the protecting the privacy of information, this is all it has to say on the matter:

> *Privacy and protection of personally identifiable information shall be ensured as required in relevant legislation and regulation where applicable.*

Personally-identifiable information (PII) is a key concern for customers and citizens, and it is worth looking at this in more depth. Some organisations will already have controls in place to ensure that data is anonymised, pseudonymised, or only available in aggregate form.

The Australian *Better Practice Guide for Big Data*[126], acknowledges that new data created through the use of data analytics provides valuable capabilities to generate enhanced information about a person. However, it cautions against compromising anonymity through the collation of a range of data that inadvertently reveals identity. This is known as the 'mosaic effect'; a concept whereby data elements that in isolation appear anonymous, and amounts to a privacy breach when combined as a whole.

The United States is at the forefront of protecting PII. The *Health Insurance Portability and Accountability Act*[127] (HIPAA) has a specific set of privacy rules. In essence, these boil down to *de-identifying* information about individuals through one of two methods:

a) Expert Determination:

This relies upon expert individuals to use high-quality scientific and statistical analysis. This approach does carry a small risk that an individual may be identifiable, however.

b) Safe Harbour:

This is useful when there is no actual requirement for knowledge about identifiable individuals, as it removes 18 personal identifier types[128], and employs techniques such as combining postal codes into single three-digit figures which has the effect of grouping around 20,000 individuals within a region. It's the transactional business data that's analysed (health information in the case of HIPAA), and the actual individuals involved are not relevant to the analysis.

---

[126] Data Analytics Centre of Excellence, (2014). *Better Practice Guide for Big Data*. Australian Federal Government.

[127] *Guidance Regarding Methods for De-identification of Protected Health Information in Accordance with the Health Insurance Portability and Accountability Act (HIPAA) Privacy Rule*. [Online]. Available at: http://www.hhs.gov/ocr/privacy/hipaa/understanding/coveredentities/De-identification/guidance.html

[128] Examples of identifiable data include names, vehicle registration details and social security numbers.

The US Department of Homeland Security[129] conducted a Government Privacy and Best Practices workshop, and this reported a number of best practice principles in great detail. In summary:

- Transparency Principle: The Government should 'be transparent and provide notice to the individual regarding its collection, use, dissemination, and maintenance of PII'

- Individual Participation Principle: The Government should 'seek individual consent for collection, use, dissemination and maintenance, and provide appropriate access for correction'

- Purpose Specific Principle: The Government should explain who is collecting the data and why, using specific purposes

- Data Minimisation Principle: The Government should 'only collect PII that is directly relevant ...' for the specified purpose(s), and 'only retain PII for as long as is necessary to fulfil the specified purpose'

- Use Limitation Principle: The Government should 'use PII solely for the purposes specified'

- Data Quality and Integrity: The Government should 'ensure that PII is accurate, relevant, timely and complete'

- Security Principle: The Government should 'protect PII through appropriate security safeguards ...'

- Accountability and Auditing Principle: The Government should 'be accountable for complying with these principles, providing training and auditing use of PII ...'

The Canadian Information and Privacy Commissioner identifies *seven* complementary principles of data privacy under the banner of 'Privacy by Design'[130]:

1) Proactive not reactive; preventative not remedial

2) Privacy as the default setting

3) Privacy embedded into design

4) Full functionality – positive sum not zero sum

5) End-to-end security – full lifecycle protection

6) Visibility and transparency – keep it open

7) Respect for user privacy – keep it user-centric

[129] Department of Homeland Security, (2009). *Government 2.0: Privacy and Best Practices*. DHS Privacy Office.
[130] *Privacy by Design*. [Online]. Available at: http://www.privacybydesign.ca [Accessed 26 June 2016].

The objective of *Privacy by Design* is to "ensure privacy and gain personal control over one's information, and for organisations, gain a sustainable competitive advantage".

At the time of writing this book, the European Union has just ratified the General Data Protection Regulation (GDPR). This European-wide regulation will come into force over the next two years, and the UK's Information Commissioner's Office (ICO) has produced the following guidance[131]:

- *Awareness* – *You should make sure that decision makers and key people in your organisation are aware that the law is changing to the GDPR. They need to appreciate the impact this is likely to have.*

- *Information you hold* – *You should document what personal data you hold, where it came from, and who you share it with. You may need to organise an information audit.*

- *Individuals' rights* – *You should check your procedures to ensure they cover all the rights that individuals have, including how you would delete personal data, or provide data electronically and in a commonly used format.*

- *Subject access requests* – *You should update your procedures, and plan how you will handle requests within the new timescales and provide any additional information.*

- *Legal basis for processing personal data* – *You should look at the various types of data processing you carry out, identify your legal basis for carrying it out, and document it.*

- *Consent* – *You should review how you are seeking, obtaining and recording consent, and whether you need to make any changes.*

- *Children* – *You should start thinking now about putting systems in place to verify individuals' ages and to gather parental or guardian consent for the data-processing activity.*

- *Data breaches* – *You should make sure you have the right procedures in place to detect, report and investigate a personal data breach.*

- *Data Protection by Design and Data Protection Impact Assessments* – *You should familiarise yourself now with the guidance the ICO has produced on Privacy Impact Assessments, and work out how and when to implement them in your organisation.*

---

[131] https://dpreformdotorgdotuk.files.wordpress.com/2016/03/preparing-for-the-gdpr-12-steps.pdf. Although the UK has decided to leave the European Union during the production of this book, the GDPR legislation draws heavily on the UK's own work in the area of data privacy. GDPR will have an impact on organisations outside the EU, directly if they are trading partners with counterparts inside the bloc.

- **Data Protection Officers** – *You should designate a Data Protection Officer, if required, or someone to take responsibility for data protection compliance and assess where this role will sit within your organisation's structure and governance arrangements.*

- **International** – *If your organisation operates internationally, you should determine the data protection supervisory authority under which you reside.*

Clearly, no matter the jurisdiction in which you operate, data privacy is set to become a *demanding* aspect of information security, and data management in general. And by 'demanding', this means that numerous Data Management disciplines need to be established in order to fulfil many of the requirements of this domain.

4.9.2 What does maturity look like?

Level 1 – Initial: Data Security practices are minimal and ad hoc. While material data breaches may not have occurred so far, this is more by luck than judgement. There is no regard for the need to protect personally identifiable information[132].

Level 2 – Repeatable: There is evidence of documented security and privacy standards, though there is no guarantee that these are sufficiently comprehensive, or that there is any consistency of implementation across departments. The built-in security features of systems are accepted as the default security position without further evaluation. Personally identifiable information is given privacy protection primarily through ad hoc staff training and common sense.

Level 3 – Defined: Organisation-wide policies and standards are defined to provide strategic direction for Information Security and Data Privacy practices across all departments. Systems have a consistent security policy, and business processes are designed with security and privacy in mind.

Level 4 – Quantitatively Managed: Data Security and Privacy practices are measured using KPIs and reported to the Data Governance team. Policies and standards are actively improved to reflect the daily impact as appropriate.

Level 5 – Optimising: Security and Privacy is regularly audited and tested through the use of ethical hacking and social engineering. The results of these tests are used as part of continual improvement of systems, processes and staff training.

---

[132] Finding organisations at this level is rare due to internationally recognised requirements for personal data privacy, both in the EU, USA, and elsewhere.

4.9.3 Value/Benefits

It's something of a challenge to describe the value of implementing robust security and privacy measures in terms of 'benefits'. This domain is very much about adopting a defensive stance against the *loss* of value, and other related risks, rather than actively *adding* value.

As we observed earlier, the scope of this subject is so wide-reaching, that it touches on many of the other Data Management domains. If the need to address risks and comply with regulatory requirements are the stimulus for effecting improvements in other areas too, then it could be argued that information security and privacy are indirectly adding value to your organisation.

The following case study underlines the potential for harm if security and privacy are not approached in a comprehensive and holistic way.

One particular government department was involved in spending large amounts of government money on one-off contracts. There was concern about the potential for collusion between individuals in the procurement function and potential vendors.

With single contracts valued in excess of one billion USD, it was thought that even the most conscientious of staff might be led astray by a vendor desperate to know overall budgets, the status of other bids, the name of the person who would make the final decision and so on.

Accordingly, the administration set out to make the process as 'clean' as possible. They commissioned an old building specifically to manage this large-bid procurement. Full access security was used on the building, with strictly required personnel identification including biometric passes.

To enter the Bid Room, you had to go through an airport-style scanner. No electronic devices of any kind were allowed to be taken into the area. The room itself contained a number of desks and PCs with 'hardened' security, in that they had no internet or intranet access at all. They were essentially glorified word processors.

Vendors had to submit their bids on CDs, which were kept securely contained inside this room where Procurement staff evaluated the competing bids. The room was monitored via CCTV cameras that continuously recorded the activity at every workstation (via audio and video).

It was an impressive operation, and the organisation managed to instil a genuine awareness for the importance of security among all the staff involved.

As the work progressed, the outcomes were recorded into an Oracle ERP system. This wasn't a one-off task; these were complex multi-phase programmes, and the differing approaches suggested by the vendors each required the budget to be allocated in various different ways.

Oracle's *own* security to manage this operation was also extremely tight. There was strict control – built into the user profiles for the system – over who could see or maintain *exactly* which data fields. A specialist security penetration testing consultancy was engaged to test the resilience of the security, which they undertook by way of 'ethical hacking' techniques, both from outside and inside the enterprise firewall.

This was an iterative process, as procedures were successively tightened until the penetration testing failed to breach the defences.

Everything was being done to stop potential vendors from finding out anything they shouldn't know – most crucially the forecast budget for the piece of work for which they were bidding. At face value, it all appeared watertight and, as far as anyone knew, there were no breaches of security.

No breaches … as far as anyone knew.

The problem is: there was a gaping hole in all these measures.

There was absolutely nothing to stop *anyone* with read-access to the Oracle system, in any non-secure building, from exporting the relevant data into Excel spreadsheets. Even though the corporate email system was carefully monitored, there were no controls to prevent such an Excel file from being saved onto a USB stick. From here, it would be a simple matter to take it home, and then email its contents to anyone in the world from an anonymous email account!

Did this happen? Did anyone abuse the system? Perhaps not, though there is absolutely no way of knowing, and this fundamentally defeated the objectives of all those costly security measures.

Crossing the *Data Delta* requires an holistic approach to every aspect of Data Management, and this most certainly includes information security.

Security is only as strong as the weakest link – apologies to re-use the simile but there really isn't an easier way to say it. Generally speaking, everyone currently has their core business systems nicely secured. The problems are more likely to exist outside or around the edges of these systems.

We have seen many cases where IT will point to their information security and governance policies and standards, and the robustness of the ERP or core operational system, but fail to recognise that a high percentage of the organisation's business moves through third party systems (such as Cloud-based SaaS[133] solutions), or processes where data is downloaded and transported around offline.

4.9.4 Impact

Our fictional company, *GoDelta*, was planning a new online portal to allow its customers to engage more readily online, with the key objective being to provide greater self-service, which would lead to increased sales and improved customer satisfaction. The following example illustrates the steps that *GoDelta* followed, in line with its Information Security and Privacy policy, to assess and mitigate the risks associated with the release of this new online capability.

This is the outline of the steps taken by *GoDelta*:

1) Catalogue the landscape – producing a diagrammatic model if necessary

2) Define the focuses of interest

3) Define the threat sources

4) Define the threat actors

5) Identify the risks and estimate Risk Levels

6) Prioritise and present the risks

7) Identify appropriate countermeasures

The first four steps focused on examining the specific context of the system in question, and were implemented in a workshop consisting of representatives from *GoDelta's* Marketing, Customer Service and IT functions (including a consultant specialising in information security and governance).

---

[133] Software-as-a-Service (SaaS) is a way of making functionality available from a centrally-hosted application (such as over the internet) rather than requiring software to be installed on local computers. If this is a 'paid-for' service, users will usually pay a subscription fee (monthly or annually, for example), and this can be based on the level of usage.

The remaining steps processed the information provided by the earlier steps, and resulted in the identification and presentation of the risks, along with possible mitigations. These latter steps were carried out by the specialist consultant.

The product of the risk assessment was a document presenting the information produced at each step of the process.

Part of the risk assessment process established that the company's appetite for risk was such that any risks identified as being at a 'Low' level could be accepted, but that anything above this level should be addressed and preferably mitigated.

The exercise identified a number of 'Low' risks and only four 'Medium' risks. No risks were identified at a higher level than 'Medium'.

In practice, the four risks can be considered as *two* risks, which are similar in nature, but which are duplicated because they apply to two geographically isolated systems. There are two such systems because *GoDelta* has decided to have a live system, and a standby 'Disaster Recovery' (DR) system for use if the primary system fails. These two systems represented the 'Focuses of interest'.

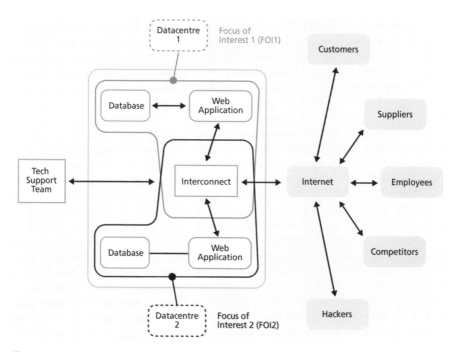

Figure 11 – Landscape and security 'focuses of interest' for GoDelta's Online Portal

The following technical components were identified. The numbers represent the impact level in terms of confidentiality, integrity and availability (the values can range from 1 to 5, with 5 representing the highest potential impact in the case of a compromise).

- Firewalls/Network Devices/Infrastructure (2 | 2 | 4)
- Primary Application Server (2 | 2 | 1)
- Primary Database (4 | 3 | 1)
- Disaster Recovery Application Server (2 | 2 | 1)
- Disaster Recovery Database (4 | 3 | 1)
- Archive (4 | 3 | 1)
- Tape Backup (4 | 3 | 1)
- Staging Server (1 | 1 | 1)

These threat assessments were aggregated to determine the maximum threat for these three categories. This was determined to be 4 | 3 | 4 for both of *GoDelta's* Primary and DR systems.

GoDelta identified the following 'threat actors'. The numbers represent the capability of the various actors (the values can range from 1 to 5, with 5 representing the highest ability to effect a breach of security).

- General Hackers (3)
- The Competition (3)
- Disgruntled Employees (3)
- Customers (3)
- Suppliers (3)

Each of these threat actors was assessed as posing a 'medium' risk of compromising the confidentiality and availability of the systems by operating through the public-facing internet.

The specialist advised that the identified risks could be mitigated by implementing measures against all the relevant security objectives described in HMG's Infosec *Manual of Level 3 Baseline Countermeasures*.

There are many security objectives in the *Level 3 Baseline Countermeasures* manual, and only a relatively small proportion are relevant to mitigating risks associated with confidentiality and availability.

Consequently, a subset of security objectives was produced by including anything that could be said to impact on confidentiality and/or availability, however marginal that impact might be.

All other security objectives were ignored. The remaining security objectives were examined in turn to assess whether they were covered by the implemented system design and/or *GoDelta*'s Managed Service provision.

GoDelta's team identified over 50 security objectives of relevance to the risks to confidentiality and availability. Of these, only one objective was not already being mitigated either by the design of the implemented system or by the Managed Service provision.

The unmitigated objective relates to the collection of evidence of a security breach. *GoDelta* discussed this with the supplier of its Managed Service provision, and the scope of the service was changed to include this element.

The point of this example is to highlight that a clear policy – plus related standards – allows your organisation to conduct systematic analyses of your security and privacy risks. Any weaknesses in the countermeasures and mitigations can be identified and addressed before it's too late.

If your organisation does not already have such a thing, you need to establish a policy around information security and privacy. At a minimum, this should address the following areas:

- Security and privacy must be adopted wholeheartedly, and done so across the entirety of the enterprise. This will require careful strategic planning and communication.

- Your Data Governance function[134] has a role in ensuring that data security and privacy concerns are understood across your organisation. This may translate into providing formal training sessions, but one-off events should be supported by a sustained awareness and communication campaign.

---

[134] Many organisations carve information security out into a separate function headed up by the Chief Information Security Officer (CISO). If this is true of your organisation, your CISO should be part of your Data Governance function, and you also need to ensure that data privacy is fully covered.

- Data Governance should also ensure that datasets are classified for data privacy and security risks, and then proactively develop appropriate risk management strategies. They should lay down checkpoints to be included within all projects to ensure compliance with privacy and security controls. This group should also ensure that 'Privacy by Design' principles are maintained within systems and projects.

- The Data Governance function should be commissioning audits and spot checks of systems to ensure compliance with data security and privacy. They will sign off on data security and privacy requirements for systems where there is an identified privacy or security risk. This is the group that monitors the processes around sharing data within the organisation – to ensure it complies with security and privacy controls – and it also approves data sharing requests from external parties.

- Data Governance will also establish the appropriate indicators and metrics suitable for the specific systems and datasets under your organisation's control. They should be monitoring security incidents and privacy breaches, but also anticipating security incidents and preparing responses using simulated scenarios.

- Data Governance should ensure that *all* the appropriate security and privacy Metadata is attached to published datasets and services in the Data Catalogue, and that it is regularly reviewed and maintained.

- Development project teams should act under the guidance of the Data Governance function in regard to data security and privacy, and should be able to provide systematic evidence of the implementation of the relevant controls.

4.9.5 Next steps

Security and Privacy represent key aspects of your journey to cross the *Data Delta*, and the Entity Method encourages everyone in your organisation to view data as an asset *all the time*. This means that data has to be made appropriately secure at every stage in its lifecycle, and not just when it sits behind firewalls and under the protection of your enterprise systems.

It's not sufficient to focus solely on the security within your core business systems. You need to ask more fundamental questions about how easy it might be to copy data into less controlled media. Also, how might live data be being used for testing purposes? Are sufficient controls in place?

There are technical solutions available for almost every security concern, but of course, these all require investment. As for any asset, your organisation needs to decide *how much* it is prepared to spend in its protection of it. Given that, organisations are adept in making cost/risk assessments about protecting every type of asset. You need to make sure *your* organisation is doing just that in relation to its data assets.

4.10 Quality – Data Quality Management and Remediation

The success of data-related implementation projects – such as Data Warehousing, BI and Analytics – significantly relies upon having a clear understanding of the quality of underlying data, and the ability to improve quality. You need to establish the capability to manage data quality across and throughout your organisation.

We always ask organisations open questions such as: 'What is your data quality like?' The responses range from: 'Okay', or 'Patchy' or 'I guess that's why *you* are here'. Sometimes, organisations have *already* invested quite heavily in data quality initiatives before they meet us, and we get a slightly different response: 'Actually, we think it's pretty good.'

None of these responses, however, represent a *Data Delta* response to the question about data quality, and that's because they are all subjective. A more objective statement might be:

> *Currently, in terms of our metadata and reference data, we are sitting at 100%, which is the only acceptable target for us. In relation to our key customer master data, we've identified 18 critical pieces of information we are monitoring against each customer. For these, we are currently at a 94.7% quality rate, which is .3% below our minimum target. However, we know the primary cause of this – our recent acquisition, and the need to merge the data of the company we bought, and bring that up to our standards – and we have a plan in place to get above 95% within three weeks. Below that, our transactional data is standing up well; we are still within all our tolerances for reported errors, which gives us confidence in the dataset.*

This type of statement hails from the other side of the *Data Delta*. The good side.

The only meaningful measure of the quality of data is its fitness for purpose.

This relies on establishing recognition for the importance of data quality as part of your organisation's culture. This stems from the notion of 'quality by design', and from a drive towards continuous improvement in *all* areas related to the quality of data.

'Quality by design' means considering data quality at every stage of the development of a system; from initial requirements elaboration, user interface design, functional specification, data design, technical design and reporting, through to implementation and operational execution.

Each of these stages represents an opportunity for assessing the implications for data quality, thereby optimising those aspects of the system that influence data quality.

Quality should be measured at each stage of the data lifecycle, and processes should be established to fix any detected data quality issues.

4.10.1 Features to consider

There are a number of key requirements for improving and managing the quality of data.

We have already underlined the importance of measurement. All data should have a quality statement that describes its level of quality. This could be expressed as a percentage – as we saw in that quantified statement in the introduction to this section – but, at the very least, it should be possible to describe data quality at the granular level of the maturity model (on a scale of 1 to 5).

The question is: what are we measuring against?

To have any value, our measurements of data quality must relate to some kind of data quality standard that relates to its 'fitness for purpose'. This, in turn, requires that we can articulate an understanding of the reason that data is captured, maintained and used.

Clearly then, the management of data quality extends beyond the Data Quality domain, and in fact spans a number of Data Management domains.

The *understanding* of data is bound up in the domains relating to the 'Description' Data Management principle, namely: Metadata, Data Modelling, Data Architecture and Data Catalogues. While the techniques and tools for monitoring and fixing data may be focused in the Data Quality domain we're considering here, other domains – such as MDM and RDM, for example – will also contribute. Further still, the *processes* and the *people* related to managing data quality rely on effective Data Governance and, as we have seen, that is the subject of yet another domain.

Having established a measurement scheme, data quality should be actively monitored and managed, with planned remediation procedures in place to handle any data that falls below the agreed quality standards.

Data quality validation – and remediation of any errors detected – should be applied at the point that data enters a system or service, or when existing data is changed in some way. Stored data should also be monitored and undertaken routinely (you should look towards automating these processes).

The following list represents some important characteristics of effective Data Quality Management:

- Data Quality is known and measureable for all operational data
- Data Quality is known and measureable for all data services
- A non-functional requirement for data quality measures is included as part of the design for any and all development projects that involve data
- Data Quality is monitored and managed effectively
- Strategic goals for data quality drive improvements across the organisation

Implicit in that quantified statement in the introduction to this section was the ability to classify data. Remember the reference to Metadata, Reference Data, Transactional Data etc?

The following picture shows how the characteristics of these various types of data are related. Note in particular: the left-most arrow, indicating the importance of data quality, resides towards the top of the hierarchy.

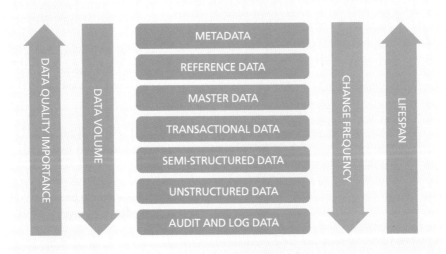

Errors in metadata and reference data could potentially have disastrous consequences for an organisation. For example, if the definition of 'sales territory' is inconsistent in Sales compared with Finance, an analysis of performance might lead your executives to invest marketing spend in the wrong region. It's worth reflecting on this if, like most organisations, yours is not actively managing its reference data today.

Metadata and reference data errors can potentially impact large groups of customers or citizens and critically, all the management information with which they are associated. For most organisations, the quality of metadata and reference data *needs to be at 100%*.

The following case study underlines the potential difference that reference data can make to the outcome of democratic elections in the modern age.

In 1997, the 'new' Labour Party, under the then-popular leadership of Tony Blair, won a landslide victory to oust the UK's incumbent governing party, the Conservatives. The size of the victory suggests that Labour might have won in any case, but leading Labour strategists believe that a key determinant for the *size* of the victory was their access to better data on which to make decisions. All modern political campaigns invest the most money in those marginal seats where the outcome appears to be at risk.

But where, in this case, were the marginal seats?

When preparing for the election, the two political parties used different approaches to determine what constituted a marginal constituency – and hence, where to focus their main campaigning efforts.

The Conservative campaign approached this using the traditional approach of looking at recent elections and applying the likely percentage vote-swings predicted by pollsters. The New Labour Party undertook a more complex analysis across the country that considered changes to constituencies in terms of population movements, population ageing and constituency boundary amendments.

One of the constituencies contended in the UK's 1997 General Election – Croydon Central – serves as an illustration of the effect. In their database, New Labour classified this as a *marginal* seat, and therefore, with appropriate campaigning, this seat was potentially winnable. In contrast, the Conservatives failed to identify the risk, and instead continued to view Croydon Central as a safe Conservative seat, and assumed they were sure to win.

On Election Night, New Labour achieved a swing of over 15% in this constituency compared to the national average of 10%, and to the considerable surprise of the

Conservatives, won the seat. One of the key factors in this instance was that New Labour campaigned with substantial resources devoted to Croydon Central, whereas the Conservatives assigned minimal resources to the area.

Both parties made their resourcing decisions based on reference data, but the New Labour classification of 'Marginal' proved more accurate in this instance than the Conservative assessment of 'Safe'[135].

If we accept that metadata and reference data need to be 100% accurate, the next important decision about data quality resides at the level of master data – the data about your customers, citizens, products, assets and the rest.

What are the factors by which quality should be assessed for each item of data? There are a number of ways to look at this, and usually a combination of factors is used. Here are some of them:

4.10.1.1 Accuracy

This is fairly self-explanatory; data must be sufficiently accurate to support the tasks at hand. It follows that the concept of accuracy is *relative* rather than absolute. For example, if your company is based in the UK, you might need to assess the economic status of your customers. You might go about doing this by using a postcode lookup against a generic marketing database, and from this determine, say, that people who live in the area with postcode 'W13 9RN' have a status of 'C1'. In terms of accuracy, such an organisation would want a very accurate postcode but if, in practice, one house out of the thirty[136] covered by a typical residential postcode was a little different in terms of its economic status, they probably would not be unduly concerned.

In this day and age, there is very little data where we can talk of 'absolute' accuracy. Age, for example, is very well defined and documented in Western countries, but is more likely to be an approximation in some other parts of the world. For example, a disproportionate number of Afghanis working for one of our Middle-Eastern clients were discovered to all have the same birthday of 1ˢᵗ of January[137]. There are neither the social

---

[135] Information on the campaign can be found in the authoritative work *The British General Election of 1997* by Butler and Kavanagh. 'We generally take a healthily sceptical view of the effect of local polling activities on the outcome of a General Election but concede that, in this instance, there is significant evidence that individual results were impacted.' See also: https://en.wikipedia.org/wiki/Geraint_Davies_(Labour_politician)

[136] In the UK postal system, a 'Postcode' narrows the area of focus to around 30 addresses, and it is possible to make this reference unique by combining this with the building number. In some cases, a single postcode can represent one building (this can cause data protection issues if 'aggregate' data is released by postcode (health statistics, crime statistics, etc).

[137] In this instance, the percentage was well over 70% on a sample of over 5,000 people. This cannot be explained by the basic statistics question 'How many people do you need in a group so that it is more likely than not that at least two of them will share the same birthday?' The purpose of this question is to raise awareness of the 'counterintuitive' nature of statistics; the answer being that any group of just 23 people is slightly more likely than not to contain at least two people that share a birthday. The same simple arithmetic shows that with 41 people in a room, there is a 90% probability of a shared birthday. 'Coincidences' are far more common than one first thinks! The arithmetic is trivial but is easy to prove using a spreadsheet. The first person can pick from 365 days and be sure not to share a birthday. The second 364, the third 363 and so on. So the probability of say three people having a shared birthday is $1 - (365/365 * 364/365 * 363/365)$. A very unlikely event at about 0.009 probability. However, by the time you add 23 terms to that series (which is why you need the spreadsheet) the odds raise to just over evens.

conventions nor the bureaucratic processes necessary in Afghanistan to record birthdates more accurately than that.

In the future, gender will need to be given more consideration than might have been the case historically. As an example, for many years, Australia has been issuing passports with three genders (M, F, X), and a number of other countries are following suit to offer more options of gender selection/choice.

4.10.1.2 Duplication

This represents one of the most common causes of poor data quality (especially within customer or citizen datasets), and indicates that you may still have quite a distance to travel to cross the *Data Delta*. Doubling up – or more – on information wastes storage space, with a moderate impact on cost, but other consequences are potentially far more damaging.

Having multiple records to represent the same information means that the data within those records can quickly become unsynchronised. If a customer changes their address (and you are in the fortuitous position to discover this), you are most likely to update just *one* of the records.

We've all been there: writing to companies or government offices to say, 'This is the third time I've informed you that I've changed my address.' Duplicate records inevitably lead to declining data quality, poor customer service and – as we discussed in the MDM section – is a huge contributory factor in those pervasive challenges: 'I don't know what products my customers have', or 'I don't know which services my citizens use'.

4.10.1.3 Completeness

It is highly likely that your data records are missing some key values, particularly if your organisation has a history that has involved mergers or acquisitions. Completeness is a measure of the degree to which a data attribute is present. It is common to define completeness in terms of how complete a full dataset is. For example, your organisation may have postcode information for 72% of your customers.

It is also valid to determine whether given data items require 100% completeness. For some older records, for example, it's possible that a data attribute was never previously recorded, or else a value has been lost over time and cannot easily be retrieved. In such cases, it can be acceptable to have a completeness target of less than 100%.

Questions relating to completeness might include:

- Do I have all the records I require?

- Do I have values for all the relevant attributes of my records?

- Do I have an audit trail of past data values for this record?

You need to assess the cost to your organisation resulting from the lack of completeness and, if appropriate, devise a cost-justified plan to redress the shortfall.

4.10.1.4 Consistency

Problems here stem from having information about the same data entity in multiple records, possibly spread across multiple datasets or systems. Inconsistencies dramatically reduce the value of your data. Is this person male or female? Do they have this product or that product?

Consistency checking should ensure that key attributes about an entity are consistent across *all* related records. An example is ensuring that a customer has the same email address in the CRM, the ERP system and all other operational systems.

The outcomes of such checks should identify any gaps in consistency between related records, and allow you to determine actions to improve consistency. Master Data Management provides capabilities to address consistency gaps.

4.10.1.5 Relevance

Data changes all the time. People get married and change their name. People move. They change their mobile number. And everyone increases their age, every year (and on that latter point, an obvious objective is to maintain a Date of Birth value as accurately as possible).

Systems will often hold data that is no longer relevant. Does it matter which warehouse shipped the first order to a customer 15 years ago? If we consider that there's a maintenance cost associated with every attribute of data you store, then the cost of *accumulating* data increases repeatedly.

There is an additional consideration when your data relates to personally identifiable data. In these cases, most territories have data protection regulations that require data processors to declare the purpose for collecting data, and then destroy the data after this purpose expires.

You should establish processes to ensure that *all* data is periodically reviewed for relevance.

4.10.1.6 Trust

Though not an objective measurement, it is important to consider the question, 'Does anyone actually believe this data is correct?' In our experience, end users are often surprisingly sophisticated in the way they interpret information supplied in report format based on data from within systems. We often hear phrases such as, 'I think the actual number is wrong, but it gives me a good general direction'.

So while trust isn't a 'black and white' binary issue, there is always a danger that reports – especially new reports with great modern BI graphics – will be taken at face value, simply because they are so aesthetically pleasing. It's the ultimate triumph of style over substance.

One of the more difficult and delicate conversations relates to trust of data within Finance systems – this is a 'red rag' topic to Finance staff if your questions aren't phrased very carefully, for very good reasons. Finance staff will argue passionately that their data is different: it is correct. On one level, they have a point – after all, for any organisation the finance system is the legal system of record.

However, in this context, it's perfectly fair to ask how many correcting journals were posted last month. How about at the last year-end? The data might be *correctable* – so that it can pass an audit – but that does not mean that, at *any* point in time, it is actually *correct*, except at the signed-off, year-end position. It might very well correctly reflect the paperwork processed, but that isn't quite the same matter.

There are also other issues with finance data. Like any system, it is only as good as the inputs it receives; if there are a stack of invoices sitting on someone's desk, they might very well not have gone anywhere near the Finance system. That's absolutely not the fault of anyone in Finance, but it means in the broader sense there are potential issues with their data.

In addition, Finance systems are, by definition, limited in the data that they hold; for example, you won't find anything there about orders or call history.

And finally, it is always one of the most isolated and guarded datasets within any organisation. The Finance department will have their definition of a customer for example, and they are going to stick with it, whatever the Sales team might argue. The Finance department has onerous legal compliance issues to face on behalf of the organisation as a whole, and this needs to rightly dominate their thinking.

From a data quality perspective, therefore, there *are* trust issues, even with Finance data. It may be accurate now, it may be complete now, but just *how* complete? These are fair questions to ask of even the best-run Finance department and do not in any way suggest that that there is anything *wrong* with the data in their Finance system.

Only a comprehensive initiative to cross the *Data Delta* can truly generate real trust in your entire organisation's data.

4.10.2 What does maturity look like?

Level 1 – Initial: There is no evidence of data quality practices external to specific systems.

Level 2 – Repeatable: Within specific functions or departments, there is evidence of documented data quality practices, though there is no guarantee that these are sufficiently comprehensive, or that there is any consistency of implementation across departments.

Level 3 – Defined: Organisation-wide policies and standards are defined to provide strategic direction for data quality practice across all function. Departments define their local practices based upon these standards.

Level 4 – Quantitatively Managed: Data quality practices are measured and controlled in accordance with organisation-wide standards, with all functions reporting compliance or exception back to the Data Governance Steering Group.

Level 5 – Optimising: Data quality practices form a core part of organisational strategy, and are considered as a material factor for every tactical project. Proactive steps are taken to improve data quality to optimise its value to all stakeholders.

4.10.3 Value

Problems occur when data does not adequately meet the standards that make it fit for purpose. Some of these problems include:

- Inefficiencies – as business processes become overly complex to compensate for poor data quality

- Lack of trust – as a result of difficulties in producing accurate reports and statistics

- Reduced opportunities to exploit information – as data sharing, in either direction, is impeded

- Increased costs – due to delays in introducing or upgrading systems

- Customer dissatisfaction – resulting from a perception of poor (costly, slow, burdensome and/or defective) service

- Failure to comply – because, by definition, compliance depends on demonstrating the capability to track processes accurately

The value of improving data quality stems from avoiding these types of problems so that the business operates efficiently. Stakeholders can place their faith in the information made available to them. The organisation benefits by being in a position to exploit information, costs are reduced, customers are happy, and your organisation is given a clean bill of health by regulators.

4.10.4 Impact

From an organisational perspective, your Data Governance Steering Group needs to be geared up to take ownership of data quality problems being raised by any data-related activities – including, but not limited to initiatives focused on improving data quality.

This means that instead of data problems being handled as risks and issues within specific self-contained development projects – this is the default position in most organisations – such problems come under the oversight of the Data Governance function.

One effect of this will be gathering together a central pool of knowledge about the types of data-related problems that face your organisation. As your Data Governance function is a group comprising senior representatives within the organisation, they are best able to use this awareness, and thus promote the benefits of addressing data quality across the management team.

This group should, in turn, establish a Data Stewardship function by co-opting key subject matter experts from across the business to take decisions about reported data issues.

An example of this data steward activity might be the discovery of a new reference data value being added to an individual business system by an administrator. In this case, following referral by the data stewards, your Data Governance function might decide that the new reference data value should be added to the overall reference dataset.

This organisational structure is well placed to establish a programme of data quality improvements. This will involve some planning based on analysis and design: to establish what needs fixing, and – most likely –several phases of execution to actually fix the problems.

We recommend that the execution is approached iteratively. In summary, these are the steps:

Planning

- Data cataloguing – to help identifying the primary datasets
- Aligning business processes – to determine what information they require
- Initial profiling of actual data values
- Assessing data findings against the needs of the business need
- Creating targets for remediation

Remediation (iterative)

- Identifying the root causes of data problems
- Improving business processes
- Applying cleanse rules

In terms of ongoing improvement, it is critical to set up an easy route to allow anyone within your organisation to report data issues, and then promote this facility. The quickest way to do this is likely to revolve around expanding the remit of your existing Helpdesk function by allowing people to report on data issues in the same way they currently do for system or hardware problems. The difference is that data issues should be routed to the appropriate Data Stewards, rather than your IT function.

We would recommend making it incumbent on *all staff members*, from your senior management downwards, to have a *duty to report data errors or concerns*, in much the same way that security concerns should be reported.

While this is initially likely to generate a reasonably long list of issues, these should be prioritised and fed into the *next data quality iteration*.

A word of caution on remediation, reflected upon earlier in our MDM example. You may well recall this real-world example:

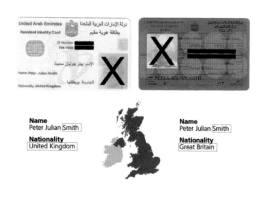

Remember, the reference data on the card on the right is wrong: Great Britain is a geographic area, not a political country. Worse, it doesn't include Northern Ireland, which is part of the United Kingdom.

As we discussed in *Section 4.4 – Master Data Management* above, there are over 250,000 UK citizens with driving licences in the UAE, and as far as we know, every one of them contains this reference data error.

Fixing the error at a data level might appear straightforward: replace all 'GB' country codes with 'UK'. However, the whole purpose of the card is to represent the data of the issuing authority, so it cannot be correct to change the underlying data but leave the cards in error. However, the costs and logistics of issuing 250,000 new cards seems prohibitive.

In this case, the only sensible option seems to be to 'live with' the data quality situation until the card needs to be re-issued – at which point it can be fixed.

Remediation is a complex topic on its own if there is an important physical record as well as an electronic one. The challenge is prevalent across much of government and the financial services sector, for example.

Let's now see how *GoDelta* set about undertaking some data remediation within their organisation.

From a planning perspective, *GoDelta* began by carrying out a data cataloguing exercise[138] identifying their existing systems, the key datasets within each system, the operational purpose for the system, and the strategic purpose for each system.

Analysis of this information allowed *GoDelta* to determine the scope of data to be assessed. They recognised that checking all data in all systems would be an impossible task within their allotted time allowance, so they focused on the data that seemed most important: the data supporting the ability to identify and contact their customers.

Next, they set about identifying the primary data source for attributes related to customers. Although some data originated from the Web Store, they determined that the CRM system was the key source of *all* customer data. Accordingly, this was targeted as the primary system for data quality assessment and cleansing.

The fields within the CRM system were then mapped to business processes, with an attempt to identify why each data field was captured, the value to the company, and what might be the cost of keeping that data maintained to an acceptable level of quality. This was used to define a prioritised set of fields for initial profiling. Profiling provides information about the actual values captured within data fields.

GoDelta then moved to profile the data values in the scope of fields they had decided were most important.

Two of the resulting observations related to customer phone numbers. They discovered that 35% of all the phone numbers *GoDelta* held about customers had at *least one duplicate*. They also found that several uses of the prefixes such as 'M', 'S' and 'F' (to indicate 'Mobile', 'SMS' or 'Fax' numbers respectively), and also instances of the suffix 'Wrong number'.

Although such occurrences were not a valid use of the telephone field, there was nothing preventing users from entering these values. However, this was causing problems with

---

the data warehouse, because the routine to transfer data from the CRM system to the data warehouse ignored telephone numbers containing incorrect values such as these.

For *GoDelta*, landline and SMS numbers are still primary mechanisms for communicating with their customers, particularly from an ongoing support perspective.

Aside from this issue, *GoDelta*'s data profiling revealed several other problems, and they set about creating targets for a number of those which they deemed to be more important.

Keeping in mind the need to fix their data iteratively, the company determined that the ability to contact customers quickly and easily was a key requirement for meeting its overall strategic and operational targets, so they decided to make this the focus of their first iteration. In line with this, they allocated a four-week 'time-box' to address the data issues relating to customer telephone and SMS details.

At this point, *GoDelta* moved into the 'Remediation' stream of their programme to improve data quality.

Their first step was to identify the root causes of the data problems.

Service Desk staff revealed that they resorted to tagging numbers with a 'wrong number' string as a work-around, because the CRM system didn't provide any facility for them to identify 'bad' phone numbers.

There was also some evidence that phone numbers were sometimes entered into the system incorrectly.

Often customers had no landline number, but sometimes gave a mobile number instead, or perhaps more than one SMS number. This led the Customer Service reps to add the 'M' and 'S' prefixes within the Landline Number field. As a result, either the 'M' or 'S' prefix could signify a mobile phone. Similarly, there was nowhere to record Fax numbers, hence the use of the 'F' prefix.

Having identified the primary causes, the team then turned their thoughts towards improving business processes to stem the tide of errors.

In order to ensure customers were reachable by phone, it was decided that the *first* thing the Customer Service agent would do before creating the application would be to call the customer back. This would confirm that the customer had given a valid phone number, and that the Service Desk had recorded it correctly.

A plan was formulated to make a change to the CRM system to allow it to capture multiple contact details of different 'contact types', and establish that the numbers adhered to a common format.

This left the thorny task of addressing the data known to be problematic. To this end, a number of database scripts were written to perform the following cleansing inside the CRM system:

- Archive all numbers with a 'wrong number' suffix

- Remove all Fax numbers marked with the 'F' prefix (these were deemed to be superfluous)

- Standardise all numbers to a unified format

- Create records with the appropriate 'contact type' to distinguish between landline, mobile, work and 'other' numbers

In addition, an external agency was engaged to validate existing numbers, which they undertook by checking the numbers against an external commercial service to determine that they were at least still valid and current.

Separately, *GoDelta* initiated a campaign to contact customers by email to inform them of the phone numbers held by the company, asking them to get in touch with any changes.

As a final step, *GoDelta* implemented a monthly automated report to show the percentage of numbers that met the various quality standards (such as '% Contact numbers confirmed as being correct in the past three months', '% Contact numbers with a non-standard format', etc). This report was presented to the Data Governance Steering Group.

At this point, the programme moved on to consider its next data issue, as the second iteration of data remediation.

Turning back to the impact on your own organisation, your Data Governance function needs to establish a programme to plan, analyse and design measures to improve the quality of your data. These measures should be implemented iteratively. As part of this activity, you will define your organisation's data quality requirements from the perspective of how data supports the day-to-day operation (a Data Quality Plan), and thus the overall strategic goals.

Ensure that this group is empowered with oversight of any data-related development projects, making sure that these comply with your organisation's data quality requirements.

Data Governance should also set up a monitoring and reporting capability that tracks data quality metrics on an ongoing basis (this is likely to entail implementing a data profiling toolset). Ensure appropriate controls exist within systems to generate alerts when data quality metrics fall below agreed thresholds.

Individual project teams should be required to ensure that data quality non-functional requirements are gathered as part of the design for any data-related development of change projects.

4.10.5 Next Steps

It can be helpful to consider the scale of the problem using some real numbers.

How many customer or citizen records do you have in your organisation? We will deal in round numbers to make things easier.

Suppose you have 250,000 customers with records about each of them in four systems. Some organisations will have many more than that, some fewer. So in this example that's one million records where you might need to be concerned about data quality. How long would it take to fix them?

Let's start off by assuming you can read, check and fix a record in one second (we'll circle round and make a better speculation on that in a moment). How much effort is involved to fix the records?

There are 3,600 seconds in an hour, and we'll assume we're working an eight-hour day. Dividing eight times 3,600 seconds into one million, gives us a fraction under 35 days. That's 35 days' effort if you could fix each of your records in one second.

What would represent a more sensible estimate? What about an average of two minutes per record?

This time, we have 120 lots of 35 days. Assuming, say, there are 220 working days per year – to allow for weekends, bank holidays, annual leave and sickness – you could complete the task in a fraction under nineteen years of manual effort. This brings us quickly to the point. We are *long* past the point of being able to fix enterprise volumes of data by hand.

Once you are dealing with hundreds of thousands of records – and that hardly makes you a large organisation – there is simply no practical way you can address data quality issues effectively by generic manual processes. It's obvious that exercises of this scale will themselves have significant error rates, and that data will change throughout the exercise: by the time you finish, it will be time to start again. We won't say, 'Just like the Forth Bridge'[139], because that's technically inaccurate, and you know how much we hate that.

The impact of activities related to improving data quality are likely to be the most challenging aspect of your journey to cross the *Data Delta*, especially when we consider that some of the solutions lie in capabilities delivered by several other Data Management domains – not least Data Governance, Master Data Management, RDM, Data Cataloguing, among others. Each of these represent significant aspects of the overall picture in their own right!

It is important to *not* be intimidated by 'a problem too large', but instead to make a start, and to approach the issue iteratively. This needs to be at the top of your list of priorities. To paraphrase an ancient saying about meditation: 'Spend at least one hour every day improving your data, and if you don't have time, spend two'.

---

[139] The main bridge over the Firth of Forth in Scotland, the Forth Bridge, was built in 1890 and for its first 120 years was subject to a continuous repair programme as it was constantly re-painted because of damage caused by adverse weather conditions, However, technology improved over the years, and on the 12th December 2011 the job was completed, at least for the next 20 years. That job came to an end. Fixing your data by hand almost certainly wouldn't. Probably ever.

4.11 Description – Data Architecture

Data architecture describes everything related to the data which supports all the 'things' that are important to your organisation (such as customers or citizens, products, suppliers, sales channels, regulatory context and market sector), your operational activities, your data systems, and your data-related technologies and tools.

If you approach your data architecture from a technical IT-centric perspective, you will struggle to engage executives, and also to make business users accept accountability for Data Governance and Data Quality. This means you will fail to realise the full potential available from effective Data Management within your organisation. Instead, you need to develop your data architecture from the perspective of your organisation's strategic objectives. This leads towards a business and operational view, which changes the dynamics completely.

Data architecture should not be a reactive activity; it should be used to map out your current data capabilities, and the shape of these capabilities in the future. In this way, data architecture becomes a key component of your organisational transformation, one that puts effective Data Management at the heart of your DNA.

This domain is closely allied to that of Data Integration and Interoperability, among many others. It provides the means for describing concepts and producing designs that are implemented in that domain. In short, data architecture lays down the blueprints for enabling information to flow freely around your organisation.

Given its central importance, you should articulate an approach – defined within your policy and standards – to allow common architecture patterns, techniques, tools and skills to be pervasive across the organisation. Your key business users and subject matter experts should become familiar with seeing and working with those data architecture artefacts of a less technical nature, and be comfortable discussing aspects of the business with reference to them.

4.11.1 Features to consider

The Data Governance function should act to help data architecture become an integral aspect of daily business life. A consistent approach to data architecture should be applied across the entire organisation. This will require the selection and adoption of an Enterprise Architecture framework, supported by both business and technical representatives throughout your organisation, who are trained to an appropriate level of skill.

Your Data Governance group also has needs to establish data architecture policy and standards, and then monitor compliance against them. This implies an ability to monitor use of the data architecture framework, and to react and improve standards, processes and toolsets as required.

The chosen data architecture approach must align with toolsets and processes related to the Data Modelling domain. Ideally, the latter should emerge from the decisions relating to your overall Architectural approach.

There are a number of well-developed architectural frameworks, such as The Open Group Application Framework (TOGAF), Zachman, the US Federal Enterprise Architecture Framework (FEAF), and Informatica's BOST. These are all Enterprise Architecture frameworks, of which data architecture is an integral part.

In choosing a framework, we are keen to emphasise that both our practical experience – and our extensive research of international best practice – indicates that the actual choice of a framework has very little bearing on the success or otherwise of architecture activities. However, the lack of a chosen framework tends to reflect negatively, while having any framework has a positive impact. The message is: 'Choose a framework, and implement it effectively'.

TOGAF has a high level of adoption within both public and private sectors, and relevant qualifications and knowledge of this framework are relatively widespread and plentiful.

We should also note that data architecture is only part of the picture. All organisations can benefit from having a broader Enterprise Architecture function, with data architecture forming part of this. It is not essential for the full Enterprise Architecture capability to be in place in the first instance. Aspects of your Data Management activities can be expanded later to form a basis for the wider scope of your Enterprise Architecture function.

It is easy to become confused about Data Architecture and Data Modelling, and this is not surprising as they are tightly bound up with each other. It might help to think of data architecture as representing the *link* with the business context – its drivers and requirements.

This context determines the data capabilities required to support its overall goals but also, the way that these data capabilities are modelled and documented (including which artefacts are to be produced). Data Modelling by contrast represents the activities required to physically produce these model and design artefacts.

These are the type of artefacts your data architecture might mandate. This is a relatively long list of documents, and your chosen architectural framework is likely to have some version of most of these (though it may attribute different names to them):

Enterprise Data Model (EDM) – Illustrating the high level relationships and concepts across your organisation's data landscape. This is a useful document for discussing the overall context of data with your business people.

Logical Data Model (LDM) – Presents data tables, fields and relationships in 'business speak', and without concern for technical system-related details. This is a useful document for discussing the actual data used within or flowing between applications and services with business people, who should be actively involved – or at the very least, consulted extensively – when producing these models.

Physical Data Model (PDM) – Presents the technical implementation-level details of the data – used within and flowing between – applications and services. This is used by technical specialists within your IT function, who will design and implement new or enhanced technical capabilities in the form of information systems and services.

Component Model – Presents the technology components that comprise your organisation's data platform and the way they relate to one another. Component Models can be 'logical' – describing the landscape in conceptual terms, or 'physical' – describing the technical details of that landscape.

Examples of components include your Enterprise Service Bus (ESB), databases, Enterprise Data Warehouse (EDW), data marts, Master Data Management (MDM) and Reference Data Management (RDM) technologies, Document Content Management, security and access control systems, and Extract-Transform-Load (ETL) tooling for moving larger batches of data between components. This is not an exhaustive list, and your organisation may have many more components.

Some people talk about this technical artefact as '*the* architecture diagram', as though to suggest this is the only concern of data architecture. Hopefully, we will have said enough within this book to paint the wider picture of the Data Architecture domain.

Data Entity/Business Service matrix – Presents *what* data is used by *which* business services. This is particularly useful for communicating how information supports the day-to-day operation of your organisation, which is useful for understanding the impact of proposed changes or diagnosing problems that occur.

Data Lifecycle Model – Presents the lifecycle (capture, storage, processing, usage, archival, disposal) of individual data entities across your various systems and services. Some data entities will be more stable or long-lived than others.

Data Security Compliance Design – Presents key security touch points and describes how the risks are mitigated.

Data Quality Compliance Design – Presents key Data Quality initiatives, such as validation and cleanse processes, and describes how the established data quality targets are implemented.

Data Model Change Process – Presents the process related to changing data entity models. This is an important concept to embed within all of your organisation's process and systems development activities. When anything changes, or is planned to be changed, that could affect the data *in any way*, and this must be considered within the context of your data policies and standards. This is a key Data Governance concern.

The Business Glossary and Data Dictionary should be regarded as required reading when developing any architectural artefacts to ensure consistency of terminology. It will often be the case that architectural development will also require changes to be made to these resources.

With such a significant number of artefacts to produce and manage, you can see why you really do need to adopt a framework that provides a readymade format for those artefacts.

It is also important to keep track of the status of your architectural artefacts in terms of their level of development.

Here is an example of how you might tag their developmental status:

- ***Emergent*** – Architectural assets that are as yet to be proven in a live environment. These components are likely to require proof-of-concept development in order to assess suitability.

- ***Current*** – Architectural assets that are in development or are being implemented.

- ***Strategic*** – Architectural assets that are expected to be available in the medium term, such as Big Data solutions, Mobile Apps, or other components that are anticipated to provide strategic advantage to your operation. Some 'Strategic' components might also be classified as 'Emergent'.

- **Retirement** – Architectural assets that no longer help you meet your strategic goals, and that are due to be decommissioned, replaced or archived.

In summary, look towards establishing a widespread data architecture approach that encourages people to share their experience, and so determine and promote best practice. Data architecture should follow a single standard methodology that's part of a well-respected Enterprise Architecture framework.

Architectural artefacts should be developed as a collaboration between business and technical experts, and relate clearly to real-world business scenarios. Ensure that data architecture activities can be subsumed into a wider Enterprise Architecture practice at an appropriate time in the future, *if not at the outset.*

4.11.2 What does maturity look like?

Level 1 – Initial: Data Architecture practices are ad hoc. Across the business, little regard is given to re-usability and standardisation. Though some definitions may be agreed, these tend to be used by people from the EA team for specific projects.

Level 2 – Repeatable: Within specific business functions or individual departments, there is evidence of documented data architecture practices, although there is no guarantee that these are sufficiently comprehensive, or that there is any consistency of implementation across functions.

Level 3 – Defined: Organisation-wide policies and standards are defined to provide strategic direction for data architecture practice across all functions. There is a defined data architecture framework (possibly part of a wider Enterprise Architecture framework). Business functions define their local practices based upon these standards and framework.

Level 4 – Quantitatively Managed: Data Architecture practices are measured and controlled in accordance with organisation-wide standards, with all functions reporting compliance – or exception – back to the Data Governance Steering Group. Data architecture is a mandated core, deliverable of all system projects, with artefacts being re-used and managed across business functions.

Level 5 – Optimising: Enterprise Architecture is an organisation-wide distributed function. All projects are reviewed and coordinated from an architectural perspective as a matter of course, both within and across business functions. There is continuous improvement to the Enterprise Architecture Development Process. All reference architecture models are established and used for all new systems, and for key legacy systems.

4.11.3 Value

As we have seen, data architecture (like architecture in the construction industry) represents the blueprint for building and sustaining assets. In this case, those assets reside within the realm of data. Data architecture is therefore a dependency for developing valuable capabilities that rely on data.

In the final analysis, can you think of any assets within your organisation to which this does *not* apply? You even rely on information to make decisions about hiring your people: your human resource assets.

With this in mind, it's essential to ensure that your data architecture activities run like a well-oiled machine. All organisations *have* a data architecture, but for many, this is an intangible nebulous design that exists only in the sense that they have physical data repositories, systems, processes, services and interfaces, and that data flows in, around and out of their organisation via these components.

For these organisations, little – or none – of this landscape is documented, which means that no one can state, with any certainty, how data supports their organisation. This also means that changes to the data landscape are riskier than they should be.

If today's pace of change – and the current climate of 'disruptive technologies' – tells us anything, it has to be: 'Prepare for change'. The organisation that is unable to innovate, to respond to changing market conditions, to be 'disruptive', will have a most difficult and uncertain future.

Data architecture is fundamentally about readying your data capabilities – and, by extension, the whole of your operation – for change.

An important aspect of this is to enable the domain experts within your organisation to collaborate on architectural tasks (and, yes, that does include business people). Given appropriate time and resources, this will lead to best practice architectures being identified through natural project cycles rather than a large initial design-time effort.

The goal is to have a stock of these readymade architectural designs standing by to bolt together, and solve business challenges in the future.

One way to remove the barriers to collaborative working is to establish a single and standard architectural framework across your organisation, allowing a common vocabulary, as well as patterns to make it easier to achieve cross-functional integration of data.

The value comes from increased cooperation between the various areas of your organisation: building relationships, identifying areas to reduce duplication and cost and, in turn, gaining ever more engagement and buy-in to the notion of improving Data Management. Data architecture will become an essential element in developing a 'virtuous cycle' of continuous improvement.

4.11.4 Impact

Your Data Governance function will need to direct some activity around selecting the framework to support your data architecture needs across the organisation. They will also need to ensure that representative subject matter experts, both from business and technical areas, are appropriately trained in getting the best value out of this *for* the business.

The group should facilitate collaboration between departments within the organisation, ensure the appropriate architectural artefacts are produced as part of project deliverables, and that these artefacts meet the defined standards (reacting to any compliance failures as required).

Part of this role should also include highlighting and propagating best practice architectures and related approaches to promote re-use.

Project teams should be alert to the existence of available architectures (eg from other projects), and actively collaborate with other relevant parties when developing new or enhanced architectural solutions.

This will require submitting architectural deliverables at appropriate checkpoints for approval by the Data Governance Steering Group (or, optionally, the Enterprise Architecture function, if one exists). Your standards might require project teams to report *any* exceptions to standards or deviations from established best practice solutions, and to justify these to the Data Governance function.

The costs of introducing or enhancing a data architecture capability are largely related to providing training for existing staff in the chosen architecture frameworks (or recruiting people who already have these skills). There are technologies that support this, but these are already covered in other Data Management domains (such as Metadata Management, Data Modelling and Data Catalogue).

The timescales for improving data architecture capabilities will be driven by your particular business needs and your active projects. We would strongly advise you to instigate a strategic review of your current Data Management maturity. This will provide a firm basis from which to consider how well-placed your organisation stands in terms of understanding its use and management of data, and the way this needs to change to support the business into the future.

If Data Maturity is low, you should think about enhancing your data architecture capabilities sooner rather than later, and to capture *as much information as possible* about the way data is used now; otherwise, how else can you know where the gaps are, and what changes need to be made?

If data-related implementation programmes are underway, or imminently so, you may be able to include a stream of work within them to develop your data architecture function. We are always keen to recommend including activities to improve Data Management within existing initiatives. This is a most effective way of making sure that improvements happen.

Ultimately, the goal is to leverage your data architecture to *reduce* the amount of time it takes to develop new capabilities. Projects using the data architecture framework and governance structure will gain through the ability to share resources, architectures and so on, but the longer-term benefit will be realised for the second and future iterations, coupled with the availability of tried-and-tested architectural patterns from across the organisation.

4.11.5 Next Steps

The first activity you need to consider in relation to data architecture is which methodology to follow. It is not so important which framework you choose, but you absolutely *must select one*. There are several good choices[140] – pick one and *work* with it.

Any data architecture methodology is going to take you through a similar journey. You'll need to baseline your current data architectures, describing your current data landscape. We would underline the need to relate this to a conceptual model of your business – the

---

[140] TOGAF, FEAF, GEAF, Zachman, Informatica BOST, and many others. At Entity, we happen to have made our investment in TOGAF and Informatica BOST.

market(s) you are in, your suppliers, customers or citizens, products and services, and any other keys aspects (such as regulatory requirements).

Once you've got where you are now – your 'current state architecture' – appropriately described using the conventions of your chosen architecture, you can move forward to define your target architecture, representing the desired data capabilities across your organisation at some point in the future.

Once you know the endgame, the trick is to work out a roadmap for all the stages in between; the so-called 'transitional architectures'. It turns out that this is not necessarily as straightforward as it might seem, and our experience is that there is no substitute for leaning on people who have experience in this area.

The architectural frameworks are of even less help in this regard, and finding a plan that works for your organisation will mean calling on people who understand the consequences and benefits of deciding to go one way over another.

It's essential to see data architecture as a business-led concern at the strategic and operational levels. IT then, in turn, supports and enables the aims of the business from the Systems and Technology levels.

To put data squarely at the centre of the picture, you need to start with a business-centric view. Build an architecture for IT *alone*, and the business won't care. You need the business to care, so build out from that perspective, and the systems/technical pieces will flow from this more naturally.

4.12 Description – Data Modelling and Design

As an organisation, you will need to find a way to represent *all* the key data entities that concern your operation on a day-to-day basis, and define them and their relationship to each other. For example, what is the relationship between Salesperson and Sales Territory, between Product and Product Group, between Person (eg Customer or Employee) and Address?

Before you can understand such relationships, you need to have a clear definition of the key terms themselves: terms such as Customer/Citizen, Supplier, Account, Revenue, Contract, Project, Programme, etc. This means agreeing these definitions within your organisation, and then writing that agreement down in a useful form.

Do not underestimate the size and scope of this task. We've already mentioned the multinational enterprise that had *eighteen* differing definitions of the term 'Account'. Standardisation was out of the question for them. The term had been devalued too much, and their only alternative was to drop it from their corporate vocabulary.

The topic of modelling can get quite technical very quickly, but we are especially keen to emphasise the importance of involving business users in defining data models. This leads to two levels of modelling – one that represents information in the language that non-technical people will understand and find useful, and the other that is used by technical staff.

In the following discussion, we separate out these two levels – so by all means, skip the techie bits if they are not your cup of tea! If you do represent the technical side, we *strongly* advise you to read all the way through. This section is just a starter on this topic, and everything here should be considered prerequisite knowledge before you get going and actually do some modelling.

4.12.1 Features to consider

Ideally, your organisation will establish a central repository and a set of recommendations for storing, publishing, and indexing data models and architectures for re-use within and across departmental boundaries.

Also, if you don't have such a thing already, you should evaluate the various leading data modelling, and design standards and approaches, and then choose one to be used for all of your data modelling activities. You should then home in on a standard modelling toolset that supports your chosen design approach.

The following list of features might be helpful in starting a discussion about your organisation's own requirements for data modelling tools. Consider whether the following would be useful in your context:

1) A central, cross-organisational repository for storage, searching and publishing of:

    a. model and architecture metadata

    b. architecture models

    c. data models

2) The ability for any authorised person to search for modelling artefacts (using appropriate metadata)

3) Storing modelling artefacts in a common format that is used by the whole organisation

4) Standardised model development tools and notations

5) Facilities to assist in migrating existing models into the new repository

6) The ability to embrace a range of modelling areas of the wider enterprise architecture, such as business process modelling, application modelling, etc

7) Recording and reporting of usage metrics

8) Reverse engineering from common database platforms

9) Representation of Conceptual, Logical, Physical models (ideally allowing relationships to be maintained between these levels)

10) Support for Data Warehouse (OLAP) modelling

11) Generic diagramming for high-level architectures

12) Versioning, change tracking and descriptive metadata

13) Comprehensive role-based access control.

Many organisations fail to provide sufficient training for those staff that will undertake the modelling. Remember: this is likely to involve business people to some extent, as well as technical staff. Though essential, this is a little unfortunate in practice, because the modelling tools themselves can be both relatively expensive and complex.

Data modelling is a hugely worthwhile endeavour – one that has lasting value – and you will want to ensure you have tools, staff, skills and approaches that can help you realise the value from this resource.

Your central modelling repository will contain all solution artefacts from new and work-in-progress designs, as well as approved and implemented designs. The repository will allow authorised users to search and re-use models that are in any state of completion or approval. It should contain design artefacts for all current systems, and these will vary in depth and detail depending on the data and knowledge available, the importance of the system, and the status of the system.

For example, it would not be appropriate to set about describing in detail a system that has been identified and planned to be *retired*, whereas a legacy system that is active with core business processes, or interacts with many other systems, should be described in more detail.

In terms of the actual modelling, there are several things you need to do.

We recommend that you:

- Standardise on modelling tools and techniques throughout your organisation
- Define the metadata to be collected as part of data modelling
- Develop a policy that enshrines a drive for the active production of data models
- Set about collecting information about your data (in line with the metadata requirements determined in a previous step)
- Develop a Business Glossary
- Develop a Data Dictionary
- Develop any other models required to clarify understanding (using standard notations such as UML[141] or Barker-Ellis[142]) – ensure these are appropriate to the intended audience

[141] Unified Modelling Language – see http://www.uml.org
[142] See http://www.entitylogic.org/home.html

As you can see, there are a number of artefacts that you'll need to produce as part of your modelling activity. You might have some of these already in one format or another. If so, that's excellent news as it will save you time. In any case, have a read through the rest of this section, as it provides practical advice about collecting information about your data.

4.12.2 What does maturity look like?

Before we look at the benefits and activities related to modelling, let's consider how to get a handle on assessing the maturity of data modelling practices.

Level 1 – Initial: There is no standardisation within or between departments for data modelling practices.

Level 2 – Repeatable: Data Modelling and Design practices within specific functions, their departments or individual projects are successfully implemented, documented and repeated. Though they have standardised on tooling and methodologies, there is no evidence that these are coordinated at a higher level, leading to inconsistent approaches or duplication of effort across the organisation.

Level 3 – Defined: Organisation-wide policies and standards are defined to provide strategic direction for Data Modelling and Design practices across all functions. Departments define their local practices based upon these standards. Tooling and methodologies are mandated for departments to enabling sharing of models across the organisation.

Level 4 – Quantitatively Managed: Data Modelling and Design practices are measured and controlled in accordance with organisation-wide standards, with all functions reporting compliance – or exception – back to the Data Governance Steering Group. There is a well-populated artefact repository, and modelling artefacts are consistently re-used across functions.

Level 5 – Optimising: Re-use of modelling artefacts in the repository go through feedback loop cycles with robust controls over versioning. Project implementations are referenced to re-usable designs.

4.12.3 Value

Walk into almost any commercial organisation and ask the Sales and the Finance teams for a definition of 'revenue', and you are almost bound to get at least two – and probably more – different answers. In such cases, modelling is a useful 'blameless' vehicle to use for getting to the bottom of what single definition you as an organisation want to use. (To be clear, the Finance definition of the word 'revenue' will undoubtedly be correct, but it needs to be clarified from other related words such as 'sales' and 'income'.)

Although modelling does take time and effort to do properly, one of the more immediate returns comes from avoiding those repeated discussions and re-workings to clarify and compensate for misunderstandings. If nothing else, there is value in undertaking an effective modelling campaign targeted at your key business terms.

Having a standard modelling tool that offers a centralised repository reduces management overhead during design activities and allows an organisation-wide visibility of the models and data available to be re-used or extended. Your data models can easily be re-used directly from the repository.

The data model repository can be analysed to highlight common uses of data usage across your organisation leading to a more informed view of synergies and gaps in the data modelled across the whole enterprise.

These benefits reduce complexity across the organisation, reducing total cost of ownership. They also increase the opportunities for re-use of data and collaborative working, as well as allowing different parts of the organisation and external stakeholders to share data.

4.12.4 Impact

The tooling related to Data Modelling can be costly, and is often charged on a per-seat basis. If the approach to Data Modelling is somewhat ad hoc in your organisation, be sure to factor in some budget to undertake a proper evaluation of the tools for establishing something more standard, and something that will provide you with a comprehensive modelling capability that includes a central repository[143].

The beauty of per-seat licensing is that you can buy more licences as and when you need them. Some tools also offer a 'floating licence' arrangement that simply restricts the number of people that can sign on concurrently.

Your costings will also need to allow for the migration of your existing models into the new standard modelling repository – though this could be tackled over a long-term period, and approached on an as-needed basis. You may also be able to save money that is currently being used to maintain licences and support with a number of modelling tool suppliers.

---

[143] Though not intended as a recommendation, we use SAP (previously Sybase) PowerDesigner within Entity (see http://go.sap.com/product/data-mgmt/powerdesigner-data-modeling-tools.html). This was largely because many of our larger clients were using it, and it made sense for us to do likewise. That said, we periodically review the latest offerings on the market, and we have yet to find anything that would cause us to change to a different tool.

Finally, there is the cost associated with training and support. You will need to have users that are appropriately skilled in Data Modelling and the related tools, but you should also ensure that business people are actively involved, and they may well benefit from some awareness training.

Here's a summary of the activities that need to be considered over the short, medium and longer terms.

In the short term, your Data Governance Steering Group should commission an assessment of the existing tools in use across your organisation – if any – and develop an understanding of your organisation's Data Modelling requirements.

The Data Governance function should use this to produce a policy and standards for developing data models, for approving and publishing modelling artefacts, and to promote the re-use of published artefacts. These standards should be backed up by appropriate KPIs. A key aspect of the standards will relate to the metadata to be collected for the various types of modelling artefacts. More on this later (See: 'How to collect modelling information' below).

The collated requirements from these activities should then be used to evaluate the various commercial offerings available.

In the medium term, turn your attention to selecting and establishing a data modelling toolset that offers a centralised repository for your models. You might consider piloting your modelling approach on a forthcoming development project. This would be a good time to carry out some training for technical users and for those business people that will be involved in modelling the data used by your operation.

In the longer term, look to integrate existing models into the new central repository, and transition towards the new standard toolset in the longer term – possibly guided by annual renewal contracts on existing tools. The Data Governance function should actively govern how Data Modelling is carried out; analysing and acting on the established KPIs to encourage re-use of artefacts across the organisation, foster collaboration of model production, and possibly even review and approve artefacts from project teams.

How to collect modelling information:

We hope it's clear that we attach a lot of importance to understanding your data fully, and to documenting this understanding. Accordingly, we have given quite a lot of thought to the kind of information that should be captured. A summary first, and then some examples.

- **Data Entities** – your business users (eg the assigned Data Owner) should describe the key information about data entities (eg Customer, Citizen, Supplier, Product, Asset, etc) such as the data entity's name, description, lifecycle dates, etc.

- **Data Entity Usage** – Another one for the business users, this defines how a given data entity is used within other entities. For example, the Customer profile may be referenced by profiles such as Order, Customer Survey, Payment, etc.

- **Data Attributes** – This is likely to require collaboration between business users and more technically inclined data modellers, and provides a detail description of all the data attributes (or 'fields') within a data entity. Attributes can be described at both business and technical levels.

- **Datasets** – All the previous types of information describe the structure or format of the data used by your organisation. You can think of this as the blueprint for how information is held. In contrast, a dataset represents an actual collection of data (irrespective of the medium used – eg a spreadsheet, an XML file, a report, a database table, etc). The idea is to record all of the instances of the data entities – such as a database table holding customer information, a spreadsheet of monthly orders, or a report about income vs expenditure. The information about datasets is likely to be captured by technical staff supported by business people.

- **Dataset Distributions** – Distributions are listed for each dataset. This includes details regarding the physical storage media used for the datasets.

Many people become overly concerned about not having appropriate tooling to capture this information. We would urge you to begin collecting information about your data even if you do not have a Data Modelling tool in place.

We often instigate a simple spreadsheet-based approach to get things started. All you need is a workbook which contains a worksheet for *each* type of information outlined above.

These are the steps required to capture information about your data entities and datasets using a spreadsheet-based approach. The first three steps are undertaken by *business users*, and the remainder by *technical people*.

- **Step 1** – Create an Entity Description containing general details about the data entity [Responsibility: Business specialists]

- **Step 2** – Define the scope of use for the data entity in an Entity Usage definition. For example, the scope of use for a data entity representing a 'Person' might include Customer, Employee or Supplier Contact. This should include a description of the core characteristics of the data entity for each of the business areas listed [Responsibility: Business specialists]

- **Step 3** – Create an Entity Attribute definition, supplying the business property values for each data attribute of the entity. Data types should be selected from a controlled list of permitted values [Responsibility: Business specialists]

- **Step 4** – A technical specialist expands on the Entity Attribute details provided by business specialists in the previous step, and appends technical-level information [Responsibility: Technical specialists]

- **Step 5** – A technical specialist (usually in collaboration with business specialists), completes a Dataset Definition listing all of the known published datasets for the data entity described [Responsibility: Technical specialists]

- **Step 6** – A technical specialist (usually in collaboration with business specialists), completes a Dataset Distribution definition supplying details of all known distributions and media types for each dataset [Responsibility: Technical specialists]

The output from these steps can be used to populate the business glossary and data dictionary, provide master and reference entities, data models and common types, and identify code lists for populating in the Data Catalogue. All of this information can be imported into a data modelling tool/repository at a later date.

Warning: the remainder of this sub-section is relatively technical. If that's not for you, you might prefer to skip to 'Next Steps', and come back to the detail when you are ready to undertake some actual modelling.

Recall that the *Entity Description* represents key information to describe a data entity. Our fictional company, *GoDelta*, defined the metadata that should be captured within its own Entity Descriptions (shown below).

In each case, there is an *optionality* indicator representing, shown within square brackets [], which indicates whether the attribute value is optional [O] or mandatory [M]:

- *Entity Title* [M] – The name given to the data entity

- *Description* [M] – A longer form description of the data entity from a business perspective

- *Creator* [M] – The name of the person or department that created the data entity

- *Date Created* [M] – The creation date, in the format YYYYMMDD

- *Version* [M] – A version number to aid in change tracking, formatted as NN.NN

- *Status* [M] – The document status: choose from 'Draft for review', 'Approved' or 'Outdated'

- *Subject Category* [M] – A categorisation to indicate the subject of the data entity

- *Other Information* [O] – Optional information to capture additional details about the data entity

- *Inherits from Entity* [O] – The name of a data entity from which this entity inherits its attributes

- *Owner* [M] – The name of the person or department that owns the data entity

- *Classification* [O] – Classifications are a means for grouping data entities and providing context

Example 1:

The following list is an example of the data that *GoDelta* captured for its Customer data entity:

- *Entity Title:* Customer
- *Description:* A customer is a domestic or business party that has already bought at least one of our products or services
- *Creator:* Sales
- *Date Created:* 20160714
- *Version:* 1.0
- *Status:* Draft for review
- *Subject Category:* Sales Customer
- *Other Information:* None
- *Inherits from Entity:* Party
- *Owner:* Sales (see John Applebaum)
- *Classification(s):* Common, Master, Subtype Profile Usage

The *Entity Usage* information provides an indication of where the data entity is used within other entities. This is *GoDelta's* definition of the metadata to be collected for Entity Usage:

- *Used in Entity* [O] – Identifies the data entities that use this entity (eg Domestic Customer, Business Customer, etc)
- *Description* [O] – Describes how this data entity is used when it comprises part of another entity

Example 2:

The following example of Entity Usage details is again for *GoDelta*, and shows where and how its Customer data entity was used within other entity definitions:

- *Used in:* *Domestic Customer* – Represents characteristics of customers who have purchased our domestic products or services

- ***Used in:*** *Business Customer* – Represents characteristics of customers who have purchased our industrial products or services

Having established a high-level description, the data entity was further defined by describing its attributes within an Entity Attribute Definition. Business experts are responsible for describing the data attributes of a data entity from a high-level business perspective. The following list shows the metadata that *GoDelta* determined should be collected when business specialists described the attributes for a data entity:

- ***Attribute Short Name*** [M] – A shortened and unique version of the attribute name. The value contains alphanumeric characters. Spaces may not be used, though underscores may be substituted for spaces

- ***Attribute Name*** [M] – The attribute name

- ***Description*** [M] – Attribute description (max 500 characters)

- ***Single or Repeating*** [M] – Determines whether the attribute occurs one or more times. The allowable value for this field is either 'Single' or 'Repeating'. 'Single' denotes cases where only one occurrence of the attribute (per record) is allowed, and 'Repeating' is used in cases where one or more occurrences may appear within the same record

- ***Optional*** [M] – Determines whether the value for this attribute must be supplied. The value must be either 'TRUE' or 'FALSE'

- ***Default Value*** [O] – Determines a default value for this attribute if appropriate

- ***Reference Data/List*** [O] – Identifies a reference data table used to control the permitted values for this attribute if appropriate

- ***Data Constraints/Business Validation Rules*** [O] – Describes any rules or data constraints and/or business validation rules. These rules and constraints should be written from a business perspective and be comprehensible by any business user

- ***Data Type*** [M] – Identifies the data type: the value is selected from a controlled list of Data Types

Example 3:

Once again, this is an example taken from GoDelta's Customer data entity. This example describes one of a number of data attributes. In this case, the focus was the properties of the 'Gender' attribute (from a business perspective):

- *Attribute Short Name:* Gender

- *Single / Repeating:* Single

- *Optional:* False

- *Reference Data/List:* See 'Gender' code list

- *Data Constraints / Business Validation Rules:* Only values within the 'Gender' code list

- *Data Type:* Code

Technical data modelling, also within the *Entity Attribute Definition*, describes the process of building on the logical data model resulting from the business-perspective information to include technical details. Data models should fulfil the purpose of aiding understanding of the appropriate audience; a technical audience necessarily requires a level of detail that would aid implementation, support and maintenance of information systems.

When undertaking modelling, the following considerations should be borne in mind:

- Investigate whether others have already described similar data

- Produce a high-level Entity Relationship Diagram (ERD)

- Encourage re-use of defined schemas/vocabularies to promote consistency and enrichment

- Use best judgment to decide whether or not to create links for Linked Data

The technical specialist expanded on the data attribute definitions provided by the business specialists (as described the previous section). *GoDelta* determined that the metadata for data attributes look like this:

- *Format* [M] – Identifies the data format – a default value is established by the Data Type selected by the business user. The default can be overridden by the technical expert.

- **Length** [O] – Identifies the length – a default value is established by the Data Type selected by the business user. The default can be overridden by the technical expert.

- **Scale** [O] – Identifies the scale (if appropriate) – a default value is established by the Data Type selected by the business user. The default can be overridden by the technical expert.

- **Allowed Values** [O] – A code list – establishes the list of allowable data values if appropriate. Values are defined within a code list referenced by a Uniform Resource Name (URN).

- **Regular Expression Validation** [O] – A formal representation of an expression that can be applied to validate this attribute's data value.

Example 4:

The following example shows how *GoDelta*'s technical data modellers went about describing two of a number of data attributes for the Customer entity. The first example is for 'Gender', and the second for 'Customer Name':

- **Attribute Short Name:** *Gender*

- **Format:** Code – fixed length character format

- **Length:** 1

- **Scale:** (not applicable)

- **Allowed Values:** urn:com:godelta:core:codelists:Gender

- **Regular Expression Validation:** (not applicable)

- **Attribute Short Name:** *Customer Name*

- **Format:** Text – variable length character format

- **Length:** 60

- **Scale:** (not applicable)

- **Allowed Values:** (not applicable)

- **Regular Expression Validation**[144]**:** ^[\\p{L} .'-]+$

The *Dataset Definition* describes an actual collection of data that make use of a data entity (remember to think of the entity as the blueprint for how data is held within

---

[144] If you are unfamiliar with Regular Expressions, these odd-looking collections of characters can seem very geeky. Don't worry, they are even geeky-looking to geeks! They can be used by computers to validate the format of values supplied as input. In this case, this expression is used to check that the value has the correct characters to represent a person or company name. The '^' denotes the start of the expression, while the '$' denotes the end. The '+' says that everything inside the [square brackets] can occur multiple times. The '\\p{L}' is a special code for any single character in any language. Finally, the space, underscore, apostrophe and hyphen allows for these characters to be included too. We did warn that this section could get technical!

a dataset). The technical specialist would usually obtain the information to describe a dataset, in collaboration with a business specialist.

The following list describes the metadata that *GoDelta* determined should be used to describe a dataset:

- *Title* [M] – The dataset title

- *Date Created* [M] – Creation date of the dataset

- *Date Issued* [M] – Date the dataset was issued

- *Date Modified* [O] – Date the dataset was last modified

- *Version* [M] – Version number of the dataset

- *Status* [M] – Status of the dataset: choose from 'Draft for review', 'Approved', 'Outdated'

- *Description* [M] – A brief description of the dataset contents

- *Source (Publisher URL)* [M] – Where the dataset may be found for access or download

- *Publisher* [M] – The *person* or department that published the dataset

- *Update Frequency* [M] –- How often this dataset is updated

- *Licence* [M] – A statement specifying restrictions on use of the dataset content

- *Subject Category* [M] – A categorisation to indicate the subject of the dataset

- *Subject Keywords* [M] – A set of key words and phrases that can be used to facilitate searching for the dataset

- *Subject Project* [O] – The name of the programme or project that caused the dataset to be created initially

- *Creator* [M] – The person or department that created the dataset

- *Language* [M] – The language in which the dataset is published

- *Other Information* [O] – Any additional information that aids understanding of the dataset, its use within business operations, etc

Example 5:

The following example shows *GoDelta's* information for one of its Customer datasets:

- *Title:* Customers Monthly
- *Date Created:* 20160702
- *Date Issued:* 20160702
- *Date Modified:* not applicable
- *Version:* 0.1
- *Status:* Draft
- *Description:* GoDelta Customers – Monthly
- *Source (Publisher URL):* sharepoint.godelta.com/customers
- *Publisher:* GoDelta Sales
- *Update Frequency:* Monthly
- *Licence:* "Commercially sensitive – only for internal use"
- *Subject Category:* Sales Customers
- *Subject Keywords:* sales, customers
- *Subject Project:* Sales BAU
- *Creator:* GoDelta Sales
- *Language:* [ISO639-2]en
- *Other Information:* (none)

The *Dataset Distribution* describes a physical instance of a dataset, and includes the medium used to hold the data. There may be several distributions for any given dataset. A technical expert would ordinarily obtain the information to describe a dataset distribution, in collaboration with business experts.

The following list describes the metadata that *GoDelta* determined should be used to describe a dataset distribution:

- *Title* [M] – The dataset title

- *Description* [M] – A brief description of the dataset contents

- *Subject Category* [O] – A categorisation to indicate the subject of the dataset distribution

- *Format* [M] – The format of the dataset distribution, eg MS Excel, MS Word, PDF, CSV, XML etc

- *Creator* [M] – The person or department that created the dataset distribution

- *Size* [M] – The file size of the dataset distribution

- *Date Created* [M] – The creation date of the dataset distribution

- *Date Issued* [M] – The date the dataset distribution was issued

- *Source (Access URL)* [O] – A URL describing the web page where a link to the dataset distribution can be found

- *Source (Download URL)* [O] – The URL via which the dataset distribution can be downloaded to the user's computer

- *Other Information* [O] – Optional information to capture additional details about the dataset distribution

Example 6:

The following example shows a Dataset Distribution entry for one of *GoDelta's* Customer datasets:

- *Title:* Customers 2016 July

- *Description:* GoDelta Customers 2016 July

- *Subject Category*: Sales Customers

- *Format:* PDF

- *Creator:* GoDelta Sales

- *Size:* 3.2MB

- *Date Created:* 20160702

- ***Date Issued:*** 20160702

- ***Source (Access URL):*** https://sharepoint.godelta.com/customers/
ReportDetails/tabid/121/Default.aspx?ItemId=2313&P-
TID=104&MenuId=1

- ***Source (Download URL):*** https://sharepoint.godelta.com/
customers/ ReportPDF/2016%20July%20Customers.pdf

- ***Other Information:*** (none)

The above discussion is intended to provide advice on the type of information you should expect to collect about your data. All of this information will be useful in terms of building your Business Glossary, your Data Dictionary, and other assets related to documenting an understanding of your data.

We have purposely dwelt on the information related to modelling in some depth. The reason? We so often see organisations that have become paralysed by a lack of confidence about what information to capture.

It is important to get started as quickly as possible on a path that will lead to a comprehensive understanding of your organisation's key data. The forthcoming chapter on Data Catalogues will touch on modelling again, but this is more from the perspective of what data to model rather than how to model it.

Next Steps

The purpose of crossing the *Data Delta* is to add measurable value to your data, and to transform it into information that has value. This is information that enables you to derive knowledge so that to make better decisions eg which customers to target with which products, which citizens are entitled to which services etc.

To do this effectively, you need to ensure that your organisation has a standardised approach towards modelling, supported by appropriate tools and skilled people.

Modelling needs to become a part of daily life in your organisation, so you must establish measures to enforce the production of data models at various and appropriate levels of detail. As part of this, ensure that you have agreement on what metadata needs to be collected within your models. Ensure too that you have an up-to-date Business Glossary and Data Dictionary, and that people are actively encouraged to use these essential resources.

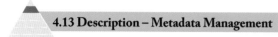

4.13 Description – Metadata Management

Metadata is often characterised as 'data about data', but if you're not technically minded, it's easy to become confused about what *exactly* this means.

Another way of thinking about this is to say: "I have some data. What do I need to know about it?" Metadata provides the answer about how to capture descriptions about data.

Though you may not have thought about it in these terms, most people use metadata throughout their working days. Every time you create or open a file, perhaps tag it with a category, or check to see when it was created, you call on metadata.

The use of metadata requires that your Data Governance function makes some decisions about what aspects of the data should be described, and when various descriptions are warranted.

Such an aspect is known as a 'data element', and is given a unique name, such as: "Dataset Name", "Creation Date", "Format", "Security Classification", etc.

The data elements tell us what aspects we want to describe. Actually *describing* a piece of data simply involves recording information for these data elements. For example:

- Dataset Name = *Population_Census_2015*
- Format = *pdf*
- Security Classification = *Confidential*

There are already many sets of recognised metadata standards. Some are generic, and contain the data elements for describing any sets of data. For example, the Dublin Core Metadata Element Set[145] includes 15 elements: Title, Creator, Subject, Description, Publisher, Contributor, Date, Type, Format, Identifier, Source, Language, Relation, Coverage, and Rights. Other standards are designed to describe specific focuses of interest or specialism, such as the METIS framework for describing statistical data[146].

Metadata can be used to describe a number of aspects for any given set of data, such as data provenance, ownership, intended use, security attributes, quality metrics, business rules, financial value, usage rights, licences, business continuity risk, and lifecycle state.

In many senses, the metadata you decide to capture will represent what makes your organisation different from every other. For example, some organisations are comprised of a group of several legal entities consolidated under a holding or central company. In this case, one use of metadata could be to describe which information belongs to the various entities, as well as the holding group itself.

Well-defined metadata elements and values can prove essential at a number of levels.

Data models and data architectures describe data, and should make use of metadata to express these descriptions. At the risk of complicating matters, for such models to be useful, they themselves rely on metadata to allow the right people to discover and use them fully.

Metadata is also essential for describing services, and thereby promoting effective interoperability, sharing and re-use. In terms of the data within systems, metadata allows users to understand aspects of the data including ownership, quality, security and usage restrictions.

4.13.1 Features

Effective management of metadata relies on a number of key features.

Your Data Governance function will need to establish a roadmap for defining the set of data elements that best serves your organisation. What information should be collected for each type of data? What are the mandatory elements that must be captured as opposed to the optional characteristic? Where, within the lifecycle of each type of data, should the various items be recorded[147]?

Clearly, the reason for going to the trouble of collecting metadata is to add value to data, and for this to be effective, knowledge about metadata should be shared as widely as possible – ensuring, of course, that any information that needs to be restricted is appropriately controlled. This includes awareness of what, how and when information should be collected, but also *knowledge* of the information that has been collected. This is ultimately where the value of metadata resides.

Where possible, metadata should be aligned with international standards (such as Dublin Core, etc) to facilitate sharing, where appropriate, outside the organisation.

We recommend that, for all the types of data used by your organisation, you should consider whether there is a role for metadata.

---

[147] This concept is referred to as 'Metadata lineage'.

From the perspective of effective governance and continuous improvement, the use, quality and coverage of metadata should be measured and monitored against appropriate KPIs.

The sets of metadata elements – representing the descriptions you choose to maintain about your data – will change over the course of time. This is most likely to amount to new metadata elements being added. Changes to your metadata should be *version controlled*, so that changes are tracked between the various versions.

As a summary of Metadata Management features, think of metadata as the means to:

- Describe the various sets of data that flow into and out of key business systems;

- Describe the services available to and from departmental functions within your organisation;

- Describe the quality of data provided by data services;

- Describe any sensitivities, such as information of a commercial or personal nature that would help to support decisions about data sharing, security and privacy;

- Support the widespread discovery of data and data services;

- Allow data capture and Data Management to be made as effective as possible, and;

- Improve users' understanding of the data, services and processes in order to promote confidence in existing data, and to ensure effective ongoing Data Management.

4.13.2 What does maturity look like?

This is our guide to the characteristics of the various levels of capability maturity in regard to Metadata Management:

Level 1 – Initial: There is no evidence of metadata being captured outside enterprise systems.

Level 2 – Repeatable: Some metadata has been captured for use within specific departments. This is likely to be as a result of specific project requirements.

Level 3 – Defined: Organisation-wide policies and standards are defined to provide strategic direction for Metadata Management practice across all departments. A centrally managed list of minimum metadata requirements is published for use by all departments.

Level 4 – Quantitatively Managed: Metadata Management practices are measured and controlled in accordance with organisation-wide standards – with all departments reporting their level of compliance – or reasons for exception – back to the Data Governance Steering Group. Metadata use and quality is managed across all departments.

Level 5 – Optimising: There is an active drive to improve the quality and the reach of metadata across the organisation.

4.13.3 Value/benefit

There are many benefits available to your organisation once it begins to apply a systematic approach towards Metadata Management. Crucially, these benefits provide greater trust in the traceability and provenance of data as it flows across your organisation, resulting in improved decision making, and more effective reporting across business units.

Metadata Management provides the key to describing all the major aspects of data including identification, purpose, ownership, permitted uses, security, quality, related services, etc. Together, these allow the entire lifecycle of the data to be governed. An example of this is to use metadata to keep track of those pieces of data that may be due for retirement to offline archives, or disposal.

Using standard descriptions makes it possible to discover areas of commonality – or even direct duplication – in data, services and workflows, and this can help in reducing waste and improving productivity.

We have seen cases where the same report is generated by individual departments within an organisation which is unaware that the information already exists elsewhere. Generating a report may not sound particularly onerous, but often most of the effort stems from preparing (or cleansing) the source data, and processing and transforming it in some way.

Doing this more than once can be avoided by capturing information about the data (metadata – possibly recorded within a Data Catalogue), and publishing its availability across the organisation.

Having established the framework for metadata, you can measure against it so see how widely data, services and workflows are re-used. As an example, you might decide you are going to record all the sets of data created by your data services. Where two or more datasets originate from a given service (eg a 'List Customers' service), this is evidence of re-use. It may also cause you to investigate whether there are differences between these various datasets. If not, this may point to unnecessary duplication of effort, which we looked at earlier in this section.

Metadata provides a foundation to categorise data in the context of sharing, and even as Open Data. This makes it easier for people to decide whether, and how, data should be published.

These represent just a few examples of how metadata benefits the operation overall. Most people would agree that it's a good thing to actively describe information, and make this available for general consumption by those who can make good use of it. Metadata provides the means for standardising how this is carried out.

This section on Metadata Management is one of the shortest discussions of any of the 14 domains, because we have been making reference to the theme of metadata throughout almost *all* of the other domains. It is worthwhile taking a moment to reflect on this, because this highlights the value of metadata.

We described how an organisation's data warehouse relies on metadata to trace the lineage of data and to clarify its owner. We also highlighted the importance of metadata for Document and Content Management; especially when linking semi-structured content – such as letters – to the structured information within your enterprise applications.

We underlined the need for standard descriptions of data service interfaces within the context of integration and interoperability, and metadata is the primary means for achieving the consistency that opens the way for data sharing and reuse. We also saw how this is of particular relevance when describing the properties of data to be published as Open Data.

The management of data storage relies on metadata to help keep track of the usefulness and relevance of data, so that it can be archived or destroyed when it no longer has value for operational reasons. Furthermore, metadata is used to describe various security and privacy characteristics of data, enabling data to be protected appropriately and used within the confines of acceptable use.

One of the most critical uses for metadata is in providing the basis for measuring and hence *improving* the quality of data. Data Modelling relates to the activity of capturing descriptions of data and encoding this as metadata, and the Data Catalogue provides the repository for making metadata available widely across – and perhaps even beyond – your organisation.

Metadata has a part to play in almost every aspect of effective Data Management, and this is the reason that we place this category of data at the top of the hierarchy. This is an appropriate place to revisit our graphic that shows how the characteristics of the various types of data are related:

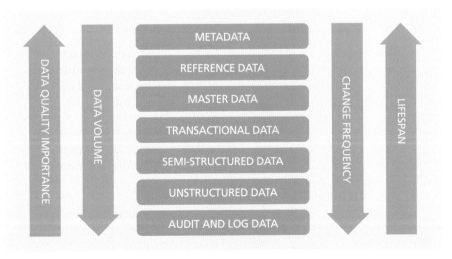

Understanding the supreme importance of metadata is vital for making progress towards stronger Data Management. Get this wrong, and your organisation's data capabilities can only suffer as a consequence.

Getting this right relies on instituting a capable and empowered Data Governance function, and it's no accident that this is where we began our discussion at the start of this chapter.

4.13.4 Impact

Defining and maintaining metadata data elements and then capturing the actual values to describe your data requires initial investment, both in terms of the people, and in establishing a suitable technical platform to host the metadata. You should expect to allow for consultation across the various functions of your organisation to ensure that metadata is as widely applicable as possible.

Your Data Governance function will need to monitor the application of metadata, ensuring that the value is fully realised.

As part of the overall awareness programme for matters related to crossing the *Data Delta*, your people also need to understand the importance and value of metadata, and the part they play in unlocking its value.

4.13.5 Next steps

Your Data Governance function should determine what types of data should be described using metadata, and indicate which data elements are mandatory or optional for each of these types.

Use metadata as a systematic way of adding structural and semantic descriptions of your data. For example, the Data Catalogue, a Business Glossary and the Data Dictionary all serve to provide and manage descriptive information, and they use metadata to achieve this.

Similarly, as we described earlier, there is a need to manage documents and contents, and an appropriate set of metadata is *crucial* to achieving this.

Once you have established *what* to capture, you need to put processes in place to ensure that the right metadata is recorded, and at the right time.

Clearly, everyone involved in using data needs to understand the importance of following the rules, but also of the value of having metadata available to them.

4.14 Description – Data Catalogue

We don't always agree with everyone else's theory about every aspect of data management. We do *try* to read it all – and we try very hard to understand it all – but sometimes, we see things differently. This is one such instance.

In pure terms, a Data Catalogue represents a list of available datasets – in the widest possible sense of the word. Your Data Catalogue entries could point to relational databases, or the tables within them, to data held in XML files, to spreadsheets, to flat files (such as CSV[148] or other text-based formats), to a report, to a CD-ROM or USB Stick containing data, to various forms of multimedia files, etc.

The point is: the catalogue is a reference to all the collections of *actual* data your organisation uses. Clearly, this could be quite an extensive list, consisting not just of major applications (or rather, the databases behind them), but all types of data, however structured they may be. This, in itself, is a valuable resource, and we would certainly agree that it's better for an organisation to have one of these than not.

But we think there's so much more useful material you could and *should* manage inside a Data Catalogue.

With the 'pure' version of a Data Catalogue, it's like having a list of what's on TV but it only contains the programme *titles*. If you simply want to know that, fine, but you will often want to know more about a particular programme, such as what it's about, whether it's a comedy or drama, and whether it's strictly for adults or aimed directly at a children's audience. Obviously, the more information provided in the programme guide, the easier it is for you to make your choice.

In a similar way, we believe that a Data Catalogue should contain a great deal more than merely a listing of the datasets. In fact, it can become the repository for much of the information relating to other data management domains (such as Data Modelling, Data Architecture, Metadata and even Data Quality and Information Security and Privacy).

Let's establish that the purpose of the Data Catalogue is to describe the data owned by your organisation in order to help you maximise its value as an asset. At a minimum, as we've said, the Catalogue should contain entries to describe your organisation's core *datasets*.

We'll explain that term in more detail, but think of it as a set of related data items that has meaning to you – maybe a customer dataset, or a citizen dataset.

---

[148] A file format, known as 'Comma Separated Variable', where each line represents a record, and the records contain a given number of data items – usually separated or 'delimited' by commas (though other delimiters can be used). The data contained between the delimiters can be of any length (including zero length).

4.14.1 Features to consider

The real value of a Data Catalogue derives from it being accessible by all parts of your organisation. One of the most wasteful practices within organisations occurs when one part of the operation duplicates the work of another unnecessarily.

This can be avoided if everyone creates an entry in the Data Catalogue for each data extract or report that is produced. Of course, this requires that people check the Data Catalogue before embarking on producing any data. This means that the Catalogue needs to be published through a centrally-hosted portal that can be accessed as a shared service across the organisation.

As a matter of course, the Catalogue should include references to all data – irrespective of whether it's intended for general consumption. Access to information about the data can be controlled using the Catalogue's access control facility.

The Catalogue should be populated with various levels of information about each dataset. Not everyone will want to see all the details, especially the more technical-ly-focused information.

At the absolute minimum, you should aim to ensure all datasets are described from a business perspective, whereby each dataset, and the data elements it contains, is described in its business context using terms that will be familiar to non-technical people.

This may include links to a business glossary, which is recommended because it ensures that descriptions make use of standard terminology. If you are feeling particularly adventurous, you could associate your datasets with a high-level data model, such as a conceptual or logical model.

Your Catalogue should also hold technical descriptions of your datasets relating to their format, structure and composition. This may include links to some form of 'data dictionary' and physical data models. This information is of less interest to business users, and is more likely to appeal to systems designers, or those involved in establishing data services.

We can't help feeling that the whole issue of data quality, though recognised as a concern, is under-represented when people think about using or sharing data. Where can you go to determine whether the data you are using is reliable? What actions could you take to measure the quality of data? If you are processing or transforming data in some way (including combining it with another source or, perhaps, undertaking some analytics), how can you be sure that you aren't doing anything to compromise the integrity of the data?

All these questions cry out for somewhere to capture details that would help in controlling and measuring the quality of data – and a Data Catalogue is the obvious place for this.

There is a similar problem when it comes to understanding the security and privacy characteristics related to data. It comes as a surprise to many people to learn that your IT Department probably has some information about the security classifications of key data within your organisation (if not, they certainly should!). But this information is mainly used to ensure that data is kept secure within *all* the enterprise systems and databases.

What about the general use of data? After all, data doesn't spend its entire life inside systems. Are all the people that use data on a day-to-day basis aware of the security concerns and other potential restrictions, not least the privacy requirements related to personally identifiable data?

Related to this, is information that describes the purpose and intended use of the data. Why are we capturing and maintaining this data? How can it be used? When *shouldn't* it be used?

Again, the Data Catalogue represents a perfect repository for registering details relating to security, privacy, purpose, and intended uses for all data, so that everyone has the information they need to ensure they minimise any risks and stay within acceptable bounds of usage. This is especially important when deciding whether to publish data, and how widely to extend its circulation.

A final consideration for the type of details stored in the Data Catalogue relates to how data is distributed. Some datasets are made available to be distributed and accessed in particular ways and – where this information is known – it should be included as part of the Catalogue entry.

Examples of how data is accessed could include: via a database management system, as a file-on-a-file share location, as a download from a given web URL, or perhaps as part of a machine-to-machine communication via a Web Service API[149].

---

[149] An Application Programming Interface is similar to a User Interface for humans, which allows people to work with systems by exchanging information and using on-screen controls. An API allows machines to exchange information by passing messages in pre-defined formats.

Aside from the types of information it can hold, you also need to look for the capability of your Data Catalogue to maintain a *version history*, so that past and current versions can be retrieved, and new versions can be built.

The full power of a Data Catalogue will be realised by those who can integrate with your other data management tools (such as Reference Data Management, Master Data Management, Metadata Management, and Document and Content Management systems).

Access to the Data Catalogue can be controlled to provide general access to anyone who needs it, but also so that *only* those who should be making updates to the Catalogue can add or change entries.

Don't overlook the need for appropriate governance and process to decide and control who should be authorised to use your Data Catalogue, and how they should use it.

4.14.2 What does maturity look like?

Having looked at some of the potential and desirable features of Data Catalogue management, let's consider the various levels of maturity in this data management domain:

Level 1 – Initial: The departments do not maintain an accurate record of datasets in the departments.

Level 2 – Repeatable: Datasets that are maintained inside enterprise systems are recorded in a 'Data Catalogue', possibly manually, such as in a spreadsheet. These Catalogues are not generally shared to the benefit of all departments.

Level 3 – Defined: Organisation-wide policy and standards are defined to provide strategic direction for Data Catalogue practices across all departments. Departments define their local practices based on these standards. There is a central Catalogue of datasets managed outside any specific department. Departments contribute to the Data Catalogue.

Level 4 – Quantitatively Managed: Practices are measured and controlled in accordance with organisation-wide standards, with all departments reporting compliance (or non-compliance) back to the Data Management Steering Group. Datasets exist in a central Catalogue, with access to the Catalogue being used to evidence re-use across departments. Departments contribute to the Data Catalogue.

Level 5 – Optimising: Departments contribute directly to maintaining the Data Catalogue. There is a well-defined process of reporting errors and improving data held in the Catalogue. The Catalogue is capable of allowing public access to selected records to support use of Open Data.

4.14.3 Value/Benefit

Managing a Catalogue of your data provides many opportunities for increasing its value.

We have discussed the value derived when it's clear who's accountable for looking after the various pieces of your data throughout its entire lifecycle.

In recognition of this, our fictitious company, *GoDelta*, decided that all the data owners would be identified against their data. Their Catalogue was made available to everyone within the company (via a web browser). This meant that whenever a data-related question or issue arose, people were able to determine whom to contact. The organisation found that this helped to reduce the errors within the records. Previously, people regarded it as too much trouble to pursue problems, but the introduction of the Catalogue removed the obstacles to identifying the appropriate person.

The availability of information about all the data also contributed to improved reporting. For example, *GoDelta*'s Finance Department and Sales Team recognised that they were using different approaches towards accounting for revenue – a constant source of tension in years gone by – but instead agreed to use an accruals basis to report their figures.

The Data Governance function mapped out a schedule both for cataloguing data, and for addressing data quality issues based on a prioritisation of the most critical data. One of these areas related to data received from one of *GoDelta*'s largest industrial customers.

This customer operates several business parks in the UAE, and buys *GoDelta*'s controller products so frequently that they established an arrangement for ordering products and spare parts using a weekly data file. The problem was that the quality of the data was habitually very poor, and required significant effort to rectify before the data could be loaded into *GoDelta*'s ERP system.

This file was subjected to some systematic modelling activity, which allowed the company to create some detailed entries about the dataset in its Data Catalogue. As part of this, they investigated what caused the ERP system to reject the file, and described various validation criteria to be applied to the various fields within this file.

They went as far as defining the validations using 'regular expressions', which are a representational form that computer systems can use to ensure that data values conform to a given pattern. For those fields where the values were taken from a controlled list (such as product codes), one of the junior Data Modellers established a link to the related reference data list.

This was all recorded within the Data Catalogue, and made it easy for *GoDelta* to develop a validation routine that can check the file (before attempting to load the file into the ERP system) and report any errors back to the customer.

BUT, there are no longer any errors!

Why? Because *GoDelta* shared carefully selected regions of its Data Catalogue with the customer – they accessed it via the internet – including the information about this file. The customer also made use of the descriptions relating to this file within the *GoDelta's* Data Catalogue, and *they too* implemented a validation routine – based on the same information.

This allowed the customer to prepare the file, check that it conformed with *GoDelta's* data quality requirements, and resolve any issues before transmitting it to them. This was a significant win for everyone involved.

As a separate activity, the Data Governance function established some automatic monitoring for any data now covered by data quality rules within the Data Catalogue. It reported the results of this at the monthly management meeting, and also used the information to help inform plans for which data to target for data remediation.

GoDelta has developed plans to replicate the use of data files to streamline interactions with other customers, and the Architecture team suggested that this should make use of Web Services rather than files. There is a desire to make these Web Services as generic and re-usable as possible, and the team stressed the importance of using the Data Catalogue to communicate the data formats to those interested in making use of the Web Services (both inside and – to a more restricted extent – outside the company).

GoDelta's Data Catalogue would in the future define all of the standard message formats use within the Web Services, so that everyone involved would be aware of how they should be used. This will underline the value of using a Data Catalogue to support other aspects of the *Data Delta*, and promotes ease of use and sharing of data.

The prospect of more data sharing galvanised *GoDelta's* IT department to revisit the information it holds on the information security classifications for each type of data.

They would, in the future, check that this was still current and relevant, and then migrate the information into the Data Catalogue, which would become the master store of data security details, and therefore be available for anyone who needed to refer to it.

Each of these advances had a reliance on understanding certain aspects about the data at hand, and describing it in various ways. Just as in the above *GoDelta* example, developing a Data Catalogue is an effective way of making this information available more widely throughout your organisation, and serves to help you unlock more of its value.

4.14.4 Impact

By now, you should have a good overview of what goes into a Data Catalogue, and why it is useful. We'll look now at what's involved in populating and maintaining the entries it contains, while allowing this information to be accessed and exploited.

A typical Data Catalogue workflow looks like this:

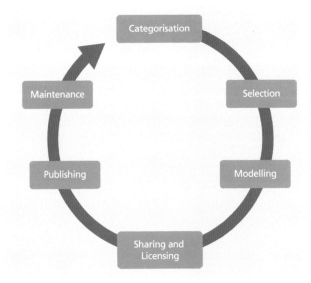

Figure 12 – Data Catalogue workflow

- *Categorisation* identifies and assigns a type, such as reference data or master data, to all data, and assists when it comes to selecting and prioritising the data to be included in the Data Catalogue.

- *Selection* takes account of a number of considerations to determine whether data should be selected for inclusion within the Data Catalogue, and helps to create an order of priority for addressing this selected data.

- *Modelling* captures information about the data: business descriptions, technical details, quality characteristics, information related to security classification, privacy requirements, purpose and intended use/s.

- *Sharing and licensing* considers whether there are – or should be – any restrictions imposed on the sharing of the actual data, or the way that shared data is used. Such restrictions should be described within the Data Catalogue. It is important to apply an explicit licence, creating one if necessary, to make it clear whether a dataset can be re-used, even when no restrictions apply.

- *Publishing* releases Data Catalogue information for use by other authorised people and systems. This includes consideration of how information is made available both in human and machine-readable forms.

- *Maintenance* ensures that existing published information within the Data Catalogue is kept up to date.

4.14.5 Next Steps

Your Data Catalogue represents the *focal point* for capturing your understanding and description of the data used by your organisation. The 'Description' principle is an essential foundation that underpins the quality and value of all your data. If you're unable to define your data, and make this definition available, your chances of maintaining or improving its quality, security, re-use and value are greatly diminished.

It's important to attach all the activities related to describing data to a more tangible initiative. It is all too easy to for this to become an end in its own right but, treated in isolation, this is unlikely to be sustained by the business for very long. Find an initiative with tangible business benefit, and attach this activity to it. Break the task down into bite-sized pieces that can be used to unlock business value.

4.15 Summary of the Data Delta model

We have now reviewed each of the fourteen Data Management domains that comprise the *Data Delta* model. Though this is necessarily high-level in a book of this nature, we have covered a lot of material and it's worth taking stock of what we have learnt.

It should be clear that in many organisations there *is* a gap between the data you have and the information you need. That gap is made up of a number of elements: missing data, badly-defined data, poor quality data, out-of-date data, duplicates and inconsistent data. Those problems are themselves caused by breakdowns in business processes and management accountability.

The attitude that no one in management has time to care if *one* record is somehow incorrect translates into an attitude whereby no one in management has time to act if a hundred thousand records are wrong. This attitude has to change. Radically.

The single most important change that must occur is the realisation at the senior executive level that *data is an asset*. Quite literally, it affects the value, and therefore the *valuation*, of your organisation. The recognition of data as an asset leads immediately to the need for enterprise-level Data Governance.

We've provided a lot of information about exactly what we mean by that. It isn't just another executive job title; it's a real role with real responsibilities, which we have spelled out in detail.

Once Data Governance is introduced, and the principal of 'Ownership' is established, the rest of the gap between the data you have and the information you need can be addressed by working your way forward with this model to inform your journey:

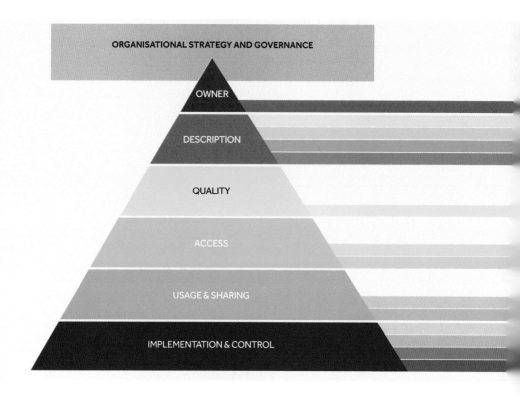

Another key learning point from our walkthrough of the Data Management domains is that there are a great many specialist issues to deal with; this is not a 'general purpose, throw it to the IT department, three-month' project. You might well find you need skills sets that aren't on your payroll today.

On the positive side, two key points should stand out. Firstly, you are extremely unlikely to be starting from scratch; almost everyone has *something*. And if it's not perfect, throw our Voltaire quote at them: '*The best is the enemy of the good*'.

Secondly, remember that the only way you will cross the *Data Delta* is in small incremental steps; with each step delivering business value. Don't fall into the trap of acknowledging all the work that has to be done, but then throwing it into a top-down monolithic programme. It will never, *ever* happen. You have to find cute, agile approaches to bring the business benefits forward. Only then can you hope to carry the organisation with you.

We've provided you with lots of examples about where other organisations have started. Many begin their journey by introducing governance around master data; managing customer and citizen data lifecycles. That isn't the only starting place, but it works for

Data Governance
Data Catalogue
Metadata Management
Data Modelling and Design
Data Architecture

Data Quality Management and Remediation

Information Security and Privacy
Data Storage

Open Data
Integration and Interoperability
Reference Data Management
Master Data Management
Document and Content Management
Enterprise Data Warehouse, BI and Analytics

many organisations. If it isn't obvious where you should start, pick up the phone and call us.

There are great moments to be enjoyed on your *Data Delta* journey. Perhaps it's the first time you go into a management meeting, when everyone agrees all the figures, and the Finance and Sales Directors exchange a smile. Or maybe it's when you get a call from the Customer Support department saying, "We see now why we couldn't find those records. We've got his name as Sir Ranulph Twisleton-Wykeham-Fiennes,[150] but in the ERP system, his customer name is Ran Fiennes – because now we can see all his data in the new 'golden view'."

Again, we have never said that crossing the *Data Delta* would be easy. There are alligators in the swamps.

We repeat: if you don't do it, believe us, your competitors will. Cross the *Data Delta*, and data becomes information, and information becomes knowledge. And knowledge is power[151].

---

[150] The full name of the great British explorer, the first person to visit both the North and South poles, who is more commonly known as Ran Fiennes. There is no global format for names that works in practice when you consider full Arabic and Sri Lankan names, as well as the various variations on Chinese names and those of many other countries. Western Europeans, in particular, often have a hopelessly optimistic expectation of address management based on their parochial experience. One of our favourite addresses, for example, is the main police station in Dubai, which has an official address of Sheikh Khalifa Bin Zayed Rd, Near Dawar Trading Center, Al Jafiliya, Dubai, United Arab Emirates.

[151] We've used that quote a couple of times – here is its full story. The quote is usually attributed to Francis Bacon, the English philosopher and statesman, although made more famous by Thomas Jefferson in a letter to George Ticknor, 25 November 1817): *'the important truths, that knolege is power, that knolege is safety, and that knolege is happiness'*. In 1597, Bacon had written wrote *'ipsa scientia potestas est'* (*'knowledge itself is power'*) in *Meditationes Sacrae*. The first known use of the actual phrase, *'scientia potestas est'* goes, however, to his apprentice, one Thomas Hobbes in the *Leviathan*. But this is all a very Western perspective, because the phase *'Knowledge is power'* was clearly first used by Imam Ali sometime in the early 7th century. We know this because the quote is documented and ascribed to him by Sharif Razi in his *Nahj al Balagha*, written in the tenth century, at least 500 years before Bacon.

5
The Future [152]

'*Change is the only constant*'. It's a saying so old that it almost seems to come from a different world[153].

The digital revolution began with the advent of commercial computing some 50 years ago and is making an impact of global and historic proportions. The world will not be the same again, the internet will not be turned off, and everyone's lives will be impacted more and more by the consequences of *data*.

Data. Because data is at the heart of the digital transformation.

Great enterprise systems and personal mobile apps that use data will come and go. Uber has become a part of everyday life for many people around the world, but would you bet your house on them still being around in another twenty years' time? The chances are that something will have replaced Uber. And there will be better ways to exploit all the data that we will have available. Apps, or perhaps technology that will replace apps, will come and go. Technology to store and manipulate data will *certainly* come and go, but *data* will remain at the heart of the ever-evolving digital revolution.

> Technology to store and manipulate data will certainly come and go, but data will remain at the heart of the ever-evolving digital revolution.

You need to be prepared to *act* as the waves of change break upon your world, in your particular sector. Stay the same and you will follow Kodak into the 'Where-are-they-now?' files. That action must be based on knowledge and insight of your organisation – its customers, markets and uniqueness. This is insight that you can only derive

---

[152] The words *caveat emptor* ('*let the buyer beware*') should be writ large over newspaper articles, technical journals, blogs and, indeed, books that deal with the future of technology. We need to thank Rhett Butler and Scarlett O'Hara for re-awakening the world's awareness of this 'shrewd' advice. Or rather, Margaret Mitchell for writing their parts in her 1936 novel. '*Gone with the Wind*' remains to this day near the top of most 'favourite American fiction book' lists. When looking for some independent technology predictions from soothsayers to support the arguments in this chapter, the thoughts of the leading industry analysts, Gartner, came right at the top of *that* list. So no apologies for quoting liberally from Gartner in this section, but not from any of the leading vendors.

[153] We believe it was first said by Heraclitus of ancient Greece, in about 500 BC.

from the data that you have available. Why aren't customers aged under 30 returning so often? Why can't you sell more to affluent over-50s?

'You can't step into the same river twice'[154]. And just as the river changes moment by moment every single day, so does your data. Your data will be different tomorrow, next week, next month, next year. What then do we know about the data of the future?

For starters, the future will involve *far* more data than any of us currently envisage. Here is an average of some of the assessments we see in pictorial form:

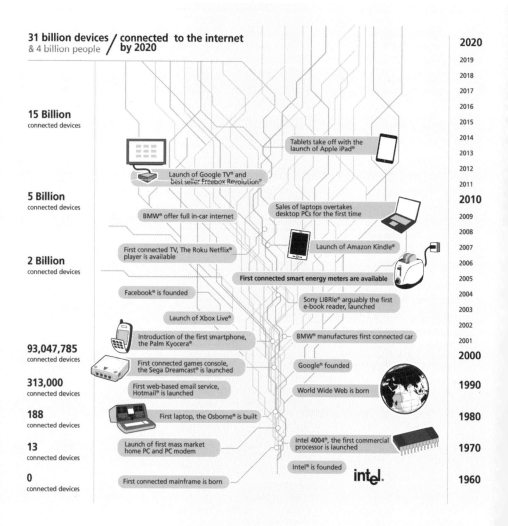

[154] Another aphorism from Heraclitus.

The growth in data needs to be understood from two related perspectives: personal and social media data on the one hand, and the Internet of Things (IoT) on the other. These worlds are closely related, and indeed, where they meet is where the *Data Delta* gap is potentially at its widest. We'll look next at these two areas individually, and then go on to examine their relationship and the challenges they bring.

5.1 The Internet of Things (IoT)

Our sincere hope is that the Internet of Things will soon cease to be known by that title. Its name proves that the idea is, even now, still the province of technologists rather than mainstream business.

IoT represents the inter-connection of 'smart' devices. This includes everything from sensors monitoring traffic flow, pressure in an oil pipe, the contents of your refrigerator, the organs and systems in your body, to just about every form of device imaginable (and, indeed, many that are currently beyond imagination).

The resulting data is going to exhibit different characteristics to those of today's social media and personal data.

5.1.1 Volume and Velocity

IoT will generate data in unparalleled volumes and ever-increasing speeds.

For example, sensors monitoring traffic flows will ultimately be capable of providing real-time data feeds. Even at a transmission rate of one data point per second, that's 3,600 transactions per hour from *every* sensor along *every* road in *every* major city.

The technology will undoubtedly develop to cater for the storage and processing aspects of this but, from a Data Management perspective, the needle-in-a-haystack problem is also set to grow, most probably at something approaching exponential rates.

Here are some important Gartner views about the future of the IoT that help focus on its scale:[155]

Through 2018, 75% of IoT projects will take up to twice as long as planned.[156]

---

[155] *Gartner quotations described herein, represent research opinion or viewpoints published, as part of a syndicated subscription service, by Gartner, Inc. ('Gartner'), and are not representations of fact. Each Gartner quotation speaks as of its original publication date (and not the date of this publication), and the opinions expressed by Gartner are subject to change without notice. Quotations from Garter are only valid in the context of the original Gartner report.*

[156] Gartner Press Release: Analysts Reveal Five Unexpected Implications Arising From the Internet of Things January 14, 2016 http://www.gartner.com/newsroom/id/3185623

By 2018
- *20% of all business content will be authored by machines.*[157]

- *6 billion connected* things will be requesting support.[158]

By 2020
- *More than 3 million workers globally will be supervised by a 'robo-boss'.*[159]

- *20% of smart buildings will have suffered from digital vandalism.*[160]

- *45% of the fastest-growing companies will have fewer employees than instances of smart machines.*[161]

- *Autonomous software agents outside of human control will participate in 5% of all economic transactions.*[162]

- *A black market exceeding $5 billion will exist to sell fake sensor and video data for enabling criminal activity and protecting personal privacy.*[163]

- *Addressing compromises in IoT security will have increased security costs to 20% of annual security budgets, from less than 1% in 2015.*[164]

- *80% of asset-intensive industry CIOs will have embraced IT/OT integration as a strategic imperative.*[165]

- *About 25 billion 'things' – not counting smartphones, tablets or computers – will be connected* to the IoT.[166]

- *More than half of major new business processes and systems will incorporate some element, large or small, of the IoT.*[167]

5.1.2 Context

With all this data streaming around at unfathomable rates, the ability to provide *context* will become a pre-eminent concern. For example, you may want to prioritise responses to those 'technical fault' alerts emanating from roadside sensors depending on the *location* of the problem and, perhaps the time of day.

---

[157] Gartner, Gartner Predicts Our Digital Future, Smarter with Gartner, October 6, 2015: http://www.gartner.com/smarterwithgartner/gartner-predicts-our-digital-future

[158] Ibid.

[159] Ibid.

[160] Ibid.

[161] Ibid.

[162] Ibid.

[163] Ibid.

[164] Ibid.

[165] Gartner Predicts 2016: *Unexpected Implications Arising From the Internet of Things* 3 December 2015.

[166] Ibid.

[167] Ibid.

However, context is often something of a weakness where machine-generated data is concerned. Manufacturers produce sensors that can become components in a wide variety of devices.

The same sensor component may play a very different role from machine to machine and indeed, the same type of machine could provide information that is immensely more important than other machines of the same type, depending upon *where they are located*, and on the role they are to *perform* at that location.

A proliferation of sensors leading to ever-increasing volumes of data will require new levels of proficiency in *converting* this data into actionable information. Context is the key ingredient of the conversion of data into actionable information. The *Data Delta* principles (especially *Ownership* and *Description)* will become more important by several degrees.

For example, a sensor detects a failure in a set of traffic lights. Are the traffic lights managing the pedestrian crossing of some isolated Scottish fishing village that sees three cars a day, or are they controlling rush-hour traffic on Times Square or Hyde Park Corner? The context dictates the action to be taken.

There's no way that a component or machine could recognise this for itself without someone configuring the contextual information, usually in the form of *metadata*. Context is a key concern of the *Data Delta* model and the Entity Method, and questions need to be asked. Questions such as:

- Who owns the sensor metadata?

- Who defines it?

- Whose job is to ensure the values are correct?

- What does 'correct' mean?

5.1.3 Variability

Commentators often talk about 'variability' in the context of Big Data. Systems will need to be able to accommodate data sources that provide data in a wide variety of formats.

This is usually discussed in relation to *semi-structured* documents, and also the influx of data from social media sources. By its nature, information needs to be discerned by analysing natural – or perhaps not-so-natural – language text.

Generally speaking, IoT devices will present their data in well-defined and structured formats[168]. However, as already noted above, the 'meaning' of data (with the same or similar message or content) could vary wildly based on context. Metadata is key to resolving this.

From the perspective of message content or 'payload', different devices and manufacturers will represent the same information in every different way imaginable eg different part numbers for the same type of part, different status codes for the same condition, etc.

This relates to the domain of Reference Data Management (RDM), and is set to become especially complex with the advent of IoT, with nested components and sub-components all talking different 'languages'. This will be one of the key drivers of the *semantic web* discussed below.

5.1.3.1 IoT – Crossing the Data Delta

Technology alone cannot provide the solution to address the characteristics of an IoT future, and the principles of the *Data Delta* model will become even more relevant. Vendors marketing Big Data solutions will focus on the enormous power of technologies such as Hadoop (and its descendants).

It is true that smarter technologies will help store, process and retrieve data, but on their own, these will not solve the context challenges of the IoT.

Here's a real-world example from the 'bleeding edge' of today's Big Data capabilities. A well-funded law enforcement agency – we can't give any clues as to who or where – was working on a high-profile case where there was a huge amount of political pressure to deliver quick results.

One promising line of enquiry concerned data relating to a group of particular people and their mobile phones, which were being used in a manner which appeared suspect. The agency had access not only to the related call and messaging logs, but also large amounts of IoT location data from cell towers which provided significant insights into the movements of these phones over a period of time.

The agency commissioned an extensive analytical effort using the latest Hadoop-based Big Data technologies, but this was unsuccessful and the investigation stalled. Entity became involved to see if we could provide some insights.

---

[168] However, a structured format could also include embedded audio and video data that would need to be analysed to extract 'meaning'.

We applied *Data Delta* principles and in this instance, highlighted a potential solution that harnessed a combination of Master Data Management and contextual information (all relating to the *Description* principle in our Data Delta model).

By analysing the location data over a period of time we were able to determine the relationships between mobile phones, and the individuals who potentially used them at specific times. From this we built an evolving matrix of potential 'ownership'. Armed with this one new piece of information that it couldn't deduce itself, the Hadoop engine was able to very rapidly identify likely suspects[169].

With the right information, Hadoop provided a whole array of insights phenomenally quickly and efficiently. Without enough of the crucial pieces, it was unable to assemble the jigsaw.

This true story highlights some fundamental points[170]. The Internet of Things is going to extend into many – if not all – parts of our lives eg health management, shopping, driving and of course, every aspect of policing and security.

The technology has enormous potential but on its own, will struggle to add value quickly. Linked to *Data Delta* principles, the value within your data can quickly be transformed into useful information.

5.2 Social Media and Personal Data

It's worth reflecting that the Facebook experience has only just celebrated its 10th birthday.

It has been an astonishing period which has seen the rise of a new communication phenomena. Also joining the party are apps such as Skype, Twitter, Instagram, WhatsApp, Snapchat, and many more. It doesn't take a crystal ball to foretell that this is the *beginning*, not the end.

Linked to this social media explosion has been the internet becoming mobile. Back at the turn of the century, early mobile internet pioneers such as AvantGo frantically wrote browsers for every available device, but the inevitable focus then of a mixed online/offline experience has already been replaced by the assumption of pervasive 24/7 access.

---

[169] Just as a message about a major new sales order will follow a specific route within your organisation generating a pattern of voice and email communication, a comparable *pattern* of usage could be identified within this group following particular events.

[170] At this stage in the book, it's worth acknowledging that two major market sectors – security and financial services – are underrepresented in terms of anecdotes. These organisations insist on absolute anonymity, and as the above example shows, it really does weaken the impact of the story when you remove anything that might give a clue as to who you are talking about. It's the details that make stories interesting, and we hope you will understand that we can't do that when discussing cases from these sectors.

Moreover, while bricks-and-clicks may still be a thing, business driven by clicks alone is increasingly winning the day.

It's also clear that there has been a profound *generational* shift in attitude, which will have a significant impact on the debates around privacy and security. There has been a widespread change in terms of the willingness to accept the internet into our lives.

Particularly led by younger generations, there is an almost unchallenged perception of the value of sharing information about ourselves, whether this be in traditional data – or indeed pictures and video clips – and this has changed the balance between openness and privacy. The genie is out of that particular bottle, and it's unlikely to be stuffed back anytime soon.

In addition, the internet is almost synonymous with 'mobile' – or 'on the move' – for many people living in the developed world today. It's a personal experience based on a device of choice, with apps selected and discarded as interest ebbs and flows.

The old concept of fixed 'real-estate', with restricting standards set by central IT functions, now seems to belong to another age. Millennials expect their chosen online experience *wherever* they happen to be ('What's your Wifi password, Grandma?'). And these young people are growing up fast.

It seems obvious that these different attitudes will be carried further and further into the business mainstream as each successive generation matures. We've already come a long way in such a short time.

For example, one Entity client uses social media to assess the impact of its advertising campaigns in each geographic area. This client then swiftly makes real-time stock decisions for its network of high street stores based on those findings. 'Sentiment analysis' in social media is developing in sophistication, and can already apply context to deal with irony and reverse meanings such as: 'That was bad' instead *translating* to: 'That was great'.[171]

The characteristics of social and personal data are very different in comparison to IoT data:

- There is a lot of social media data, but nowhere near as much as that generated by IoT. Even the most avid blogger posts a frankly insignificant amount of data compared to a single traffic-light sensor.

---

[171] Inversion – particularly in this case – is not a modern phenomenon. 'Bad' meaning 'good' stems not from the Michael Jackson era, but was first recorded in the 3rd edition of the Oxford English Dictionary (OED) in 1897. What's more, we only had to wait one further edition (1920) for the OED to acknowledge the use of 'wicked' in its alternate sense!

- Social media data is essentially unstructured (or, more accurately, *semi-structured*, as discussed in *Document and Content Management*). It's usually tied to a person – if not several – in some way.

- Data quality is exceptionally variable, and not only in terms of social media commentary. Personal data is notoriously unreliable; names and addresses are among the most inaccurate data an organisation holds. Consider the example of the Dubai driving license we've used several times in this book.

However, the potential value of social media data to organisations is immense. Insights into what customers truly think of your organisation, or why they choose – or pass over – particular products, etc are literally invaluable to any organisation. An analysis of social media data gives organisations the best opportunity ever known to listen to their customers.

Social media and personal data will doubtless extend in terms of usage. For instance, Gartner tells us that: 'By 2018, customer digital assistants will recognise individuals by face and voice across channels and partners'.[172]

It is inconceivable that you would not have a social media strategy so that you can listen and talk to your customers, whether you are in the public or private sector. How exactly you do that effectively is at the very heart of the *Data Delta* model.

You won't be allowed to do whatever you like, however. Organisations in the European Union are already facing regulation via the General Data Protection Regulation (GDPR), which has a wide-ranging scope, and applies not only to EU organisations themselves, but also to those *outside* the EU that deal with 'data citizens' within the region.

The deadline for compliance falls in 2018, and regulations include coverage of the collection, storage *and use* of information about data citizens. This is backed up with punitive fines for non-compliance of up to 4% of an organisation's turnover.

This reaffirms the behaviour that data-aware organisations should be exhibiting already, as well as providing a pretty clear indication as to the direction of forthcoming legislation around the world.

New social media apps will come and go. Already we see the possibility of a shift away from Facebook because 'That's used by the *olds*'. Perhaps that means that no social media app should ever be expected to last more than a generation. Many of us were witness to the 'deaths' of MySpace and AOL Chat, for example.

The constants though will be change, data, regulation (obligation) and opportunity. An agile approach towards crossing the *Data Delta* is the *only* way you will be able to balance these tensions going forward.

5.3 The Big Data Future

> *Big Data is high-volume, high-velocity and high-variety information assets that demand cost-effective, innovative forms of information processing for enhanced insight and decision making. Gartner defines 'dark data' as the information assets organizations collect, process and store during regular business activities, but generally fail to use for other purposes (for example, analytics, business relationships and direct monetizing). Similar to dark matter in physics, dark data often comprises most organizations' universe of information assets. Thus, organizations often retain dark data for compliance purposes only. Storing and securing data typically incurs more expense (and sometimes greater risk) than value.*[173]

It should be clear by now that we see the storage and physical management of data as just one aspect of the *Data Delta* model. Earlier, we presented the analogy of car washing, and the idea that the bucket that holds the water is the least important consideration when washing a car. The quality of the water, brush and detergent, not to mention the skills and attitude of the person *doing* the washing, are of far greater consequence to the job itself.

In all probability, Big Data means you keep your existing warehouse, but augment it with a separate Big Data architecture and technology stack. However, given the increases in data volume, velocity and variety, we believe that the monolithic data warehouse that acts as the place where all data is physically integrated will, in all likelihood, *not* be the dominant model for the future.

We expect to see more Logical Data Warehouses (LDWs), in which there are multiple data sources, types and structures integrated in a federated way. Significantly, most analytic use cases will still need the traditional Data Warehouse platform. The LDW will lean heavily on Master and Reference Data Management to act as the indices of a virtualised data store.

The landscapes of the Internet of Things and social media are clearly going to continue to develop and interact, and the future for most organisations will rest with the effective

[173] Gartner IT Glossary, Dark Data, http://www.gartner.com/it-glossary/dark-data

management of Big Data. Effective management *does* include the technical 'bucket' side, but it relies on so much more. In short, it relies on crossing the *Data Delta*.

The concepts of *Digital Disruption* arising from Clayton Christensen's work that we quoted right back in *Section 1 Introduction* are here to stay: data and digital technology will *change* the core value within businesses. Booksellers will no longer need a warehouse of books, movie sellers no longer need a cinema, and airlines and hotels do not need travel agents to sell their services. And the company selling you a taxi ride doesn't even need to own any taxis.

We should assume that the level of disruption will increase. There will be increases in terms of scope – in areas such as health and education – but also, as we have access to more and more data, new trends and new opportunities will certainly also emerge.

5.4 Algorithms as an Asset

That great philosopher, Alanis Morissette, once opined that '*Rain on your wedding day*' was ironic. In this, she was mistaken, unless you happened to be marrying a weather forecaster who had picked that particular day for your festivities based on their in-depth analysis of weather patterns. Otherwise, rain on your wedding day is best viewed simply as bad luck.

However, it may be ironic that just as BI tools begin to deliver on their long-heralded promise of true end-user reporting, these capabilities may be arriving just a little too late.

The challenges posed by the *data-driven* digital age call for a new approach to data analytics, and vendors have begun to respond by introducing a new class of automated – some are using the term *robotic*[174] – tools that mimic the cognitive processes of humans. Data is inherently passive, so what is it that provides the 'drive' – the action – for a data-driven organisation? A key aspect of the answer to this is found in the science of algorithms.[175]

Algorithm is a word that has so far been somewhat absent from the vernacular – confined to use within research labs, academic circles, and school maths class – but it is set to pervade our modern business vocabulary. The reason is that algorithms are, and always have been, all around us. Interestingly, given the right data, machines can make very effective use of them.

Algorithms are instructions. Put simply: 'If you want that to happen, then do this'. A baking recipe is an example of an algorithm. So too, are turn-by-turn driving

---

[174] We are using the term 'robot' in the context of an artificial mechanism or process that is able to perform non-trivial tasks.

[175] The word *algorithm* is a Latinised version of the name of the great Arab mathematician *Al Kwarizme*. He also first recognised the benefit of using the decimal number system, and defined algebra so fundamentally that the very word is derived from one of his works *Al-Jabr*. Western science, mathematics and computing owe a huge and largely unrecognised debt to the pioneering work of the great Arab mathematicians led by Al Kwarizme.

instructions. Then, of course, we have the traditional concept of algorithms in mathematics (formalised functions) and computer coding (programs).

Indeed, over time, there has been a gradual convergence of these two worlds, as the 'scientific' algorithm has begun to demonstrate its relevance to the *real world*.

If you do see a six-foot plus android wearing sunglasses as he walks down your high street muttering 'I'll be back', we recommend buying shares in Skynet.

We have mobile apps that help us follow instructions – algorithms – to navigate from Point A to Point B, and, in the future of self-driving vehicles, those same algorithms will increasingly be carried out by our cars themselves.

However, long before the advent of such apps, algorithms had already taken up residence in our homes eg consider electronic/ programmable washer/dryers or automatic breadmakers.

Given the huge and increasing amounts of data today, it is already beyond the capacity of humans to organise and manipulate this in anything close to 'real time', and to see what's changing. Though today's algorithms are being developed by people, researchers are already looking at the possibility of making algorithms self-improving.

Cognitive algorithms that make use of advanced 'machine learning' techniques are already with us, and few would argue with the notion that computers handle certain types of problem better than humans[176] eg identifying trends in customer purchase patterns based on huge volumes of transaction data; optimising traffic flows in response to a major traffic incident during rush-hour; and complex diagnoses of the health of a patient.

As machines become increasingly involved in our lives at the level of digital information, crossing the *Data Delta* will become ever more important. We are not suggesting a Terminator 'rise of the machines' scenario, although if you *do* see a six-foot plus android wearing sunglasses as he walks down your high street muttering 'I'll be back', we recommend buying shares in Skynet.

In the context of a private company or government administration, all operations are, by definition, algorithmic. Operations are generative in nature, and they employ processes – some automated, some manual, and some combining both manual and automated steps – to deliver an outcome (such as a service, product, or an answer to a question).

[176] Indeed, Alanis Morissette's weather forecast is most likely to have been made by a computer.

In our experience of working to help private and public sector organisations improve their management of data, it's surprising how many are unable to describe these processes – let alone their data – with any clarity.

Though it requires some cross-organisational effort to achieve, working towards a comprehensive and common understanding of your key processes is, in itself, hugely beneficial. It's about bringing those anonymous functions to light.

Organisations will become increasingly dependent on their ability to work with algorithms. Those that already struggle, or simply neglect to articulate – to 'encode' – the inner workings of their processes today, are likely to flounder in the face of developments waiting just around the corner.

The algorithms of the next generation will combine both traditional business processes and new, dynamic and predictive, models of operation. Indeed, *'meta-algorithms'* will emerge, whereby algorithms will be able to generate new algorithms to respond to specific situations.

The future implications of meta-algorithms are enormous. Organisations will be able to transform the execution of their business based on 'machine thought'. However, for this to be successful, the fundamentals of the organisation's operation, including its vision, objectives, processes and data, will need to be clearly and unambiguously described. In short, to take advantage of these technological marvels, organisations must have *already* crossed the *Data Delta*.

The following example – anonymised, but real – illustrates the importance of addressing issues of Data Management in preparation for a cognitive and algorithmic future.

The client organisation in question realised that they had a data quality problem relating to their master data. Common sense told them they had far too many customer records because they had many more records than the entire population of the country they served. Each customer record was associated with a large number of transactions, events and emails, and the business wanted to unlock the value from this data.

They spent a lot of time and money resolving their data quality issues and they were very pleased with the outcome, which eliminated duplication, and reduced the number of records from 76 to 67 million. At the point they approached the Entity Group to discuss implementing new systems to maintain their data, they were very confident of its quality.

However, shortly after we were engaged, our analysts became suspicious. We demonstrated, by using more advanced matching techniques, that there should only be *53 million records*. This implied an error rate in this crucially important master data that still exceeded 20%, even *after* the client's intensive and expensive clean-up exercise.[177]

---

[177] The story had a happy ending. We worked with the client to remove the remaining duplicate records, and continued with the engagement as planned.

Feeding a cognitive tool with data carrying this level of error can only lead to confusion. The algorithm will develop its thinking and identify trends and insights incorrectly because it is working on poor quality data. There is a greater risk that people will accept the results *because* they are generated by a 'smart' piece of technology.

No matter how smart cognitive tools become – and they are going to become *very* smart – they will always be limited by the quality of data they are using. They will be able to cater for errors when the error rate is very low amongst millions of data items, but if major data elements are wrong by 20% they are only going to succeed at getting to the wrong answers more quickly.

Only by applying *Data Delta* principles can you establish the right conditions for algorithms to deliver valuable results.

5.5 Emerging Technologies

How does the *Data Delta* model help in the face of emerging technologies? What if there were a technological advancement so powerful that it could transform the very basic pillars of society? A technology that could fundamentally shift our economy, governing systems and business operations? A technology that could disrupt our conceptual understanding of trade, ownership and trust?

There is no Big Data lifeboat that is going to come and save you, because that lifeboat is moored right inside the Data Delta itself.

Many informed observers believe such a technology already exists.

When we hear the word *Bitcoin,* we usually focus only on virtual money or a transaction system. But if you look closer, you'll see that the monetary aspect is just the tip of the iceberg. That's because Bitcoin is built on some ground-breaking internet technology for which money is only one of the possible applications.

Money exists to facilitate trade. But through the centuries, trade has become incredibly complex.

Everyone trades with everyone, worldwide. Trade is recorded in bookkeeping systems, and this information is often isolated and closed to the public. For this reason, we use third parties that we trust to facilitate and approve our transactions. Think of governments, banks, accountants, notaries, and the paper money in your wallet. We call these *Trusted Third Parties*, which brings us to the essence of Bitcoin.

Bitcoin's software enables a network of computers to maintain a collective bookkeeping ledger via the internet. This ledger is neither closed, nor under the control of one party. Rather, it's public and available as a single digital ledger which is fully distributed across the network.

This is called a *blockchain*.

In the blockchain, all transactions are logged, and include information such as the date, time, participants and amount of every single transaction (or other details if non-financial).

Each node[178] in the network owns a full copy of the blockchain and, on the basis of complicated state-of-the-art mathematical principles, the transactions will be verified.

The mathematical principles also ensure that these nodes automatically and continuously agree with the current state of the ledger and every transaction in it. If anyone attempts to corrupt a transaction, the nodes will not arrive at a consensus, and hence will refuse to incorporate the transaction in the blockchain.

Every transaction is public, and thousands of nodes unanimously agree that a transaction has occurred on date X at time Y. It's like having a notary present at each transaction. This way, everyone has access to a shared single version of truth. This is why we can *always* trust a public blockchain.

The ledger doesn't care whether a Bitcoin represents a certain amount of euros or dollars, or anything else of value for that matter. Users can decide for themselves what a unit on the blockchain represents.

Each unit is both individually identifiable and programmable. This means that we can assign properties to each unit. We could program a unit to represent a monetary amount – like a penny – or a share in a company, a kilowatt-hour of energy, an air mile, or a digital certificate of ownership.

Because of this, blockchain is much *more* than just money and payments. It can represent many kinds of property, such as a thousand barrels of oil, award credits, or a vote during elections. Moreover, blockchain allows us to make our currency systems smarter, and it completely automates our cash and money flows.

---

[178] A network node is simply a connection, redistribution or end-point within a network. Examples would include both Data Communication Equipment (DCE) eg modems, hubs, bridges and switches and Data Terminal Equipment (DTE) eg digital telephone handsets, printers, routers or servers.

Imagine a healthcare allowance in some real currency; one that can only be used to pay for healthcare with certain providers. Ordinarily, a bureaucratic process would be applied after the fact to verify that all the rules are being followed in terms of permissions and authorisation. If, instead, we introduce a blockchain, we could simply program these particular rules into it, and potentially have compliance confirmation in advance and up front.

A company can control its spending in the same way, by programming budgets for salaries, machinery, materials and maintenance so that the respective money is specified, and cannot be spent on other things. Automating such things leads to a considerable *decrease* in bureaucracy, which saves accountants, managers, and the organisation in general, an incredible amount of time.

The programmable and open characteristics of blockchain could allow us to completely rebuild and innovate our financial sector and administrative processes, making them more efficient and transparent, and significantly decreasing bureaucracy. Blockchain is being hailed by many as the technology of *decentralisation and democratisation*.

In her address to the Dubai Keynote 2016 Blockchain Technology Conference, H.E. Dr. Aisha Bin Bishr (Director General of Smart Dubai) said:

> *Blockchain technology is one of the most elegant and advanced technologies to automate cross-industry processes, and presents a huge opportunity to increase efficiency, save time and reduce costs. The smart economy is a leading dimension for Dubai, and we believe that blockchain will have an important role to play in promoting entrepreneurship, boosting productivity, increasing competitiveness, and in securing our economic infrastructure – with Dubai as a global case study for blockchain.*

In an Internet of Things, our economy will be dealing with machines that actively participate in the economic traffic. In fact, they're already here. Think of a vending machine which dispenses milk. Or drones delivering packages. Or indeed, very soon, drones delivering milk to vending machine stockists!

Blockchain provides the logical capability to link these individual vending machines and drones together so that the concept of *trust* can be developed. A successful transaction requires action from both the drone and the vending machine, but neither 'knows' the actions of the other. However, blockchain means that the drone can be 100% certain that it will deliver the package to the right recipient, and know for sure that it's been paid for.

Internet technology is disruptive and shifts the status quo. It opens markets and breaks the positions of middlemen all the time. Bitcoin and other cryptocurrencies provide the potential – not just for a shift – but a real *break* in the paradigm. The *Data Delta* model helps to examine such developments systematically from the perspective of Data Management.

Accuracy and integrity, fitness-for-purpose, appropriate use, and security and privacy, may well become handled outside the organisation. The dynamic is set to become one of organisations – and primary data owners, such as individuals – agreeing on the parameters of sharing access to the primary data *source*.

The primary vehicle for this agreement is the '*Smart Contract*', which is made possible by the blockchain. The basic premise is that of a computerised agreement, one that not only describes the terms of the agreement, but also executes these terms autonomously and faultlessly.

The role of the 'traditional' data owner within an organisation will need to expand to handle the transition towards a relationship with primary data owners that is mediated by Smart Contracts. Clearly, this involves acquiring new skills for many people. It also requires that data owners are able to manage the transition in the context of how data 'owned' by their organisation is currently used, and what this will mean into a new digitally linked world.

5.6 The Data Delta in the Future

The need for an understanding of the *Data Delta* model only increases as the volume, velocity and variety of data within your organisation increases. And it will increase *exponentially* through changes brought about by movements such as social media and IoT.

Indeed, it is clear that the various challenges presented by these drivers are better addressed proactively and as early as possible, well before the volumes of data make retrospective corrective activity more difficult and costly.

IoT will call for better Metadata Management to help provide context – building on the ideas of hierarchical components and sub-components – in much the same way as the concept of a 'parts explosion' impacted the automation of the automotive industry in the 1980s.

Social media will heighten the need for effective Master and Reference Data Management, together with significant improvements in sentiment analysis and other forms of natural language processing (applied not only to text, but also to images as well as video and audio streams).

However, the use of personal data will need to be set against the privacy rights of the individual, and here, complex cultural, ethical and legal issues will come into play. And all this will be informed by the attitudes of a 'Millennial Generation' that has been sharing life through social media for their entire lives.

On a broader front, two quotes from one of the most important figures in Information Technology of the 20th century, Bill Gates, demonstrate the way.

Firstly, on the inevitability of Digital Disruption:

> *The successful companies of the next decade will be the ones that use digital tools to reinvent the way they work. These companies will make decisions quickly, act efficiently and directly touch their customers in positive ways. Going digital will put you on the leading edge of a shock wave of change. A digital nervous system will let you do business at the speed of thought-the key to success in the 21st century.*[179]

And secondly, on the importance of effectively managing your organisation's data:

> *The most meaningful way to differentiate your organisation from the competition, the best way to put distance between you and the crowd, is to do an outstanding job with information. How you gather, manage and use information will determine whether you win or lose.*[180]

These quotes from 'Business @ the Speed of Thought', show that Gates has no doubt of the importance of managing your increasingly complex, exponentially growing data. Indeed, he argues that it's the *only* way to succeed in the future.

Our experience agrees with and reinforces this perspective. It is this very experience that motivated the development of the Entity Method as the most effective way to cross the *Data Delta*.

From a technologist to a philosopher, and the words of George Santayana: 'Progress, far from consisting in change, depends on retentiveness. When change is absolute there remains no being to improve and no direction is set for possible improvement: and

---

[179] Excerpted from Business @ The Speed of Thought: Using a Digital Nervous System (Warner Books, March 1999).
[180] Ibid

when experience is not retained, infancy is perpetual. *Those who cannot remember the past are condemned to repeat it.'*

Having read this far, you are recognising that the solution for crossing the *Data Delta* rests with *you* and your organisation – your people, your culture, your operation, and your tools and technologies.

It has been accepted for far too long that data isn't 'sexy', and that somehow it's a 'detail' topic that shouldn't concern senior staff. These views are antiquated and have helped sow the seeds of the challenges so many organisations face today.

If data is not only an asset, but one of your organisation's most important assets then clearly, it has to be a key focus for all senior staff, and that *makes* it sexy. Of course, directors won't be discussing the data of an individual customer, but they do need to be discussing the quality of *all* their customers' data, and they will need to develop an objective, fact-based language to do so. Only by describing data meaningfully and applying objective principles of quality can your data assets be effectively managed.

And if you want to *succeed* in the 21st century, that is what you have to do.

6

Putting it together

We hope we've got the message across about what *Data Delta* is all about, and that you are bursting with ideas as to how to cross the *Data Delta* in your own organisation.

What we are saying is both rather old *and* very new. A lot of people have pointed out *parts* of the gaps between data and information over the years. 'Garbage in, garbage out'[181] was a data quality call *fifty* years ago.

But in this book, we've articulated three very important ideas.

Firstly, we've defined the *totality* of the gap, and we've provided an absolute and detailed definition of the 14 domains that together make up the *Data Delta*. This is a definition which is unambiguous, complete and altogether new. And it's a necessary and sufficient definition.

Secondly, we've provided heaps of advice on how to cross the *Data Delta*. We provided this at an organisational level, at a programme level, and in terms of the six principles of Data Management.

Finally, we've made the linkages from the *Data Delta* to the Digital Revolution which is washing over us all now very clearly. It's a tide where the waves are only going to get stronger throughout this century. To succeed in this new environment, your organisation will need to quickly and *repeatedly* take actions based on insight into your evolving world. How are your customers changing? How are your customers' *needs* changing? And where is your unique proposition in this fast-moving world?

Those insights will need to be based on an analysis of your data, an analysis of so much data that you will need advanced algorithms to help you do it. *Data is an asset*. And algorithms will *become* an asset, if they aren't already.

---

[181] It was back in 1963 that the phrase 'garbage in, garbage out' was first coined in relation to the early computerisation of the US Internal Revenue Service. One aspect of the problem represented by the *Data Delta* was recognised back then, and yet in all the intervening years the *Data Delta* has sadly grown wider, despite IT product vendors promoting a series of solutions to close the gap.

Only by crossing the *Data Delta* can your organisation prepare itself to withstand the tides of the digital revolution. If you don't cross the *Data Delta* properly, you run a very real risk that the waves and currents of the Digital Revolution will wash you away. There is no Big Data lifeboat that is going to come and save you, because that lifeboat is moored right inside the *Data Delta* itself.

Implementing the *Data Delta* message rests on a change programme that impacts many aspects of people, process and technology. It can't be seen as a technical project. Many people have tried that, and to the best of our knowledge, every single one of them has failed. Don't add your organisation to that list. The change you need to bring about is to get your organisation to treat *data as an asset*, because it's worth the effort.

The proof of this is everywhere – the frustrations of everyday life when data *isn't* treated as an asset. Time wasted in meetings on meaningless discussions on whose numbers are right; broken web links when trying to find a product you'd like to buy, companies offering you products you've already bought from them.

So why isn't change happening faster?

There have been two barriers to organisations moving towards treating *data as an asset*. Firstly, there is still a legacy hangover that all this is somehow IT's problem – an idea that IT are not blameless for encouraging. As IT's place in the corporate boardroom declined, particularly after the Y2K fiascos, IT has been looking to justify its continuing leadership role. Consequently, a lot of IT hands shot up when the organisation asked: 'Whose job is it to sort out the data?'

However, the principles expressed in the *Data Delta* model indicate that this was a mistake. IT can help; indeed, it *has* to help a great deal. But IT cannot *own* the problem.

IT represents a huge power for good in helping an organisation manage its data effectively. Not least, many of the people who first get the *data is an asset* message have an IT background. They've spent a large part of their lives thinking about data and have a huge number of relevant skills.

But IT don't own the asset. The only people who care enough about *procurement* data – and get it absolutely right – will be found in your *procurement department*. Likewise, sales data is in Sales. And it's the same story with Production, with Logistics, and with Finance.

Data is *owned* by the relevant line of business within your organisation. Only *they* can define it, and assess whether its quality is good enough for the task in hand. IT can be a key enabler in this process, but it cannot take absolute responsibility.

The second barrier to progress has been that *the gap between the data you have and the information you need* has been too difficult to understand. No one is quite sure how to define the gap, what to do about the it or how to bridge it. And that is the barrier that inspired us to write this book.

With the enormous amount of data that your organisation has today, there is no doubt that crossing the *Data Delta* represents a major organisational challenge. But if you think it's a big task today, ask yourself: will you have more or less data tomorrow?

It's only going to get more difficult the longer you delay starting. Your data is currently atrophying, declining in quality – and therefore value – as different business applications pull it in different directions. You are simply going to have more data, and more poor quality data, if you don't start your journey now.

How do you get started?

The great news is that over the last fifty years or so, we've all learned a huge amount about complex change programmes within an organisation. We know that monolithic 'five-year plan' top-down thinking is now consigned to the dustbin of history. No one serious is interested in playing that game anymore.

But what are the alternatives?

The concept of bimodal[182] IT is gaining a great deal of traction of late, and it is straight-forward to map bimodal concepts into our advice on crossing the *Data Delta*. Separating out steady state, predictable initiatives from exploratory, ground-breaking work is *exactly* what we have advised.

Your first few 'vertical slice' implementations could be referred to in bimodal language as the 'minimum viable product' (MVP[183]) of 'Mode 2[184]', the innovative mode. But once you have proved this technique works for you by repeated delivery of business value, and all the new technologies are de-risked as your organisational capabilities increase, further initiatives can be run in the more traditional predictable pattern of 'Mode 1'.

---

[182] Bimodal IT is being championed by many leading IT thought leaders as an approach to help balance the potential conflicting pressures on IT. It argues for the establishment of separate disciplines with IT; one manging steady-state 'keeping the lights on', and the other under-taking organisational-change work, often as part of *Digital Disruption* initiatives.

[183] The term Minimal Viable Product was coined by Frank Robinson in SyncDev methodology, and popularised by Erik Ries, Steve Blank and others. However, for the authors, MVP will always represent Most Valuable Player. We agree that our 'thin slice' might not be as elegant a phrase, but outside the pizza world, we think it's less likely to cause confusion!

[184] Bimodal theory defines Mode 1 as traditional and safe standard operations, and Mode 2 as innovative, agile developments.

Bimodal IT is just one response to the conflicting pressures facing organisations in the new digital age, and it's necessary to understand these pressures in more detail to help you find the right 'MVP' or 'vertical slice' at the start of your journey.

Many organisations, for example, are facing pressures between obligation and opportunity.

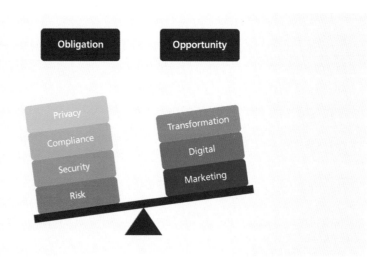

The regulatory environment is moving faster than it has ever done before as international bodies analyse past failings and risks – and seek to establish better working paradigms – in the context of a rapidly changing and growing technical environment.

Regulations such as GDPR, BCBS239, IDMP, ITAR, SOx and BCR[185] will change your business environment, and there is no choice about that. But at the same time the opportunities of the digital age are fast evolving. New apps are released every day; new channels seem to be invented almost every week. So which drives your first slice? Both obligation and opportunity would, of course, be the ideal answer.

Obligations and opportunities aren't the only conflicting pressures. Sales opportunities have never been more global, but at the same time location has never been more important. You might be able to run a sales campaign in Dubai, but how many of your staff speak Arabic or understand the local legal and cultural trading conditions?

---

[185] We could have picked from dozens of major standards. We decided that referencing the Trans Pacific Partnership Agreement (TPPA) was too controversial at the current stage of the US elections, but it will have major data implications around the world. In a similar way, GDPR will impact every organisation that holds any personal data about EU citizens, no matter where they are. BCBS applies to all systemically-important banks (SIB) – those 'too big to fail' in another language – whether that is globally or domestically. IDMP cuts across 'pharma' globally as the world finally standardises on harmonised specifications of medical products, whereas although ITAR only technically relates to standards of the imports and export of US munitions, the dominance of the US in this sector has far-reaching implications globally. Sarbanes-Oxley (SOx) has been with us some time now, but its implications are still being felt in organisations around the world, as more international bodies seek to prove compliance to facilitate US trade. And finally in our short list, BCRs represent the EU version of US 'safe harbour' legislation, enabling multinationals to transfer staff and staff data across borders in a way which is legally compliant but contains with less bureaucracy.

Global trading means you must understand your customers in their local conditions and business environment.

And the older conflicts are still with us, not least the need to do everything in the context of budget constraints. Or urgent versus important. Or thinking better versus thinking different.[186]

Somehow you need to balance all these conflicting pressures when finding those first steps. Finding early 'thin slices' that help you innovate for both obligation and innovation drivers is key.

Successful change programmes are always led by a small team of committed individuals. Early on in the process, you need to convince senior executives that *data is an asset*, and the *only way* to progress from the data they have to the information they need is to cross the *Data Delta*.

One topic you might want to explore when looking at senior staff engagement is the question: 'Who answers the door when the regulator comes knocking?'

With fines of up to 4% of turnover for non-compliance, GDPR *alone* is going to require not just a Senior Compliance Officer, but a significant team of people supporting them. Indeed, the whole CxO debate needs review – Chief Risk Officer? Chief Information Security Officer? Chief Data Officer?

It's worth investing a significant amount of time and effort to get this first step of senior executive engagement right, because if you do, everything follows naturally. Once top people in your organisation truly understand that data is an asset the right questions will start to flood out, just as with any other asset. Do you have enough? Is it of the right quality? Who is responsible for it?

You need to direct the key questions towards *value*. The value proposition for every organisation is different. The best people to find the value of *your* data is *your* staff who understand *your* business in detail. All that we outsiders can do is help you through that process.

---

[186] We aren't, in truth, entirely sure why Steve Jobs rejected the correct adverbial form, but who are we to argue with him? He asked his staff and customers to 'Think different', and the results speak for themselves.

331

As you get started, you only need to convince just one or two other people. That is how revolutions start. You need to find people who will *communicate* the vision to the absolute top decision makers in your organisation, if you aren't one of those yourself.

Different people will respond to different types of argument. Some people are inherently rationalist and will appreciate the logic of the *data is an asset* case. They will quickly grasp that anything which impacts the value of their organisation needs to be properly managed, and there is a significant gap today in how the data asset is being treated.

Other types of people might better respond to the visionary argument. People who express frustration at the current situation – whether it be trying to find all the services a local authority provides to a household, or all the products that your company has sold to a customer. Paint a different world for them where there is a 'single version of truth', and all the data about a customer or a citizen can be found with one enquiry. Emphasise that the journey doesn't start with huge data cleansing tasks of dubious outcome. Show them a twenty-minute demonstration of a 360-degree view of citizens/customers.

In terms of where to start, don't be daunted by the size of the task. Devour that elephant, one bite at a time.

Remember the concepts of 'slicing' though the *Data Delta* vertically, and don't be trapped into top-down thinking. Identify a small amount of data which is of particularly high value. This could might be a subset of customer or citizens, but it could be products or services, assets or vendors.

Start by working out how you can introduce the principles of Data Governance on this limited dataset – who owns it, how it is described, and you can objectively define, manage and improve its quality. Identify the smallest possible programme that will add measurable value to your business, and which is consistent with *Data Delta* principles. This is where you should start.

And here, as you would expect, is our final advert. We do think we've demonstrated both the clarity of our understanding of the challenges you are facing and our real world experience of working and solving similar problems.

We hope we've convinced you of the *commonality* of data challenges through industries and sectors. As a point of principal, we never claim to be experts in *your* field. We actually think that would be insulting to you. If you're not a bank, you shouldn't pretend that you are. And similarly, if you're not in the police or security services, or an NGO or a pharmaceutical company, or in transportation or local government or … This list goes on.

The point is: we are experts in *data*. And arguably, we know more about how to cross the *Data Delta* than anyone else. After all, we named it. It's our trademark.

We have provided you with a clear understanding of the underlying business problem, the broken link in so many organisations between the data they have, and the information they need. We have addressed this challenge with an holistic combination of people, process, change and technology. It's a comprehensive solution coupled to a credible implementation approach. It's isn't easy, but each day you delay getting started, the wider your delta will be.

Now is the time for you to *Cross the Data Delta*. Good luck!

Index

N

O

About the authors

This book was written through contributions from an extensive team working for the Entity Group in 2016. The four primary authors were Jason Edge, Steve Parry, Dave Wilkinson and Pete Smith.

Jason Edge[187] is passionate about everything related to data, with a career constantly ahead of the curve in terms of the *next generation* of data 'thinking' and products. One of Jason's most important successes was as the Principal Author for the ground-breaking Abu Dhabi Government Data Management Strategy.

Juggling work commitments with a busy family life, Jason is also an accomplished musician and musical director who enjoys directing groups of musicians to inspire them to lift music off the page and bring it to life. At the age of twelve, he was recognised as the UK's youngest official church organist.

Steve Parry[188] has an MBA from Cranfield, and his career in information management has seen him working around the world with some of the largest global corporations.

Companies are fond of changing the way they are organised, and the way they work, on a frequent basis. However, data is much more durable. Spending a great deal of time understanding how corporations are powered by data seemed to make sense to Steve, who's now been doing just that for over thirty years.

Meanwhile the family are growing up fast. The two eldest have both set out on an entrepreneurial path with their own internet-driven businesses, while the youngest is still studying.

---

[187] Jason is at www.linkedin.com/in/jasonedge; or Jason.Edge@EntityGroup.com
[188] Steve is at www.linkedin.com/in/steveparry; or Steve.Parry@EntityGroup.com

Dave Wilkinson[189] was born and raised in the UK but his career in Information Management has taken him around the globe, building and deploying products for various large software companies. Prior to joining the Entity Group, Dave ran IBM development for the entire MDM and Information Integration and Governance product suite. Dave's experience spans most continents, and he now resides in Austin, Texas, where crossing the language delta has definitely been a challenge.

Pete Smith[190] was born in Brixton, South London. His family migrated towards prosperity through suburbs and class barriers in a sequence of moves that were in strict synchronicity with the release of successive Rolling Stones albums. The timing of the moves was not in any way a coincidence, though the exact causality remains, as they say, 'another story'. By the time Pete was 18, his family had moved a distance of eight miles, two class barriers and eleven Stones albums. He wrote the best-selling Project Management book 'All You Need Is Love' to explain what happened next.

Pete's extensive information management career has taken him around the world many times over, and provides an enormous breadth and depth of experience across a variety of private sector organisations, governmental institutions and non-governmental agencies. He, like Steve, Dave and Jason, has helped organisations cross the *Data Delta* more times than most.

[189] Dave is at www.linkedin.com/in/dawilkinson; or Dave.Wilkinson@EntityGroup.com
[190] Pete is at www.linkedin.com/in/pete-smith-448819b; or Pete.Smith@EntityGroup.com

36788639R00209

Printed in Poland
by Amazon Fulfillment
Poland Sp. z o.o., Wrocław